5.
Ca A

THE COLD WAR

A Book of Documents

The Cold War

A BOOK OF DOCUMENTS

EDITED, WITH AN INTRODUCTION BY

H. L. Trefousse

G. P. Putnam's Sons   New York

ACKNOWLEDGMENTS

The excerpts from *Triumph and Tragedy* by Sir Winston Churchill are reprinted by courtesy of Houghton Mifflin Company; those from *The Public Papers and Addresses of Franklin D. Roosevelt*, edited by Samuel Rosenman, by courtesy of Harper & Row, Publishers; and those from Sir Winston Churchill's Fulton, Missouri, address by courtesy of *Vital Speeches of the Day*.

Library of Congress Catalogue
Card Number 65-13298

Contents

29456

THREE: THE COLD WAR IN EUROPE, 1945–1950   72

DOCUMENT:

FOUR: COLD AND HOT WAR IN ASIA, 1945–1953   130

DOCUMENT:

FIVE: THE COLD WAR AND THE EISENHOWER ADMINISTRATION   167

SIX: THE COLD WAR AND LATIN AMERICA   228

DOCUMENT:

SEVEN: THE NEW FRONTIER AND THE COLD WAR   251

DOCUMENT:

Introduction

Ever since the end of World War II, the world has lived in fear—fear of the bomb, fear of missiles, fear of complete annihilation. The Cold War has become so much a part of our consciousness that we have almost taken it for granted. And yet, it was not so long ago that people foresaw the emergence of a better world, one in which the United Nations would be able to solve mankind's most pressing problems, and the partners in war would be able to live together in peaceful cooperation. Why were these hopes disappointed? Why is the world engaged in a Cold War that seems to have no end? Who is responsible for the troubled turn of events since 1945?

The failure of the world to realize the hopes of the founders of the United Nations could have been predicted in 1942. In the light of its guiding philosophy, the Soviet Union, which emerged from World War II as one of the two super-powers, could hardly be expected to give up its hostility toward the West. "We are not pacifists," said Lenin in 1917. "We are opposed to imperialist wars for the division of spoils among capitalists, but we have always declared it to be absurd for the revolutionary proletariat to renounce revolutionary wars that may prove necessary in the interests of socialism." Stalin, too, evidently considered conflict with the West inevitable; the best that could be done, he seemed to think, was to acquire as much territory as possible to prepare for any eventual showdown. Given these beliefs, the Soviets approached their differences with the West from a point of view entirely at variance with that of their allies.

And wartime disagreements were legion. Questions of ideology; Stalin's demand for a second front in 1942 and 1943; the borders and government of Poland; the disposition of Germany after the war; the division of spheres of influence in the Balkans; Russian entry into the Pacific war with suitable compensations—all these created tension between the wartime partners. Franklin D. Roosevelt tried hard to overcome these points of friction. Adopting a policy designed to dispel Stalin's suspicions of the West, the President saw to it that aid was freely given to the Russians and that no onerous conditions for its acceptance were imposed upon them. Though Winston Churchill disagreed with his transatlantic partner on some matters, he too was inclined to seek a *modus vivendi* with the Communists.

Stalin, however, never reciprocated. Whether he knew that his allies were really trying to improve relations, or whether he considered their repeated assertions of friendliness mere camouflage, is not known. In view of his actions, however, it is likely that he never took Roosevelt's or Churchill's overtures of friendliness seriously. Apparently regarding all negotiations with the West as mere jockeying for power, he was careful to realize maximum strategic advantages in every agreement he concluded. Thus his arrangements with the West could be interpreted as efforts to seek positions of strength in the expected struggle with the non-Communist powers.

It is against this background that the wartime agreements must be assessed. Stalin found no difficulty in joining with his partners in the Declaration by the United Nations pledging a common war effort; but it is doubtful that he ever believed in the United Nations as anything more than a device by which he could be outvoted. He was not a party to the Casablanca demand for unconditional surrender of the enemy; however, the formula could be useful to him by preventing negotiations between the German opposition and the Western powers. At the Moscow Conference in October, 1943, he endorsed what must have seemed to him a highly theoretical statement of principles, and it was not until November that he finally met with both Roosevelt and Churchill at Teheran. Here his underlying resentment against the failure to establish a Western front was barely hidden;

nevertheless, finding Roosevelt's attitude useful, he encouraged the President in the belief that real allied unity could be maintained and even promised eventually to enter the war against Japan. Accordingly, a European Advisory Commission in 1944 succeeded in dividing Germany into three zones of occupation before any major allied forces had reached German soil. From Russia's point of view, the eastern zone was pushed as far forward as possible, although neither the Soviets nor their allies knew at the time that the zonal boundaries would become political frontiers as well. They had not even decided whether there was to be one Germany or many after the war.

When Winston Churchill came to Moscow in October, 1944, Stalin quickly settled down to business. The Balkans had long been a zone of conflict between Russia and the West; now the peninsula's fate was to be settled during an after-dinner conversation. The conferees easily marked out zones of influence; all that they lacked was American consent, but they must have hoped to obtain it later. In effect, the division gave Russia a preponderant influence everywhere in the Balkans except in Greece, and for the moment, the Soviet leader seemed satisfied.

The high point of allied wartime cooperation was reached at Yalta. Despite considerable argument, broad agreements were reached on such thorny questions as the borders and government of Poland, reparations and the treatment of Germany, and the structure and procedure of the United Nations. Stalin again promised to enter the war against Japan, after Germany's defeat, in return for territorial and economic concessions in the Far East. He proved fairly tractable on issues affecting the United Nations, and even signed an idealistic declaration promising free elections in liberated countries. But, as before, he made sure of his strategic bases. By insisting upon the retention of Polish territory seized in 1939 and the transfer of northern East Prussia to the Soviet Union, the Russian leader secured his western flank; moreover, military occupation of neighboring countries would create a buffer of satellite states. Russia's eastern borders were made secure by the promise of the transfer of the Kurile Islands, Southern Sakhalin, and bases and concessions in Manchuria. Russian troops were eventually to occupy all of these areas.

The more idealistic provisions of the Yalta agreement soon broke down. Wherever Soviet or Communist troops took over, pro-Soviet governments were installed and Western influence was reduced to almost zero. Rumania, Poland, Yugoslavia, Albania, and eventually Hungary and Czechoslovakia, all fell within the Soviet orbit. The Declaration on Liberated Europe was simply ignored by the Communists, and all the Western powers were able to do was to protest. This situation was most serious in Poland, where Soviet policy brought about a near break with Great Britain and the United States. Disregarding their pledges at Yalta to permit free and unfettered elections, the Soviets thoroughly communized the country in spite of Western disapproval. Stalin's intransigence was such that even Franklin D. Roosevelt, who had staked his entire policy on the hope of coming to an agreement with the Soviet leader, lost patience. Refusing to be intimidated when Stalin accused him of secret negotiations with the Germans, he wrote a vigorous reply. Two weeks later, on April 12, 1945, the President was dead.

Harry S. Truman, his successor, was unable to oppose Stalin effectively at first because Russian help against the Japanese was still deemed essential. Asked by Churchill not to withdraw from central Germany into previously delineated zones of occupation until agreements had been reached with the Communists, Truman felt compelled to refuse, and the Soviet Union's military sphere was pushed more than one hundred miles farther to the west.

Shortly afterward, the last wartime summit conference was held at Potsdam. With Russian troops in possession of virtually every disputed area in Europe except Greece, where British forces had prevented a Communist take-over, the Western leaders were unable to do much more than to postpone final decisions by referring them to their foreign ministers. The resulting agreements in effect conceded to Russia, pending the final conclusion of a peace treaty, the borders she had desired for Poland. Arrangements had already been made with the Soviets for moving Western troops into Berlin and Vienna; air corridors to supply them were eventually worked out, but few definite agreements were signed concerning the status of access routes to the former German capital. When the war with Japan ended in September, after two atom bombs had been dropped and Russia had belatedly entered the conflict, the Soviets seized the Far Eastern areas promised to them. They also occupied that part of Korea lying north of the thirty-eighth parallel.

In spite of all previous disagreements, the end of the war opened up new possibilities for peace. Although the United States was then the world's only nuclear power, it announced its willingness to share its atomic strength with the rest of the world. When the Baruch Plan for this purpose was presented in June, 1946, however, the Russians, wholly adverse to cooperation with the democratic world, rejected it. They continued to rely on their military control of conquered areas, which they sealed off completely from the West. An "iron curtain" descended upon Europe, as Winston Churchill correctly pointed out in March, 1946. It had become clear that the Soviet Union was as distrustful as ever.

This development created a difficult situation for the United States, now the strongest of the non-Communist nations. America's traditional pragmatic approach to world problems, with its emphasis on limited countermeasures against widely separated challenges, was ill suited for dealing with an opponent dedicated to long-range planning based on a more or less rigid ideology. The United States reply was the policy of containment. As viewed by its author, George Kennan, this approach would interpose American force between the Communists and their targets wherever needed; with time, the Soviet regime would become less rigid, and ultimately peace might be secured.

The new policy was foreshadowed by a change in America's attitude toward Germany, when Secretary of State James F. Byrnes, at Stuttgart, in September, 1946, said that the defeated country would eventually have to resume its place among the nations of the world. The real turning point in American foreign policy, however, came in 1947. Informed by Great Britain that she was no longer able to support Greece against Communist subversion, President Truman set forth his doctrine of aid to countries menaced by Soviet aggression. Then Secretary of State George C. Marshall outlined his plan to help Europe economically. And when the Czech Republic fell to the Communists in February, 1948, Congress was induced to vote the necessary funds to help non-Communist nations help themselves. The Russian effort to choke off West Berlin by blockade was met with the highly successful airlift of 1948–49. Soviet threats caused the Western powers to agree to a strong military alliance in the North Atlantic Treaty Organization; and Stalin's refusal to cooperate in Germany induced the allies to set up the West German Federal Republic. All Stalin could do in reply was to establish a Communist state in East Germany. His days of expansion in Europe were over.

The policy of containment had thus worked in Europe. But it had a fatal flaw. By emphasizing countermoves against Communist pressures, the policy tended to identify the United States with the status quo everywhere, not only in western Europe, where existing forms of social organization were viable, but also in underdeveloped countries of the world, where they were not. Consequently, in these areas, the Soviets benefited from local dissatisfaction with existing regimes, while the United States, with its lack of a formal ideology, suffered from its support of unpopular governments. Until America came forward with a strong, well-defined philosophy for underdeveloped lands, she would be seriously handicapped.

This weakness became most apparent in Asia, where the Communists were much more successful than in Europe. Despite the fact that he had signed a treaty of friendship with Chiang Kai-shek, the leader of the Chinese Nationalists, Stalin used his strategic position to help Chiang's Communist enemies, who eventually conquered the entire mainland. America was unable to persuade Chiang to bring about much-needed reforms; short-lived truces gained by American negotiators were soon broken; and the Chinese civil war ended in a Communist triumph. Chiang Kai-shek was forced to withdraw to Formosa, which became the refuge of the Nationalist government.

Undoubtedly, Soviet plans for Korea were similar. Divided at the thirty-eighth parallel for the sake of military convenience at the end of the war, the peninsula became a victim of the Cold War when the Soviets communized the North and transformed their zone into a satellite. They refused entry to the United Nations Commission to supervise voting in North Korea, so that free elections were held in the South only, where a non-Communist government was set up under Syngman Rhee. As in Germany, the Russians promptly countered with a Communist government in the North. Though the United States was known to be prepared for the use of force in case of an attack upon West Germany, there was some doubt about American intentions in South Korea. Possibly emboldened by the withdrawal of American troops in 1948 and Secretary of State Dean Acheson's failure to designate Korea as a part of the American defense perimeter, the North Koreans crossed the border in force on June 20, 1950.

American reaction was prompt. Authorizing naval and air forces to repel the attack, President Truman showed the world that he was determined to resist aggression. The United Nations called for a police action against North Korea, and the United States shouldered the greatest burden in ensuing operations. The attempted take-over of South Korea failed; the Communists had made a serious miscalculation.

The war in Korea lasted some three years. The North Koreans were defeated by the late fall of 1950, but with the entry of the Chinese Communists, the conflict developed into a stalemate which was resolved only after the death of Stalin. The fighting ended with a truce at Panmunjom, where the status quo was largely restored. Korea remained divided.

In 1953, the Cold War might have been expected to enter upon a new phase. A Republican administration pledged to avoiding the errors of the past had come to power in the United States, and Joseph Stalin died in March. While the new leaders of the Soviet Union were preoccupied with their struggle for succession to Stalin's power, the time seemed ripe for a new approach.

Surprisingly, however, no great changes occurred. To be sure, President Eisenhower "unleashed" Chiang Kai-shek, and the new Secretary of State, John Foster Dulles, spoke of a possible "agonizing reappraisal" and "massive" reatliation; but in reality, Eisenhower's policies were not too different from those of his predecessors. As before, the United States, a fundamentally satiated nation, tended to favor the status quo, while the Soviet Union, impelled by its messianic ideology, sought to alter it.

This attitude served the Soviets well in underdeveloped areas caught up in the anticolonialist upsurge. Communism scored gains especially in Southeast Asia, where France was defeated in Indo-China. Communist participation in the national uprising was rewarded by another partition; Northern Vietnam became a satellite, while the southern part, as well as Laos and Cambodia, became independent. Soviet influence and guerrilla forces, however, remained strong in all portions of Indo-China, where new wars were soon to break out.

Although the United States did not sign the Geneva accord, the Eisenhower administration was to become the main prop of anti-Communist forces in Southeast Asia. To meet the danger of further Soviet penetration, the United States entered into the Southeast Asia Treaty Organization; but the pact had little strength, and direct aid to the pro-Western factions became necessary. The situation was further complicated by the state of affairs in China, where an aggressive Communist government controlled the mainland, while the Nationalists on Formosa, now protected by the United States, continued to occupy China's seat at the United Nations. Intermittent warfare for the control of Nationalist-held offshore islands and frequent crises about Chinese representation at the world organization created constant friction. With the exception of Japan, where a viable social order existed, the Far East remained a veritable tinderbox.

As in previous years, the West was again much more successful in Europe. Although plans for a Defense Community that would have included West Germany went awry, the former enemy nation was admitted to membership in NATO in 1955. The Russians countered with the Warsaw Pact, linking the satellites and East Germany, but the economic development of western Europe was so great that Communist propaganda was not very effective. Stalin's successors were no more successful than he had been in extending Soviet power beyond the Iron Curtain.

Possibly for internal reasons, the new leaders of the Soviet Union permitted a slight thaw in the Cold War in 1955 and early 1956. Austria was neutralized after ten years of wrangling; the first postwar summit conference was held at Geneva, and Nikita S. Khrushchev delivered a secret speech denouncing Stalin for various excesses. Optimism was in the air.

But the Soviet leaders had by no means given up their notions of hegemony. When, in the fall of 1956, Poland and Hungary seemed about to break loose from Soviet domination, Khrushchev moved with great dispatch. Quickly stabilizing the situation in Poland by the installation of a more liberal Communist regime under Wladyslaw Gomulka, he reacted with extreme harshness to Imre Nagy's effort to neutralize Hungary. Russian tanks quelled the revolution; Nagy was arrested and finally executed, and a more pliant regime under Janos Kadar was installed in Budapest. Despite popular sentiment favoring the Hungarian uprising, the United States could do little to help. President Eisenhower was wholly unwilling to assume the risks of nuclear war.

The blow to Soviet prestige might have been more severe if, once again, it had not been for a new crisis in the underdeveloped world—this time in the Middle East, where Soviet agitation against existing regimes had made local revolutionaries receptive to Communist aid. President Gamal Abdel Nasser of Egypt, who had risen to power after the overthrow of a corrupt monarchy, was perfectly willing to obtain Western support. Secretary Dulles extended economic assistance to build the Aswan High Dam in the Nile Valley, but suddenly withdrew it when Nasser accepted aid from Russia as well. The result was that the Egyptian leader seized the Suez Canal, in order to finance the High Dam with canal revenues. The Government of Israel, which Nasser had vowed to destroy, seized the opportunity presented by the disorders in the Middle East and Central Europe. Quickly invading Egypt, the Israelis sought to open up the Gulf of Aqaba and the Suez Canal to Israeli shipping. Britain and France intervened to safeguard their interests at Suez, and Nasser seemed close to collapse. The Soviets, however, posing as defenders of anti-imperialist nations despite their aggression in Hungary, threatened to intervene to help Egypt. The world seemed close to World War III.

The United States was now faced with a difficult decision. Should it call the Soviet bluff and hazard nuclear war? Reluctant to assume such risks and loath to sanction aggression, even in its own interest, America joined its adversary in a United Nations resolution for a cease-fire in Egypt. As a general consequence, Nasser was saved, Hungary was reconquered, and America's Western allies were alienated. Soviet anticolonialist propaganda had payed rich dividends.

During the next four years, the Cold War continued in spite of temporary "thaws." To prevent the dangerous Middle Eastern situation from erupting again, President Eisenhower issued the doctrine that bears his name, and intervened in Lebanon to maintain the peace. Khrushchev, having strengthened his position at home, in 1959 provoked another crisis in Berlin by threatening unilateral action in the beleaguered city. The peril subsided when he came to visit President Eisenhower at Camp David, Maryland, only to flare up again the following year when the Soviets caught a U-2 pilot after shooting down his American observation plane deep inside Russia. Refusing to be mollified by confused American statements about the affair, Khrushchev broke up the summit conference in Paris in 1960, and the Cold War was on again in full force.

Because of American preoccupation with Europe and Asia, Latin-American affairs had received less attention at Washington than they deserved. In the Western Hemisphere as elsewhere in the underdeveloped world, Soviet propaganda was well attuned to popular dissatisfaction, while American policies were hampered by close ties with unpopular regimes. It is true that the Monroe Doctrine had been transformed from a unilateral pronouncement to an all-American principle by means of the Act of Chapultepec, the Inter-American Treaty of Mutual Assistance, and the Organization of American States; but the fundamental problem of Latin America—poverty and lack of economic development—had not been met. Accordingly, Communist blandishments found a willing echo south of the Rio Grande, where their anti-American tone increased their effectiveness. In 1954, arms from the Soviet bloc were shipped to the leftist government of President Jacobo Arbenz Guzmán in Guatemala. Although the Arbenz regime was overthrown by a timely coup, the United States had received a serious warning of troubles to come.

It was in Cuba that the Communists were to achieve their first successes in the Western Hemisphere. When, on January 1, 1959, Fidel Castro overthrew the dictatorship of Fulgencio Batista, American observers at first believed that the revolution signified a triumph for democracy; within two years, however, it had become evident that precisely the reverse was true. Probably encouraged by the certainty of Soviet support for any anti-American revolutionary, Castro drifted further and further toward the left; his non-Communist supporters began to lose faith, and political persecution became the order of the day. After Cuba signed a trade agreement with the Soviet Union and confiscated American property, President Eisenhower reduced the Cuban sugar quota in July, 1960, preliminary to an embargo in October. Khrushchev publicly proclaimed the demise of the Monroe Doctrine, while the American states, at San José, condemned Soviet interference; but Castro finally declared himself to be a full-fledged Marxist-Leninist. The Cold War had come to the doorstep of the United States.

The beginning of the seventh decade of the twentieth century witnessed another change of administrations in Washington. President John F. Kennedy inherited the problems of the Cold War; during his administration the focal points of the struggle would be in Berlin, Cuba, Southeast Asia, and newly independent Africa. Within a few months of his inauguration, an effort to liberate Cuba failed at the Bay of Pigs after the President had refused to provide air cover and the Soviets had threatened to intervene. Thereafter, steady Communist propaganda in Latin America remained a constant threat to the United States. In Europe, Chairman Khrushchev revived the Berlin crisis after a brief meeting with President Kennedy at Vienna; the President replied with a program of military preparedness including partial mobilization of the reserves, and the situation was further complicated by the Communists' erection of a wall separating East from West Berlin.

Elsewhere in the world, conditions continued to remain unstable. Quarreling factions in the newly independent Congo found supporters in Washington and Moscow, and Communist guerrillas and separate armies pushed forward in both Laos and South Vietnam. To stop the fighting in Laos, a precarious truce was signed at Geneva in 1962, but the Vietcong rebellion in South Vietnam continued unabated. Finally, in October, 1962, President Kennedy risked a showdown with the Soviet Union in Cuba, after discovering Soviet missiles on the island. Khrushchev agreed to withdraw his weapons, but the Castro regime remained staunchly Communist.

In spite of these troubles, the overall picture was changing by this time. Russia, having made great economic progress, was no longer so bellicose, while China, in the midst of great economic difficulties, was becoming ever more restive. Led by the fanatical Mao Tse-tung, the Chinese Communists accused the Soviet government of apostasy and preached unrelenting struggle against the Western powers whom they considered mere "paper tigers." The split between the two Communist giants facilitated the signing of the treaty banning nuclear tests in 1963 and the gradual subsidence of the Berlin crisis. China now denounced the treaty; an uneasy world watched while Mao Tse-tung perfected his own bomb, a new Russian government failed to heal the Sino-Soviet rift, and Chinese warmongering became the greatest threat to world peace. The Cold War was entering an entirely new phase.

The following documents are designed to facilitate the study of the diplomatic history of the Cold War and to answer some of the questions raised by it. If America and Russia seem to occupy a disproportionate share of space in these documents, it must be remembered that these two countries have been the foci of the Cold War since 1945. Whether they will continue to occupy this position remains to be seen.

THE COLD WAR

A Book of Documents

ONE

Origins: Efforts at Cooperation

Faced with a common enemy during World War II, the United States, Great Britain and the Soviet Union cooperated to the extent of presenting a united front to the world. They bound themselves to a common war effort in the Declaration of the United Nations, but deep differences based on power politics and ideology existed between them. In an effort to overcome some of these, Franklin D. Roosevelt and Winston Churchill, at Casablanca, pledged themselves to seek the enemy's unconditional surrender. The allied Foreign Ministers conferred at Moscow in October, 1943, emphasized their unity, and agreed to set up a European Advisory Commission which eventually produced plans for occupation zones in Germany. Not until later in 1943, after they had stopped at Cairo to promise the return of lost territories to China, did the President and the Prime Minister meet with Marshal Stalin at Teheran, where they tried hard to smooth over the Soviet leader's pique about their failure to open a second front by promising a landing in spring. In October, 1944, Churchill saw Stalin again, this time at Moscow, and the two allies sought to divide the Balkans into spheres of influence. Finally, when the entire range of postwar problems was discussed at Yalta by all three wartime leaders, Stalin was not only awarded several Far Eastern territories in return for a promise to enter the war against Japan, but he also procured a favorable settlement in Europe because of the swift advance of the Red Army. He did, however, promise to conduct free elections in Eastern Europe and cooperated in the founding of the United Nations. Whether the tenuous unity barely preserved in war could be maintained in peace was questionable.

DOCUMENT 1

DECLARATION BY THE UNITED NATIONS, JANUARY 1, 1942

The alliance between the three major powers was formalized on January 1, 1942, by the Declaration by the United Nations, to which the lesser powers at war with the Axis eventually adhered.

A Joint Declaration by the United States, the United Kingdom, the Union of Soviet Socialist Republics, China, Australia, Belgium, Canada, Costa Rica, Cuba, Czechoslovakia, Dominican Republic, El Salvador, Greece, Guatamela, Haiti, Honduras, India, Luxembourg, Netherlands, New Zealand, Nicaragua, Norway, Panama, Poland, South Africa, Yugoslavia

The Governments signatory hereto,

Having subscribed to a common program of purposes and principles embodied in the Joint Declaration of the President of the United States of America and the Prime Minister of the United Kingdom of Great Britain and Northern Ireland dated August 14, 1941, known as the Atlantic Charter.

Being convinced that complete victory over their enemies is essential to defend life, liberty, independence and religious freedom, and to preserve human rights and justice in their own lands as well as in other lands, and that they are now engaged in a common struggle against savage and brutal forces seeking to subjugate the world,

---

A Decade of American Foreign Policy, Basic Documents, 1941–49, Senate Document No. 123, 81st Cong., 1st Sess. (Washington, 1950), 2–3 (hereafter cited as *Decade*).

DECLARE:

(1) Each Government pledges itself to employ its full resources, military or economic, against those members of the Tripartite Pact and its adherents with which such government is at war.

(2) Each Government pledges itself to cooperate with the Governments signatory hereto and not to make a separate armistice or peace with the enemies.

The foregoing declaration may be adhered to by other nations which are, or which may be, rendering material assistance and contributions in the struggle for victory over Hitlerism.

Done at Washington

January First, 1942

[The signatories to the Declaration by United Nations are as listed above.

The adherents to the Declaration by United Nations, together with the date of communication of adherence, are as follows:

Mexico	June 5, 1942	Peru	Feb. 11, 1945
Philippines	June 10, 1942	Chile	Feb. 12, 1945
Ethiopia	July 28, 1942	Paraguay	Feb. 12, 1945
Iraq	Jan. 16, 1943	Venezuela	Feb. 16, 1945
Brazil	Feb. 8, 1943	Uruguay	Feb. 23, 1945
Bolivia	Apr. 27, 1943	Turkey	Feb. 24, 1945
Iran	Sept. 10, 1943	Egypt	Feb. 27, 1945
Colombia	Dec. 22, 1943	Saudi Arabia	Mar. 1, 1945
Liberia	Feb. 26, 1944	Lebanon	Mar. 1, 1945
France	Dec. 26, 1944	Syria	Mar. 1, 1945]
Ecuador	Feb. 7, 1945		

DOCUMENT 2

THE CASABLANCA CONFERENCE, JANUARY 14–24, 1943

When President Roosevelt and Prime Minister Churchill met at Casablanca in January, 1943, they endorsed the principle of "unconditional surrender" for the Axis powers. Not included in the official communiqué,

Samuel I. Rosenman, ed., *The Public Papers and Addresses of Franklin D. Roosevelt* (New York, 1950), XII, 39.

this decision was announced by the President during a press conference on January 24, 1943.

The Eight Hundred and Seventy-Fifth Press Conference. Joint Conference by the President and Prime Minister Churchill at Casablanca. January 24, 1943

THE PRESIDENT:

Another point. I think we have all had it in our hearts and our heads before, but I don't think that it has ever been put down on paper by the Prime Minister and myself, and that is the determination that peace can come to the world only by the total elimination of German and Japanese war power.

Some of you Britishers know the old story—we had a General called U. S. Grant. His name was Ulysses Simpson Grant, but in my, and the Prime Minister's, early days he was called "Unconditional Surrender" Grant. The elimination of German, Japanese, and Italian war power means the unconditional surrender of Germany, Italy, and Japan. That means a reasonable assurance of future world peace. It does not mean the destruction of the population of Germany, Italy, or Japan, but it does mean the destruction of the philosophies in those countries which are based on conquest and the subjugation of other people."

DOCUMENT 3

THE MOSCOW CONFERENCE, OCTOBER 19–30, 1943

The Foreign Ministers of the United States, the United Kingdom and the Union of Soviet Socialist Republics met at Moscow late in October, 1943. The resulting communiqués, in part co-signed by the Chinese Ambassador at Moscow, seemed to emphasize their cooperation. Providing for the setting up of a European Advisory Commission to deal with political affairs of Europe, they threatened punishment for war crimes, promised independence to Austria, and called for a new order for Italy.

Anglo-Soviet-American Communiqué, November 1, 1943

The Conference of Foreign Secretaries of the United States of America, Mr. Cordell Hull, of the United Kingdom, Mr. Anthony

Eden, and of the Soviet Union, Mr. V. M. Molotov, took place at Moscow from the 19th to the 30th of October 1943. There were twelve meetings.

[A list of participants in addition to the Foreign Secretaries follows here in the original.]

The agenda included all the questions submitted for discussion by the three Governments. Some of the questions called for final decisions and these were taken. On other questions, after discussion, decisions of principle were taken: these questions were referred for detailed consideration to commissions specially set up for the purpose, or reserved for treatment through diplomatic channels. Other questions again were disposed of by an exchange of views.

The Governments of the United States, the United Kingdom and the Soviet Union have been in close cooperation in all matters concerning the common war effort. But this is the first time that the Foreign Secretaries of the three Governments have been able to meet together in conference.

In the first place there were frank and exhaustive discussions of measures to be taken to shorten the war against Germany and her satellites in Europe. Advantage was taken of the presence of military advisers, representing the respective Chiefs of Staff, in order to discuss definite military operations, with regard to which decisions had been taken and which are already being prepared, and in order to create a basis for the closest military cooperation in the future between the three countries.

Second only to the importance of hastening the end of the war was the unanimous recognition by the three Governments that it was essential in their own national interests and in the interest of all peace-loving nations to continue the present close collaboration and cooperation in the conduct of the war into the period following the end of hostilities, and that only in this way could peace be maintained and the political, economic and social welfare of their peoples fully promoted.

This conviction is expressed in a declaration in which the Chinese Government joined during the Conference and which was signed by the three Foreign Secretaries and the Chinese Ambassador at Moscow on behalf of their governments. This declaration, published today, provides for even closer collaboration in the prosecution of the war and in all matters pertaining to the surrender and disarmament of the enemies with which the four countries are respectively at war. It sets forth the principles upon which the four governments agree that a broad system of international cooperation and security should be based. Provision is made for the inclusion of all other peace-loving nations, great and small, in this system.

The Conference agreed to set up machinery for ensuring the closest cooperation between the three Governments in the examination of European questions arising as the war develops. For this purpose the Conference decided to establish in London a European Advisory Commission to study these questions and to make joint recommendations to the three Governments.

Provision was made for continuing, when necessary, tripartite consultations of representatives of the three Governments in the respective capitals through the existing diplomatic channels.

The Conference also agreed to establish an Advisory Council for matters relating to Italy, to be composed in the first instance of representatives of their three governments and of the French Committee of National Liberation. Provision is made for the addition to this council of representatives of Greece and Yugoslavia in view of their special interests arising out of the aggressions of Fascist Italy upon their territory during the present war. This Council will deal with day-to-day questions, other than military operations, and will make recommendations designed to coordinate Allied policy with regard to Italy.

The three Foreign Secretaries considered it appropriate to reaffirm, by a declaration published today, the attitude of their Governments in favor of restoration of democracy in Italy.

The three Foreign Secretaries declared it to be the purpose of their Governments to restore the independence of Austria. At the same time they reminded Austria that in the final settlement account will be taken of efforts that Austria may make towards its own liberation. The declaration on Austria is published today.

The Foreign Secretaries issued at the Conference a declaration by President Roosevelt, Prime Minister Churchill and Premier Stalin containing a solemn warning that at the time of granting any armistice to any German Government those German officers and men and members of the Nazi party who have had any connection with atrocities and executions in countries overrun by German forces will be taken back to the countries in which their abominable crimes were committed to be charged and punished according to the laws of those countries.

In the atmosphere of mutual confidence and understanding which characterized all the work of the Conference, consideration was also given to other important questions. These included not only questions of a current nature, but also questions concerning the treatment of Hitlerite Germany and its satellites, economic cooperation and the assurance of general peace. . . .

DOCUMENT 4

THE CAIRO CONFERENCE, NOVEMBER 22–26, 1943

On their way to Teheran, President Roosevelt and Prime Minister Churchill met with Generalissimo Chiang Kai-shek at Cairo. The resulting communiqué, underlining the Western allies' resolve to grant great power status to China, expressed their determination to restore to that country all possessions lost to Japan and promised eventual independence to Korea. Since the Soviet Union was not at war with Japan at the time, no Soviet representative was present.

PRESS COMMUNIQUÉ

President Roosevelt, Generalissimo Chiang Kai-Shek and Prime Minister Churchill, together with their respective military and diplomatic advisers, have completed a conference in North Africa. The following general statement was issued:

"The several military missions have agreed upon future military operations against Japan. The three great Allies expressed their resolve to bring unrelenting pressure against their brutal enemies by sea, land and air. This pressure is already rising.

"The three great Allies are fighting this war to restrain and punish the aggression of Japan. They covet no gain for themselves and have no thought of territorial expansion. It is their purpose that Japan shall be stripped of all the islands in the Pacific which she has seized or occupied since the beginning of the first World War in 1914, and that all the territories Japan has stolen from the Chinese, such as

Foreign Relations of the United States: *The Conferences at Cairo and Teheran,* Department of State Publication No. 7187 (Washington, 1961), 448–449.

Manchuria, Formosa, and the Pescadores, shall be restored to the Republic of China. Japan will also be expelled from all other territories which she has taken by violence and greed. The aforesaid three great powers, mindful of the enslavement of the people of Korea, are determined that in due course Korea shall become free and independent.

"With these objects in view the three Allies, in harmony with those of the United Nations at war with Japan, will continue to persevere in the serious and prolonged operations necessary to procure the unconditional surrender of Japan."

DOCUMENT 5

THE TEHERAN CONFERENCE, NOVEMBER 28–DECEMBER 1, 1943

The first meeting of all three principal allied leaders took place at Teheran between November 28 and December 1, 1943. Stalin was promised a second front in May, 1944, and an attempt was made to induce Turkey to join with the United Nations. The original communiqué was issued on December 1, 1943; a declaration regarding Iran, promising the extension of economic aid and the maintenance of political independence, was published on December 7, 1943 (here omitted); while the secret military "conclusions" were not made public until March 27, 1947. The following original text was slightly altered in the final release.

DECLARATION OF THE THREE POWERS

We—The President of the United States, The Prime Minister of Great Britain, and the Premier of the Soviet Union, have met these four days past in this, the capital of our ally, Iran, and have shaped and confirmed our common policy.

We express our determination that our nations shall work together in war and in the peace that will follow.

As to war—Our military staffs have joined in our round table discussions, and we have concerted our plans for the destruction of the German forces. We have reached complete agreement as to the scope

---

Foreign Relations of the United States: *The Conferences at Cairo and Teheran*, 640–641, 652.

and timing of the operations which will be undertaken[1] from the East, West and South.

The common understanding which we have here reached guarantees that victory will be ours.

And as to peace—we are sure that our concord will make it an enduring peace.[2] We recognize fully the supreme responsibility resting upon us and all the United Nations, to make a peace which will command the good will of the overwhelming mass of the peoples of the world, and banish the scourge and terror of war for many generations.

With our diplomatic advisers we have surveyed the problems of the future. We shall seek the cooperation and the active participation of all nations, large and small, whose peoples in heart and mind are dedicated, as are our own peoples, to the elimination of tyranny and slavery, oppression and intolerance. We will welcome them, as they may choose to come, into a world family of democratic nations.

No power on earth can prevent our destroying the German armies by land, their U-boats by sea, and their war plants from the air.

Our attack will be relentless and increasing.

Emerging from these friendly[3] conferences we look with confidence to the day when all peoples of the world may live free lives, untouched by tyranny, and according to their varying desires and their own consciences.

We came here with hope and determination. We leave here, friends in fact, in spirit and in purpose.

Signed at Teheran, December 1, 1943.[4]

ROOSEVELT
STALIN
CHURCHILL[5]

Text agreed to by the P. M. & the Marshall [Marshal] *W. A. H.*

---

[1] This passage reads, in the release text, "operations to be undertaken."

[2] This passage reads, in the release text, "our concord will win an enduring peace."

[3] The fourth word in the paragraph, in the release text, is "cordial" instead of "friendly."

[4] The release text gives this line below, rather than above, the names of the Heads of Government.

[5] The names in the agreed text are typewritten. The three Heads of Government do not appear to have signed any copy of this document, which was intended primarily as a press release. The release text reads as follows, on one line: "Signed: Roosevelt, Churchill and Stalin."

SECRET

MILITARY CONCLUSIONS OF THE TEHERAN CONFERENCE

The Conference:—

(1) Agreed that the Partisans in Yugoslavia should be supported by supplies and equipment to the greatest possible extent, and also by commando operations:

(2) Agreed that, from the military point of view, it was most desirable that Turkey should come into the war on the side of the Allies before the end of the year:

(3) Took note of Marshal Stalin's statement that if Turkey found herself at war with Germany, and as a result Bulgaria declared war on Turkey or attacked her, the Soviet would immediately be at war with Bulgaria. The Conference further took note that this fact could be explicitly stated in the fourthcoming negotiations to bring Turkey into the war:

(4) Took note that Operation OVERLORD would be launched during May 1944, in conjunction with an operation against Southern France. The latter operation would be undertaken in as great a strength as availability of landing-craft permitted. The Conference further took note of Marshal Stalin's statement that the Soviet forces would launch an offensive at about the same time with the object of preventing the German forces from transferring from the Eastern to the Western Front:

(5) Agreed that the military staffs of the three Powers should henceforward keep in close touch with each other in regard to the impending operations in Europe. In particular it was agreed that a cover plan to mystify and mislead the enemy as regards these operations would be concerted between the staffs concerned.

F. D. R.
I. S.
W. S. C.

TEHERAN, December 1, 1943.

DOCUMENT 6

PROTOCOL ON ZONES OF OCCUPATION OF GERMANY AND ADMINISTRATION OF THE "GREATER BERLIN"

AREA, SEPTEMBER 12, 1944, AND AMENDING AGREEMENT OF NOVEMBER 14, 1944

On September 12, 1944, the European Advisory Commission established at the Moscow Conference agreed upon a division of Germany into three zones of occupation and the partition of Berlin into three additional sectors. Not until November 14, 1944, did Great Britain and the United States determine that they were to occupy the northwestern and southwestern zones, respectively. The protocols were approved by the United States on February 2, 1945; the United Kingdom, on December 5, 1944, and the Soviet Union, on February 6, 1945. This division became the basis of the later partition of Germany into an eastern and western state.

Protocol

The Governments of the United States of America, the United Kingdom of Great Britain and Northern Ireland, and the Union of Soviet Socialist Republics have reached the following agreement with regard to the execution of Article 11 of the Instrument of Unconditional Surrender of Germany:

1. Germany, within her frontiers as they were on the 31st December, 1937, will, for the purposes of occupation, be divided into three zones, one of which will be allotted to each of the three Powers, and a special Berlin area, which will be under joint occupation by the three Powers.

2. The boundaries of the three zones and of the Berlin area, and the allocation of the three zones as between the U.S.A., the U.K. and the U.S.S.R. will be as follows:—

> *Eastern Zone ...*
> The territory of Germany (including the province of East Prussia) situated to the East of a line drawn from the point on Lübeck Bay where the frontiers of Schleswig-Holstein and Mecklenburg meet, along the western frontier of Mecklenburg to the frontier of the province of Hanover, thence, along the eastern frontier of Hanover, to the frontier of Brunswick; thence along the western frontier of the Prussian province of Saxony to the western frontier of An-

---

Documents on Germany, 1944–1961, 87th Cong., 1st Sess. Committee Print for Senate Committee on Foreign Relations (Washington, 1961), 1–5.

halt, thence along the western frontier of Anhalt; thence along the western frontier of the Prussian province of Saxony and the western frontier of Thuringia to where the latter meets the Bavarian frontier; then eastwards along the northern frontier of Bavaria to the 1937 Czechoslovakian frontier, will be occupied by armed forces of the U.S.S.R., with the exception of the Berlin area, for which a special system of occupation is provided below.

North-Western Zone . . .

The territory of Germany situated to the west of the line defined above, and bounded on the south by a line drawn from the point where the western frontier of Thuringia meets the frontier of Bavaria; thence westwards along the southern frontiers of the Prussian provinces of Hessen-Nassau and Rheinprovinz to where the latter meets the frontier of France will be occupied by armed forces of * * *

South-Western Zone . . .

All the remaining territory of Western Germany situated to the south of the line defined in the description of the North-Western Zone will be occupied by armed forces of * * *

The frontiers of States (Länder) and Provinces within Germany, referred to in the foregoing descriptions of the zones, are those which existed after the coming into effect of the decree of 25th June, 1941 (published in the Reichsgesetzblatt, Part I, No. 72, 3rd July, 1941).

Berlin Area . . .

The Berlin area (by which expression is understood the territory of "Greater Berlin" as defined by the Law of the 27th April, 1920) will be jointly occupied by armed forces of the U.S.A., U.K., and U.S.S.R., assigned by the respective Commanders-in-Chief. For this purpose the territory of "Greater Berlin" will be divided into the following three parts:—

North-Eastern part of "Greater Berlin" districts of Pankow, Prenzlauerberg, Mitte, Weissensee, Friedrichshain, Lichtenberg, Treptow, Köpenick) will be occupied by the forces of the U.S.S.R.:

North-Western part of "Greater Berlin" (districts of Reinickendorf, Wedding, Tiergarten, Charlottenburg, Spandau, Wilmersdorf) will be occupied by the forces of * * *

Southern part of "Greater Berlin" (districts of Zehlendorf, Steglitz, Schöneberg, Kreuzberg, Tempelhof, Neukölln) will be occupied by the forces of * * *

The boundaries of districts within "Greater Berlin," referred to in the foregoing descriptions, are those which existed after the coming into effect of the decree published on 27th March, 1938 (Amtsblatt der Reichshauptstadt Berlin No. 13 of 27th March, 1938, page 215).

3. The occupying forces in each of the three zones into which Germany is divided will be under a Commander-in-Chief designated by the Government of the country whose forces occupy that zone.

4. Each of the three Powers may, at its discretion, include among the forces assigned to occupation duties under the command of its Commander-in-Chief, auxiliary contingents from the forces of any other Allied Power which has participated in military operations against Germany.

5. An Inter-Allied Governing Authority (Komendatura) consisting of three Commandants, appointed by their respective Commanders-in-Chief, will be established to direct jointly the administration of the "Greater Berlin" Area.

6. This Protocol has been drawn up in triplicate in the English and Russian languages. Both texts are authentic. The Protocol will come into force on the signature by Germany of the Instrument of Unconditional Surrender. . . .

Amending Agreement

1. In place of the description of the North-Western Zone given in paragraph 2 of the above-mentioned Protocol, the description of the North-Western Zone will read as follows:—

"North-Western Zone . . .

The territory of Germany situated to the west of the line defined in the description of the Eastern zone, and bounded on the south by a line drawn from the point where the frontier between the Prussian provinces of Hanover and Hessen-Nassau meets the western frontier of the Prussian province of Saxony; thence along the southern frontier of Hanover; thence along the north-western, western and southern frontiers of Hessen-Nassau to the point where the River Rhine leaves the latter; thence along the center of the navigable channel of the River Rhine to the point where it leaves Hessen-Darmstadt; thence along the western frontier to Baden to the point where this frontier becomes the Franco-German frontier will be occupied by armed forces of the United Kingdom."

2. In place of the description of the South-Western Zone given in paragraph 2 of the above-mentioned Protocol, the description of the South-Western Zone will read as follows:—

"South-Western Zone . . .

The territory of Germany situated to the south of a line commencing at the junction of the frontiers of Saxony, Bavaria, and Czechoslovakia and extending westward along the northern frontier of Bavaria to the junction of the frontiers of Hessen-Nassau, Thuringia and Bavaria; thence north, west and south along the eastern, northern, western and southern frontiers of Hessen-Nassau to the point where the River Rhine leaves the southern frontier of Hessen-Nassau; thence southwards along the center of the navigable channel of the River Rhine to the point where it leaves Hessen-Darmstadt; thence along the western frontier of Baden to the point where this frontier becomes the Franco-German frontier will be occupied by armed forces of the United States of America."

3. The following additional paragraph will be inserted after the description of the South-Western Zone:—

"For the purpose of facilitating communications between the South-Western Zone and the sea, the Commander-in-Chief of the United States forces in the South-Western Zone will

(a) exercise such control of the ports of Bremen and Bremerhaven and the necessary staging areas in the vicinity thereof as may be agreed hereafter by the United Kingdom and United States military authorities to be necessary to meet his requirements;

(b) enjoy such transit facilities through the North-Western Zone as may be agreed hereafter by the United Kingdom and United States military authorities to be necessary to meet his requirements."

4. At the end of the description of the North-Western part of "Greater Berlin" given in paragraph 2 of the above-mentioned Protocol, insert the following words:—

"the United Kingdom"

5. At the end of the description of the Southern part of "Greater Berlin" given in paragraph 2 of the above-mentioned Protocol, insert the following words:—

"the United States of America"

6. In the English text of the sub-paragraph in paragraph 2 of the above-mentioned Protocol beginning with the words "The frontiers of States (Länder) and Provinces," the words "descriptions to the zones" will read "descriptions of the zones." . . .

DOCUMENT 7

CHURCHILL–STALIN MEETING AT MOSCOW, OCTOBER 9, 1944: ATTEMPTED DIVISION OF THE BALKANS

When Winston Churchill arrived in Moscow in October, 1944, he sought to settle the question of spheres of influence in the Balkans. Stalin agreed, but the United States later refused to be bound by the arrangement.

We alighted at Moscow on the afternoon of October 9, and were received very heartily and with full ceremonial by Molotov and many high Russian personages. This time we were lodged in Moscow itself, with every care and comfort. I had one small, perfectly appointed house, and Anthony another near by. We were glad to dine alone together and rest. At ten o'clock that night we held our first important meeting in the Kremlin. There were only Stalin, Molotov,

---

Winston Churchill, *Triumph and Tragedy* (Boston, 1953), 226–228.

Eden, and I, with Major Birse and Pavlov as interpreters. It was agreed to invite the Polish Prime Minister, M. Romer, the Foreign Minister, and M. Grabski, a grey-bearded and aged academician of much charm and quality, to Moscow at once. I telegraphed accordingly to M. Mikolajczyk that we were expecting him and his friends for discussions with the Soviet Government and ourselves, as well as with the Lublin Polish Committee. I made it clear that refusal to come to take part in the conversations would amount to a definite rejection of our advice and would relieve us from further responsibility towards the London Polish Government.

The moment was apt for business, so I said, "Let us settle about our affairs in the Balkans. Your armies are in Rumania and Bulgaria. We have interests, missions, and agents there. Don't let us get at cross-pusposes in small ways. So far as Britain and Russia are concerned, how would it do for you to have ninety per cent predominance in Rumania, for us to have ninety per cent of the say in Greece, and go fifty-fifty about Yugoslavia?" While this was being translated I wrote out on a half-sheet of paper:

Rumania	
Russia	90%
The others	10%
Greece	
Great Britain	90%
(in accord with U.S.A.)	
Russia	10%
Yugoslavia	50–50%
Hungary	50–50%
Bulgaria	
Russia	75%
The others	25%

I pushed this across to Stalin, who had by then heard the translation. There was a slight pause. Then he took his blue pencil and made a large tick upon it, and passed it back to us. It was all settled in no more time than it takes to set down.

Of course we had long and anxiously considered our point, and were only dealing with immediate war-time arrangements. All larger questions were reserved on both sides for what we then hoped would be a peace table when the war was won.

After this there was a long silence. The pencilled paper lay in the centre of the table. At length I said, "Might it not be thought rather cynical if it seemed we had disposed of these issues, so fateful to millions of people, in such an offhand manner? Let us burn the paper." "No, you keep it," said Stalin.

I also raised the question of Germany, and it was agreed that our two Foreign Ministers, together with Mr. Harriman, should go into it. I told Stalin that the Americans would be outlining to him during the course of our future discussions their plan of operations in the Pacific for 1945.

We then sent a joint message to Roosevelt on our first talk.

DOCUMENT 8

PROTOCOL OF PROCEEDINGS OF THE CRIMEA CONFERENCE, FEBRUARY 4–11, 1945

At the Yalta conference, the three principal allied leaders attempted to settle the issues which had arisen between them. The West granted economic and territorial concessions to Russia in Europe and Asia; the Soviets, in turn, promised to enter the war against Japan within three months after the defeat of Germany and signed the Declaration on Liberated Europe. The three powers agreed to give territorial compensation in the north and west to Poland, where they provided for the establishment of a government of national unity. Germany's future was left vague, although the Russians received promises of reparations in labor and kind. Finally, all three pledged cooperation in the United Nations. Only portions of the protocol were made public at the time; the agreement on the Far East was not published until February 11, 1946, and the full protocol was not released by the United States until March 24, 1947.

The Crimea Conference of the Heads of the Governments of the United States of America, the United Kingdom, and the Union of Soviet Socialist Republics which took place from February 4th to 11th came to the following conclusions.

Foreign Relations of the United States: *The Conferences at Malta and Yalta*, Department of State Publication 6199 (Washington, 1955), 975–982, 984.

I. WORLD ORGANIZATION

It was decided:

(1) that a United Nations Conference on the proposed world organisation should be summoned for Wednesday, 25th April, 1945, and should be held in the United States of America.

(2) the Nations to be invited to this Conference should be:

(*a*) the United Nations as they existed on the 8th February, 1945 and

(*b*) such of the Associated Nations as have declared war on the common enemy by 1st March, 1945. (For this purpose by the term "Associated Nation" was meant the eight Associated Nations and Turkey). When the Conference on World Organization is held, the delegates of the United Kingdom and United States of America will support a proposal to admit to original membership two Soviet Socialist Republics, i.e. the Ukraine and White Russia.

(3) that the United States Government on behalf of the Three Powers should consult the Government of China and the French Provisional Government in regard to the decisions taken at the present Conference concerning the proposed World Organization.

(4) that the text of the invitation to be issued to all the nations which would take part in the United Nations Conference should be as follows:

INVITATION

"The Government of the United States of America, on behalf of itself and of the Governments of the United Kingdom, the Union of Soviet Socialist Republics, and the Republic of China and of the Provisional Government of the French Republic, invite the Government of ————— to send representatives to a Conference of the United Nations to be held on 25th April, 1945, or soon thereafter, at San Francisco in the United States of America to prepare a Charter for a General International Organization for the maintenance of international peace and security.

"The above named governments suggest that the Conference consider as affording a basis for such a Charter the Proposals for the Establishment of a General International Organization, which were made public last October as a result of the Dumbarton Oaks Conference, and which have now been supplemented by the following provisions for Section C of Chapter VI:

" 'C. *Voting*

'1. Each member of the Security Council should have one vote.

'2. Decisions of the Security Council on procedural matters should be made by an affirmative vote of seven members.

'3. Decisions of the Security Council on all other matters should be made by an affirmative vote of seven members including the concurring votes of the permanent members; provided that, in decisions under Chapter VIII, Section A and under the second sentence of paragraph 1 of Chapter VIII, Section C, a party to a dispute should abstain from voting.'

"Further information as to arrangements will be transmitted subsequently.

"In the event that the Government of ————— desires in advance of the Conference to present views or comments concerning the proposals, the Government of the United States of America will be pleased to transmit such views and comments to the other participating Governments."

TERRITORIAL TRUSTEESHIP

It was agreed that the five Nations which will have permanent seats on the Security Council should consult each other prior to the United Nations Conference on the question of territorial trusteeship.

The acceptance of this recommendation is subject to its being made clear that territorial trusteeship will only apply to (*a*) existing mandates of the League of Nations; (*b*) territories detached from the enemy as a result of the present war; (*c*) any other territory which might voluntarily be placed under trusteeship; and (*d*) no discussion of actual territories is contemplated at the forthcoming United Nations Conference or in the preliminary consultations, and it will be a matter for subsequent agreement which territories within the above categories will be placed under trusteeship.

II. DECLARATION ON LIBERATED EUROPE

The following declaration has been approved:

"The Premier of the Union of Soviet Socialist Republics, the Prime Minister of the United Kingdom and the President of the

United States of America have consulted with each other in the common interests of the peoples of their countries and those of liberated Europe. They jointly declare their mutual agreement to concert during the temporary period of instability in liberated Europe the policies of their three governments in assisting the peoples liberated from the domination of Nazi Germany and the peoples of the former Axis satellite states of Europe to solve by democratic means their pressing political and economic problems.

"The establishment of order in Europe and the re-building of national economic life must be achieved by processes which will enable the liberated peoples to destroy the last vestiges of Nazism and Fascism and to create democratic institutions of their own choice. This is a principle of the Atlantic Charter—the right of all peoples to choose the form of government under which they will live—the restoration of sovereign rights and self-government to those peoples who have been forcibly deprived of them by the aggressor nations.

"To foster the conditions in which the liberated peoples may exercise these rights, the three governments will jointly assist the people in any European liberated state or former Axis satellite state in Europe where in their judgment conditions require (*a*) to establish conditions of internal peace; (*b*) to carry out emergency measures for the relief of distressed peoples; (*c*) to form interim governmental authorities broadly representative of all democratic elements in the population and pledged to the earliest possible establishment through free elections of governments responsive to the will of the people; and (*d*) to facilitate where necessary the holding of such elections.

"The three governments will consult the other United Nations and provisional authorities or other governments in Europe when matters of direct interest to them are under consideration.

"When, in the opinion of the three governments, conditions in any European liberated state or any former Axis satellite state in Europe make such action necessary, they will immediately consult together on the measures necessary to discharge the joint responsibilities set forth in this declaration.

"By this declaration we reaffirm our faith in the principles of the Atlantic Charter, our pledge in the Declaration by the United Nations, and our determination to build in co-operation with other peace-loving nations world order under law, dedicated to peace, security, freedom and general well-being of all mankind.

"In issuing this declaration, the Three Powers express the hope that the Provisional Government of the French Republic may be associated with them in the procedure suggested."

III. DISMEMBERMENT OF GERMANY

It was agreed that Article 12(*a*) of the Surrender Terms for Germany should be amended to read as follows:

"The United Kingdom, the United States of America and the Union of Soviet Socialist Republics shall possess supreme authority with respect to Germany. In the exercise of such authority they will take such steps, including the complete disarmament, demilitarisation and the dismemberment of Germany as they deem requisite for future peace and security." . . .

IV. ZONE OF OCCUPATION FOR THE FRENCH AND CONTROL COUNCIL FOR GERMANY.

It was agreed that a zone in Germany, to be occupied by the French Forces, should be allocated to France. This zone would be formed out of the British and American zones and its extent would be settled by the British and Americans in consultation with the French Provisional Government.

It was also agreed that the French Provisional Government should be invited to become a member of the Allied Control Council for Germany.

V. REPARATION

The following protocol has been approved:

1. Germany must pay in kind for the losses caused by her to the Allied nations in the course of the war. Reparations are to be received in the first instance by those countries which have borne the main burden of the war, have suffered the heaviest losses and have organized victory over the enemy.

2. Reparation in kind is to be exacted from Germany in three following forms:

a) Removals within 2 years from the surrender of Germany or the cessation of organized resistance from the national wealth of Germany located on the territory of Germany herself as well as outside her territory (equipment, machine-tools, ships, rolling stock, German

investments abroad, shares of industrial, transport and other enter-
prises in Germany etc.), these removals to be carried out chiefly for
the purpose of destroying the war potential of Germany.

b) Annual deliveries of goods from current production for a period
to be fixed.

c) Use of German labour.

3. For the working out on the above principles of a detailed plan
for exaction of reparation from Germany an Allied Reparation Commission will be set up in Moscow. It will consist of three representatives—one from the Union of Soviet Socialist Republics, one from
the United Kingdom and one from the United States of America.

4. With regard to the fixing of the total sum of the reparation as
well as the distribution of it among the countries which suffered from
the German aggression the Soviet and American delegations agreed
as follows:

"The Moscow Reparation Commission should take in its initial
studies as a basis for discussion the suggestion of the Soviet Government that the total sum of the reparation in accordance with the
points (*a*) and (*b*) of the paragraph 2 should be 20 billion dollars
and that 50% of it should go to the Union of Soviet Socialist Republics."

The British delegation was of the opinion that pending consideration of the reparation question by the Moscow Reparation Commission no figures of reparation should be mentioned.

The above Soviet-American proposal has been passed to the Moscow Reparation Commission as one of the proposals to be considered
by the Commission.

VI. MAJOR WAR CRIMINALS

The Conference agreed that the question of the major war criminals should be the subject of enquiry by the three Foreign Secretaries
for report in due course after the close of the Conference.

VII. POLAND

The following Declaration on Poland was agreed by the Conference:

"A new situation has been created in Poland as a result of her
complete liberation by the Red Army. This calls for the establish-

ment of a Polish Provisional Government which can be more broadly based than was possible before the recent liberation of the Western part of Poland. The Provisional Government which is now functioning in Poland should therefore be reorganised on a broader democratic basis with the inclusion of democratic leaders from Poland itself and from Poles abroad. This new Government should then be called the Polish Provisional Government of National Unity.

"M. Molotov, Mr. Harriman and Sir A. Clark Kerr are authorised as a commission to consult in the first instance in Moscow with members of the present Provisional Government and with other Polish democratic leaders from within Poland and from abroad, with a view to the reorganisation of the present Government along the above lines. This Polish Provisional Government of National Unity shall be pledged to the holding of free and unfettered elections as soon as possible on the basis of universal suffrage and secret ballot. In these elections all democratic and anti-Nazi parties shall have the right to take part and to put forward candidates.

"When a Polish Provisional Government of National Unity has been properly formed in conformity with the above, the Government of the U.S.S.R., which now maintains diplomatic relations with the present Provisional Government of Poland, and the Government of the United Kingdom and the Government of the U.S.A. will establish diplomatic relations with the new Polish Provisional Government of National Unity, and will exchange Ambassadors by whose reports the respective Governments will be kept informed about the situation in Poland.

"The three Heads of Government consider that the Eastern frontier of Poland should follow the Curzon Line with digressions from it in some regions of five to eight kilometres in favour of Poland. They recognise that Poland must receive substantial accessions of territory in the North and West. They feel that the opinion of the new Polish Provisional Government of National Unity should be sought in due course on the extent of these accessions and that the final delimitation of the Western frontier of Poland should thereafter await the Peace Conference."

VIII. YUGOSLAVIA

It was agreed to recommend to Marshal Tito and to Dr. Subasic:
(*a*) that the Tito-Subasic Agreement should immediately be put

into effect and a new Government formed on the basis of the Agreement.

(*b*) that as soon as the new Government has been formed it should declare:

(i) that the Anti-Fascist Assembly of National Liberation (AUNOJ) will be extended to include members of the last Yugoslav Skupstina who have not compromised themselves by collaboration with the enemy, thus forming a body to be known as a temporary Parliament and

(ii) that legislative acts passed by the Anti-Fascist Assemb[l]y of National Liberation (AUNOJ) will be subject to subsequent ratification by a Constituent Assembly;

and that this statement should be published in the communiqué of the Conference.

IX. ITALO-YUGOSLAV FRONTIER
ITALO-AUSTRIAN FRONTIER

Notes on these subjects were put in by the British delegation and the American and Soviet delegations agreed to consider them and give their views later.

X. YUGOSLAV-BULGARIAN RELATIONS

There was an exchange of views between the Foreign Secretaries on the question of the desirability of a Yugoslav-Bulgarian pact of alliance. The question at issue was whether a state still under an armistice regime could be allowed to enter into a treaty with another state. Mr. Eden suggested that the Bulgarian and Yugoslav Governments should be informed that this could not be approved. Mr. Stettinius suggested that the British and American Ambassadors should discuss the matter further with M. Molotov in Moscow. M. Molotov agreed with the proposal of Mr. Stettinius.

XI. SOUTH EASTERN EUROPE

The British Delegation put in notes for the consideration of their colleagues on the following subjects:

(*a*) the Control Commission in Bulgaria.

(*b*) Greek claims upon Bulgaria, more particularly with reference to reparations.

(*c*) Oil equipment in Roumania.

XII. IRAN

Mr. Eden, Mr. Stettinius and M. Molotov exchanged views on the situation in Iran. It was agreed that this matter should be pursued through the diplomatic channel.

XIII. MEETINGS OF THE THREE FOREIGN SECRETARIES

The Conference agreed that permanent machinery should be set up for consultation between the three Foreign Secretaries; they should meet as often as necessary, probably about every three or four months.

These meetings will be held in rotation in the three capitals, the first meeting being held in London.

XIV. THE MONTREUX CONVENTION AND THE STRAITS

It was agreed that at the next meeting of the three Foreign Secretaries to be held in London, they should consider proposals which it was understood the Soviet Government would put forward in relation to the Montreux Convention and report to their Governments. The Turkish Government should be informed at the appropriate moment.

The foregoing Protocol was approved and signed by the three Foreign Secretaries at the Crimean Conference, February 11, 1945.

E. R. STETTINIUS, JR.
V. MOLOTOV
ANTHONY EDEN

Agreement Regarding Entry of the Soviet Union Into the War
Against Japan

TOP SECRET

AGREEMENT

The leaders of the three Great Powers—the Soviet Union, the United States of America and Great Britain—have agreed that in two or three months after Germany has surrendered and the war in Europe has terminated the Soviet Union shall enter into the war against Japan on the side of the Allies on condition that:

1. The *status quo* in Outer-Mongolia (The Mongolian People's Republic) shall be preserved;

2. The former rights of Russia violated by the treacherous attack of Japan in 1904 shall be restored, viz:

(*a*) the southern part of Sakhalin as well as all the islands adjacent to it shall be returned to the Soviet Union,

(*b*) the commercial port of Dairen shall be internationalized, the preeminent interests of the Soviet Union in this port being safeguarded and the lease of Port Arthur as a naval base of the U.S.S.R. restored,

(*c*) the Chinese-Eastern Railroad and the South-Manchurian Railroad which provides an outlet to Dairen shall be jointly operated by the establishment of a joint Soviet-Chinese Company it being understood that the preeminent interests of the Soviet Union shall be safeguarded and that China shall retain full sovereignty in Manchuria;

3. The Kuril islands shall be handed over to the Soviet Union.

It is understood, that the agreement concerning Outer-Mongolia and the ports and railroads referred to above will require concurrence of Generalissimo Chiang Kai-Shek. The President will take measures in order to obtain this concurrence on advice from Marshal Stalin.

The Heads of the three Great Powers have agreed that these claims of the Soviet Union shall be unquestionably fulfilled after Japan has been defeated.

For its part the Soviet Union expresses its readiness to conclude with the National Government of China a pact of friendship and alliance between the U.S.S.R. and China in order to render assistance to China with its armed forces for the purpose of liberating China from the Japanese yoke.

I. STALIN
FRANKLIN D. ROOSEVELT
WINSTON S. CHURCHILL

FEBRUARY 11, 1945.

TWO

Origins: Failure of Cooperation

The strained wartime cooperation between the Soviets and the Western allies came to an end when victory was in sight. As early as December, 1944, British troops had to intervene to prevent the overthrow of the Greek government by Communist elements warring upon it. And although the Russians had agreed to the democratic principles of the Declaration on Liberated Europe, they soon showed that they had no intention of living up to them. The ink was hardly dry on the Yalta accords when the Soviets toppled the government of Rumania. Communist regimes were gradually established all over Eastern Europe, even in Poland, where no Western protests sufficed to protect the opposition, bring about free elections, or safeguard fundamental human rights. On the other hand, when German officers attempted to arrange for negotiations for a surrender with Western representatives in Switzerland, Stalin reacted with such ill grace that even President Roosevelt became disillusioned. Two weeks later he was dead, and Harry S. Truman, his successor, was left to deal with a rapidly deteriorating situation.

The following months brought little improvement. Winston Churchill sought to induce Stalin to honor his pledges concerning Poland, and when these efforts failed, the Prime Minister suggested that, pending further negotiations, Western troops remain in East Germany instead of withdrawing to previously defined zones of occupation. President Truman, however, refused. Although he had terminated lend-lease to Russia immediately after the end of the war with Germany, he was unwilling to risk a complete break with the Soviets while Japan remained undefeated. Occupation zones were worked out for Austria; France received a sector of her own, and arrangements were made for Western entry into Berlin and Vienna. The allied leaders met for the last time at Potsdam, but although the conference seemed successful, the differences between them were so great that in effect only a series of makeshift agreements were concluded, largely postponing crucial issues. These arrangements, by and large, provided the setting for the period of the Cold War which followed.

DOCUMENT 9

PARLIAMENTARY DISCUSSION OF BRITISH INTERVENTION IN GREECE, DECEMBER, 1944

After British forces liberated Greece in September and October, 1944, the Communist controlled E.A.M. and its military arm, E.L.A.S., attempted to overthrow the coalition government of the country by force. British intervention led to a debate on the subject in the House of Commons.

Dr. Haden Guest (*by Private Notice*) asked the Prime Minister whether he can give the House any information on the occurrences in Athens on Sunday, 3rd December, when the Greek police are reported to have fired on a demonstration of children and youths, and what are the casualties, in killed and wounded?

The Prime Minister: So far as has been ascertained, the facts are as follow: The Greek organisation called E.A.M. had announced their intention of holding a demonstration on 3rd December. The Greek Government at first authorised this but withdrew their permission when E.A.M. called for a general strike to begin on 2nd December. The strike, in fact, came into force early on 3rd December. Later in the morning the E.A.M. demonstration formed up and moved to the principal square of Athens, in spite of the Government ban. On the evidence so far available I am not prepared to say who started the firing which then took place. The police suffered one fatal casualty and had three men wounded. The latest authentic reports give the demonstrators' casualties as 11 killed and 60 wounded. The demonstration continued during the afternoon but there was no further shooting, and by 4.30 the crowd had dispersed and tranquility was restored.

It is deplorable that an event like this should take place in Athens scarcely a month after the city's liberation and feeding. Greece is faced with the most desperate economic and financial problems apart from the civil war which we are trying to stop. We and our American Allies are doing our utmost to give assistance and our troops are acting to prevent bloodshed. [HON. MEMBERS: "Oh," and "Hear, hear."] Sometimes it is necessary to use force to prevent greater bloodshed. The main burden falls on us, and the responsibility is within our sphere. That is the military sphere agreed upon with our principal Allies. Our plans will not succeed unless the Greek Government and the whole Greek people exert themselves on their own behalf. If the damage of four years of war and enemy occupation is to be repaired, and if Greek life and economy are to be rebuilt, internal stability must be maintained and, pending a general election under fair conditions, the authority of the constitutional Greek Government must be accepted and enforced throughout the country. The armed forces must be dependent on the Greek Government. No Government can have a sure foundation so long as there are private armies owing allegiance to a group, a party or an ideology instead of to the State and the nation.

Although these facts should be clear to all, the Left Wing and Communist Ministers have resigned from the Greek Government at this dangerous crisis rather than implement measures, to which they had already agreed, for the replacement of the E.A.M. police and guerrillas by regular national services.

Mr. Gallacher: Why did they resign?

The Prime Minister: I say they have resigned. I am stating facts in answer to the Question. I thought the House would rather like to have a full answer. In addition, the E.A.M. leaders have called a general strike, which is for the time being preventing the bread which we and the Americans are providing reaching the mouths of the hungry population whom we are trying to feed.

Our own position, though as I have said it is a burden, is extremely clear. Whether the Greek people form themselves into a monarchy or a republic is for their decision; whether they have a Government of Left or Right is a matter for them. But until they are in a position to decide, we shall not hesitate to use the considerable British Army now in Greece, and being reinforced, to see that law and order are maintained. It is our belief that in this course His Majesty's Government have the support of an overwhelming majority of the Greek people. Their gaping need is to receive relief for their immediate requirements and conditions which give them a chance of earning a livelihood. In both of these ways we wish to help them, and we are working with experts, financial and otherwise, to do so; but we cannot do so if the tommy guns which were provided for use against the Germans are now used in an attempt to impose a Communist dictatorship without the people being able to express their wishes.

Mr. Pethick-Lawrence: While appreciating the great delicacy of the situation, I desire to ask the Prime Minister two questions arising out of his statement. Is he aware of the very grave anxiety felt in all sections in this country with regard to what has taken place, and will he undertake to keep the House informed from time to time in the immediate future so that we may know what the situation is from day to day? Will he also take care that the Government watch their step in this matter, so that their action in suppressing disorder shall not take the form of support of any one faction? . . .

Sir H. Williams: Are we not engaged in a Debate rather than asking questions?

The Prime Minister: The answer to the first part of the question is that the newspapers give full and continuous reports from Greece and, in the event of anything important occurring which is not public property, I shall always be ready to answer any questions. I have no other wish than to keep the House fully informed. I quite agree that we take a great responsibility in intervening to preserve law and order in this capital city which was so lately delivered by our troops from the power of the enemy. It would be very much easier for us to stand aside and allow everything to degenerate, as it would very quickly, into anarchy or a Communist dictatorship, but, having taken the position that we have, having entered Athens and brought food and made great efforts to restore its currency, and done our utmost to give it those conditions of peace and tranquility which will enable the Greek people as a whole to vote on their future, we do not feel that we should look back or take our hands from the plough. We shall certainly not be able to do so but we shall certainly take care that the Greek Government, which we are supporting—or perhaps acting in conjunction with would be a better expression, because General Scobie is for the moment in charge of order—is not used to fasten any rule of a faction—I think that is the word—on the Greek people. They will have the fullest opportunity of a free election. The Government of Mr. Papandreou three days ago represented all parties, including the Communists and E.A.M., whose representatives left suddenly on the eve of a quite evident attempt to overthrow the settled Government.

DOCUMENT 10

CHURCHILL'S ACCOUNT OF THE RUMANIAN CRISIS, FEBRUARY 27–MARCH 2, 1945

The Yalta agreements had hardly been signed when the Soviet Union furnished irrefutable evidence of its utter disregard for the Declaration on Liberated Europe by intervening in Rumania. The following consists of Churchill's account of these events.

On the very evening when I was speaking in the House of Commons upon the results of our labours at Yalta the first violation by the Russians both of the spirit and letter of our agreements took place in Rumania. We were all committed by the Declaration on Liberated Europe, so recently signed, to see that both free elections and democratic Governments were established in the countries occupied by Allied armies. On February 27 Vyshinsky, who had appeared in Bucharest without warning on the previous day, demanded an audience of King Michael and insisted that he should dismiss the all-party Government which had been formed after the royal *coup d'état* of August 1944 and had led to the expulsion of the Germans from Rumania. The young monarch, backed by his Foreign Minister, Visoianu, resisted these demands until the following day. Vyshinsky called again, and, brushing aside the King's request at least to be allowed to consult the leaders of the political parties, banged his fist

Churchill, *Triumph and Tragedy*, 419–420.

on the table, shouted for an immediate acquiescence, and walked out of the room, slamming the door. At the same time Soviet tanks and troops deployed in the streets of the capital, and on March 2 a Soviet-nominated Administration took office.

DOCUMENT 11

CORRESPONDENCE BETWEEN ROOSEVELT AND STALIN CONCERNING DIFFERENCES BETWEEN THEM, APRIL 1945

By March, 1945, it had become apparent to President Roosevelt that his policy of attempting to win Stalin's trust was not entirely successful. The Soviets' disregard of democratic procedures in eastern Europe and their violent reaction to exploratory talks concerning the surrender of German troops in Italy had created an atmosphere of tension between the two leaders. The following three letters between Roosevelt and Stalin are indicative of these developments.

Received on April 1, 1945

PERSONAL AND TOP SECRET FOR MARSHAL STALIN
FROM PRESIDENT ROOSEVELT

I cannot conceal from you the concern with which I view the developments of events of mutual interest since our fruitful meeting at Yalta. The decisions we reached there were good ones and have for the most part been welcomed with enthusiasm by the peoples of the world who saw in our ability to find a common basis of understanding the best pledge for a secure and peaceful world after this war. Precisely because of the hopes and expectations that these decisions raised, their fulfillment is being followed with the closest attention. We have no right to let them be disappointed. So far there has been a discouraging lack of progress made in the carrying out, which the world expects, of the political decisions which we reached at the conference particularly those relating to the Polish question. I am frankly puzzled as to why this should be and must tell you that I do

Ministry of Foreign Affairs of the Soviet Union: *Correspondence Between the Chairman of the Council of Ministers of the Union of Soviet Socialist Republics and the Presidents of the United States and the Prime Ministers of Great Britain During the Great Patriotic War* (Moscow, 1957), II, 201–205, 205–208 (hereafter cited as *Stalin Correspondence*).

not fully understand in many respects the apparent indifferent attitude of your Government. Having understood each other so well at Yalta I am convinced that the three of us can and will clear away any obstacles which have developed since then. I intend, therefore, in this message to lay before you with complete frankness the problem as I see it.

Although I have in mind primarily the difficulties which the Polish negotiations have encountered, I must make a brief mention of our agreement embodied in the Declaration on Liberated Europe. I frankly cannot understand why the recent developments in Roumania should be regarded as not falling within the terms of that Agreement. I hope you will find time personally to examine the correspondence between our Governments on this subject.

However, the part of our agreements at Yalta which has aroused the greatest popular interest and is the most urgent relates to the Polish question. You are aware of course that the commission which we set up has made no progress. I feel this is due to the interpretation which your Government is placing upon the Crimea decisions. In order that there shall be no misunderstanding I set forth below my interpretations of the points of the Agreement which are pertinent to the difficulties encountered by the Commission in Moscow.

In the discussions that have taken place so far your Government appears to take the position that the new Polish Provisional Government of National Unity which we agreed should be formed should be little more than a continuation of the present Warsaw Government. I cannot reconcile this either with our agreement or our discussions. While it is true that the Lublin Government is to be reorganized and its members play a prominent role, it is to be done in such a fashion as to bring into being a new government. This point is clearly brought out in several places in the text of the Agreement. I must make it quite plain to you that any such solution which would result in a thinly disguised continuance of the present Warsaw régime would be unacceptable and would cause the people of the United States to regard the Yalta agreement as having failed.

It is equally apparent that for the same reason the Warsaw Government cannot under the Agreement claim the right to select or reject what Poles are to be brought to Moscow by the Commission for consultation. Can we not agree that it is up to the Commission to select the Polish leaders to come to Moscow to consult in the first instance and invitations be sent out accordingly. If this could be done I see no great objection to having the Lublin group come first in order that they may be fully acquainted with the agreed interpretation of the Yalta decisions on this point. It is of course understood that if the Lublin group come first no arrangements would be made independently with them before the arrival of the other Polish leaders called for consultation. In order to facilitate the agreement the Commission might first of all select a small but representative group of Polish leaders who could suggest other names for the consideration of the Commission. We have not and would not bar or veto any candidate for consultation which Mr Molotov might propose, being confident that he would not suggest any Poles who would be inimical to the intent of the Crimea decision. I feel that it is not too much to ask that my Ambassador be accorded the same confidence and that any candidate for consultation presented by any one of the Commission be accepted by the others in good faith. It is obvious to me that if the right of the Commission to select these Poles is limited or shared with the Warsaw Government the very foundation on which our agreement rests would be destroyed.

While the foregoing are the immediate obstacles which in my opinion have prevented our Commission from making any progress in this vital matter, there are two other suggestions which were not in the agreement but nevertheless have a very important bearing on the result we all seek. Neither of these suggestions has been as yet accepted by your Government. I refer to:

(1) That there should be the maximum of political tranquility in Poland and that dissident groups should cease any measures and counter-measures against each other. That we should respectively use our influence to that end seems to me eminently reasonable.

(2) It would also seem entirely natural in view of the responsibilities placed upon them by the Agreement that representatives of the American and British members of the Commission should be permitted to visit Poland. As you will recall Mr Molotov himself suggested this at an early meeting of the Commission and only subsequently withdrew it.

I wish I could convey to you how important it is for the successful development of our program of international collaboration that this Polish question be settled fairly and speedily. If this is not done all of the difficulties and dangers to Allied unity which we had so much in mind in reaching our decisions at the Crimea will face us in an even more acute form. You are, I am sure, aware that the genuine popular support in the United States is required to carry out any government policy, foreign or domestic. The American people make up their own mind and no government action can change it. I mention this fact because the last sentence of your message about Mr. Molotov's attendance at San Francisco made me wonder whether you give full weight to this factor.

PERSONAL, MOST SECRET

FROM MARSHAL J. V. STALIN
TO THE PRESIDENT, MR. ROOSEVELT

I am in receipt of your message on the Berne talks.

You are quite right in saying, with reference to the talks between the Anglo-American and German Commands in Berne or elsewhere, that "the matter now stands in an atmosphere of regrettable apprehension and mistrust."

You affirm that so far no negotiations have been entered into. Apparently you are not fully informed. As regards my military colleagues, they, on the basis of information in their possession, are sure that negotiations did take place and that they ended in an agreement with the Germans, whereby the German Commander on the Western Front, Marshal Kesselring, is to open the front to the Anglo-American troops and let them move east, while the British and Americans have promised, in exchange, to ease the armistice terms for the Germans.

I think that my colleagues are not very far from the truth. If the countrary were the case the exclusion of representatives of the Soviet Command from the Berne talks would be inexplicable.

Nor can I account for the reticence of the British, who have left it to you to carry on a correspondence with me on this unpleasant matter, while they themselves maintain silence, although it is known that the initiative in the matter of the Berne negotiations belongs to the British.

I realize that there are certain advantages resulting to the Anglo-American troops from these separate negotiations in Berne or in some other place, seeing that the Anglo-American troops are enabled to advance into the heart of Germany almost without resistance; but why conceal this from the Russians, and why were the Russians, their Allies, not forewarned?

And so what we have at the moment is that the Germans on the Western Front have in fact ceased the war against Britain and America. At the same time they continue the war against Russia, the Ally of Britain and the U.S.A.

Clearly this situation cannot help preserve and promote trust between our countries.

I have already written in a previous message, and I think I must repeat, that I and my colleagues would never in any circumstances have taken such a hazardous step, for we realise that a momentary advantage, no matter how great, is overshadowed by the fundamental advantage of preserving and promoting trust between Allies.
April 3, 1945

Received on April 5, 1945

PERSONAL AND TOP SECRET FOR MARSHAL STALIN
FROM PRESIDENT ROOSEVELT

I have received with astonishment your message of April 3 containing an allegation that arrangements which were made between Field Marshals Alexander and Kesselring at Berne "permitted the Anglo-American troops to advance to the East and the Anglo-Americans promised in return to ease for the Germans the peace terms."

In my previous messages to you in regard to the attempts made in Berne to arrange a conference to discuss a surrender of the German army in Italy I have told you that: (1) No negotiations were held in Berne, (2) The meeting had no political implications whatever, (3) In any surrender of the enemy army in Italy there would be no violation of our agreed principle of unconditional surrender, (4) Soviet officers would be welcomed at any meeting that might be arranged to discuss surrender.

For the advantage of our common war effort against Germany, which today gives excellent promise of an early success in a disintegration of the German armies, I must continue to assume that you have the same high confidence in my truthfulness and reliability that I have always had in yours.

I have also a full appreciation of the effect your gallant army has had in making possible a crossing of the Rhine by the forces under

General Eisenhower and the effect that your forces will have hereafter on the eventual collapse of the German resistance to our combined attacks.

I have complete confidence in General Eisenhower and know that he certainly would inform me before entering into any agreement with the Germans. He is instructed to demand and will demand unconditional surrender of enemy troops that may be defeated on his front. Our advances on the Western Front are due to military action. Their speed has been attributable mainly to the terrific impact of our air power resulting in destruction of German communications, and to the fact that Eisenhower was able to cripple the bulk of the German forces on the Western Front while they were still west of the Rhine.

I am certain that there were no negotiations in Berne at any time and I feel that your information to that effect must have come from German sources which have made persistent efforts to create dissension between us in order to escape in some measure responsibility for their war crimes. If that was Wolff's purpose in Berne, your message proves that he has had some success.

With a confidence in your belief in my personal reliability and in my determination to bring about, together with you, an unconditional surrender of the Nazis, it is astonishing that a belief seems to have reached the Soviet Government that I have entered into an agreement with the enemy without first obtaining your full agreement.

Finally I would say this, it would be one of the great tragedies of history if at the very moment of the victory, now within our grasp, such distrust, such lack of faith should prejudice the entire undertaking after the colossal losses of life, material and treasure involved.

Frankly I cannot avoid a feeling of bitter resentment toward your informers, whoever they are, for such vile misrepresentations of my actions or those of my trusted subordinates.

DOCUMENT 12

ROOSEVELT'S NOTE TO CHURCHILL, APRIL 12, 1945

After his exchanges with Stalin concerning the difficulties with the Soviets, President Roosevelt wrote the following letter to Prime Minister Churchill. A few hours later, the President was dead.

Churchill, *Triumph and Tragedy*, 454.

President Roosevelt to Prime Minister   12 Apr. 45

I would minimize the general Soviet problem as much as possible, because these problems, in one form or another, seem to arise every day, and most of them straighten out, as in the case of the Berne meeting.

We must be firm however, and our course thus far is correct.

DOCUMENT 13

CORRESPONDENCE BETWEEN PRIME MINISTER CHURCH-ILL AND MARSHAL STALIN CONCERNING THEIR DIFFER-ENCES, APRIL–MAY, 1945

The differences which had developed between the allies in the spring of 1945 were many, but the main problem confronting them concerned Poland. Soviet refusals to accord elementary democratic rights to the Poles, arrests of members of the underground who had come to Moscow to negotiate—these and other Soviet acts created indignation in the West. In a frank exchange of letters, Churchill and Stalin discussed the differences between them. The Soviet version reprinted here contains slight editorial variations from the excerpts in Churchill's memoirs, including a change of dates from April 29 to April 28 for the first, and from May 5 to May 4, 1945, for the second letter.

PERSONAL AND MOST SECRET MESSAGE
FOR MARSHAL STALIN FROM MR. CHURCHILL

I thank you for your message of April 24th. I have been much distressed at the misunderstanding that has grown up between us on the Crimea agreement about Poland. I certainly went to Yalta with the hope that both the London and Lublin Polish Governments would be swept away and that a new government would be formed from among Poles of goodwill, among whom members of M. Bierut's government would be prominent. But you did not like this plan, and we and the Americans agreed, therefore, that there was to be no sweeping away of the Bierut government but that instead it should become a "new" government "reorganised on a broader democratic

Stalin Correspondence, I, 339–343, 347–348.

basis with the inclusion of democratic leaders from Poland itself and from Poles abroad." For this purpose, M. Molotov and the two Ambassadors were to sit together in Moscow and try to bring into being such a government by consultations with members of the present Provisional Government and with other Polish democratic leaders from within Poland and from abroad.

2. The Commission then would have to set to work to select Poles who were to come for the consultations. We tried in each case to find representative men, and in this we were careful to exclude what we thought were extreme people unfriendly to Russia. We did not select for our list anyone at present in the London Polish Government, but three good men, namely M. Mikolajczyk, M. Stanczyk and M. Grabski, who went into opposition to the London Polish Government because they did not like its attitude towards Russia, and in particular its refusal to accept the eastern frontier which you and I agreed upon, now so long ago, and which I was the first man outside the Soviet Government to proclaim to the world as just and fair, together with compensations, etc., in the West and North. It is true that M. Mikolajczyk at that time still hoped for Lvov, but as you know he has now publicly abandoned that claim.

3. Our names for those from inside and outside Poland were put forward in the same spirit of helpfulness by the Americans and ourselves. The first thing the British complained of is that after nine weeks of discussion on the Commission at Moscow, and any amount of telegrams between our three Governments, not the least progress has been made, because M. Molotov has steadily refused in the Commission to give an opinion about the Poles we have mentioned, so that not one of them has been allowed to come even to a preliminary round table discussion. Please observe that these names were put forward not as necessarily to be members of a reorganised Polish Government but simply to come for the round table talk provided for in the Crimea declaration, out of which it was intended to bring about the formation of a united provisional government, representative of the main elements of Polish life and prepared to work on friendly terms with the Soviet Government, and also of a kind which we and all the world could recognise. That was and still is our desire. This provisional government was then, according to our joint decision at the Crimea, to pledge itself to hold "free and unfettered elections as soon as possible on the basis of universal suffrage and secret

ballot" in which "all democratic and anti-Nazi parties shall have the right to take part and put forward candidates." Alas! none of this has been allowed to move forward.

4. In your paragraph 1 you speak of accepting "the Yugoslav precedent as a model for Poland." You have always wished that our private personal series of telegrams should be frank and outspoken. I must say at once that the two cases are completely different. In the case of Poland, the three Powers reached agreement about how we should arrange the emergence of a new government. This was to be by means of consultations before our Commission between representatives of the Bierut government and democratic Polish leaders from inside and outside Poland. In the case of Yugoslavia there was nothing of this kind. You seem now to be proposing, after your representative on the Moscow Polish Commission has made it impossible to start the conversations provided for in our agreement, that the agreed procedure should be abandoned. Thus we British feel that after all this time absolutely no headway has been made towards forming a "new" and "reorganised" government while on the contrary the Soviet Government have made a twenty years' treaty with the present Provisional Government under M. Bierut although it remains neither new nor reorganised. We have the feeling that it is we who have been dictated to and brought up against a stone wall upon matters which we sincerely believed were settled in a spirit of friendly comradeship in the Crimea.

5. I must also say that the way things have worked out in Yugoslavia certainly does not give me the feeling of a fifty-fifty interest as between our countries. Marshal Tito has become a complete dictator. He has proclaimed that his prime loyalties are to the Soviet Union. Although he allowed members of the Royal Yugoslav Government to enter his government they only number six as against twenty-five of his own nominees. We have the impression that they are not taken into consultation on matters of high policy and that it is becoming a one-party régime. However, I have not made any complaint or comment about all this, and both at Yalta and at other times have acquiesced in the settlement which has been reached in Yugoslavia. I do not complain of any action you have taken there in spite of my misgivings and I hope it will work out smoothly and make Yugoslavia a prosperous and free people friendly to both Russia and ourselves.

6. We could not however accept "the Yugoslav model" as a guide to what should happen in Poland. Neither we nor the Americans have any military or special interest in Poland. All we seek in material things is to be treated in the regular way between friendly States. Here we are all shocked that you should think we would work for a Polish Government hostile to the U.S.S.R. This is the opposite of our policy. But it was on account of Poland that the British went to war with Germany in 1939. We saw in the Nazi treatment of Poland a symbol of Hitler's vile and wicked lust of conquest and subjugation, and his invasion of Poland was the spark that fired the mine. The British people do not, as is sometimes thought, go to war for calculation, but for sentiment. They had a feeling, which grew up in the years, that with all Hitler's encroachments and preparations he was a danger to our country and to the liberties which we prize in Europe and when after Munich he broke his word so shamefully about Czechoslovakia even the extremely peace-loving Chamberlain gave our guarantee against Hitler to Poland. When that guarantee was invoked by the German invasion of Poland the whole nation went to war with Hitler, unprepared as we were. There was a flame in the hearts of men like that which swept your people in their noble defense of their country from a treacherous, brutal, and as at one time it almost seemed, overwhelming German attack. This British flame burns still among all classes and parties in this island and in its self-governing Dominions, and they can never feel this war will have ended rightly unless Poland has a fair deal in the full sense of sovereignty, independence and freedom on a basis of friendship with Russia. It was on this that I thought we had agreed at Yalta.

7. Side by side with this strong sentiment for the rights of Poland, which I believe is shared in at least as strong a degree throughout the United States, there has grown up throughout the English-speaking world a very warm and deep desire to be friends on equal and honourable terms with the mighty Russian Soviet Republic and to work with you, making allowances for our different systems of thought and government, in the long and bright years for all the world which we three Powers alone can make together. I, who in my years of great responsibility, have worked methodically for this unity, will certainly continue to do so by every means in my power, and in particular I can assure you that we in Great Britain would not work for or tolerate a Polish Government unfriendly to Russia. Neither

could we recognise a Polish Government that did not truly correspond to the description in our joint declaration at Yalta with proper regard for the rights of the individual as we understand these matters in the Western world.

8. With regard to your reference to Greece and Belgium, I recognise the consideration which you gave me when we had to intervene with heavy armed forces to quell the E.A.M.-E.L.A.S. attack upon the centre of government in Athens. We have given repeated instructions that your interest in Roumania and Bulgaria is to be recognised as predominant. We cannot however be excluded altogether, and we dislike being treated by your subordinates in these countries so differently from the kind manner in which we at the top are always treated by you. In Greece we seek nothing but her friendship, which is of long duration, and desire only her independence and integrity. But we have no intention of trying to decide whether she is to be a monarchy or a republic. Our only policy there is to restore matters to normal as quickly as possible and to hold fair and free elections, I hope within the next four or five months. These elections will decide the régime and later on the constitution. The will of the people expressed in conditions of freedom and universal franchise must prevail; that is our root principle. If the Greeks were to decide for a republic it would not affect our relations with them. We will use our influence with the Greek Government to invite Russian representatives to come and see freely what is going on in Greece, and at the elections I hope that there will be Russian, American and British Commissioners at large in the country to make sure that there is no intimidation or other frustration of freedom of choice of the people between the different parties who will be contending. After that our work in Greece may well be done.

9. As to Belgium we have no conditions to demand though naturally we should get disturbed if they started putting up V-weapons, etc., pointed at us, and we hope they will, under whatever form of government they adopt by popular decision, come into a general system of resistance to prevent Germany striking westward. Belgium, like Poland, is a theatre of war and corridor of communication, and everyone must recognise the force of these considerations, without which the great armies cannot operate.

10. As to your paragraph 3, it is quite true that about Poland we have reached a definite line of action with the Americans. This is be-

cause we agree naturally upon the subject, and both sincerely feel we have been rather ill-treated about the way the matter has been handled since the Crimea Conference. No doubt these things seem different when looked at from the opposite point of view. But we are absolutely agreed that the pledge we have given for a sovereign, free, independent Poland with a government fully and adequately representing all democratic elements among the Poles, is for us a matter of honour and duty. I do not think there is the slightest chance of any change in the attitude of our two Powers, and when we are agreed we are bound to say so. After all, we have joined with you, largely on my original initiative early in 1944, in proclaiming the Polish-Russian frontier which you desired, namely the Curzon Line including Lvov for Russia. We think you ought to meet us with regard to the other half of the policy which you equally with us have proclaimed, namely the sovereignty, independence and freedom of Poland, provided it is a Poland friendly to Russia. Therefore, His Majesty's Government cannot accept a government on the Yugoslav precedent in which there would be four representatives of the present Warsaw Provisional Government to every one representing the other democratic elements. There ought to be a proper balance and a proper distribution of important posts in the government; this result should be reached as we agreed at the Crimea by discussing the matter with true representatives of all different Polish elements which are not fundamentally anti-Russian.

11. Also difficulties arise at the present moment because all sorts of stories are brought out of Poland which are eagerly listened to by many members of Parliament and which at any time may be violently raised in Parliament or the press in spite of my deprecating such action and on which M. Molotov will vouchsafe us no information at all in spite of repeated requests. For instance, there is talk of fifteen Poles who were said to have met the Russian authorities for discussion over four weeks ago, and of M. Witos about whom there has been a similar, but more recent report; and there are many other statements of deportations, etc. How can I contradict such complaints when you give me no information whatever and when neither I nor the Americans are allowed to send anyone into Poland to find out for themselves the true state of affairs? There is no part of our occupied or liberated territory into which you are not free to send delegations, and people do not see why you should have any reasons

against similar visits by British delegations to foreign countries liberated by you.

12. There is not much comfort in looking into a future where you and the countries you dominate, plus the Communist parties in many other States, are all drawn up on one side, and those who rally to the English-speaking nations and their Associates or Dominions are on the other. It is quite obvious that their quarrel would tear the world to pieces and that all of us leading men on either side who had anything to do with that would be shamed before history. Even embarking on a long period of suspicions, of abuse and counter-abuse and of opposing policies would be a disaster hampering the great developments of world prosperity for the masses which are attainable only by our trinity. I hope there is no word or phrase in this outpouring of my heart to you which unwittingly gives offence. If so, let me know. But do not, I beg you, my friend Stalin, underrate the divergencies which are opening about matters which you may think are small to us but which are symbolic of the way the English-speaking democracies look at life.

April 28th, 1945

PERSONAL AND SECRET MESSAGE
FROM PREMIER J. V. STALIN
TO THE PRIME MINISTER, MR. W. CHURCHILL

I am in receipt of your message of April 28 on the Polish question.

I must say that I cannot accept the arguments put forward in support of your stand.

You are inclined to regard the proposal that the Yugoslav precedent be accepted as a model for Poland as renunciation of the procedure agreed between us for setting up a Polish Government of National Unity. I cannot agree with you. I think that the Yugoslav precedent is important first of all because it points the way to the most suitable and practical solution of the problem of forming a new United Government based on the governmental agency at present exercising state power in the country.

It is quite obvious that, unless the Provisional Government now functioning in Poland and enjoying the support and trust of a majority of the Polish people is taken as a basis for a future Government of National Unity, it will be impossible to count on successful fulfillment of the task set by the Crimea Conference.

2. I cannot subscribe to that part of your considerations on Greece where you suggest three-Power control over the elections. Such control over the people of an allied country would of necessity be assessed as an affront and gross interference in their internal affairs. Such control is out of place in relation to former satellite countries which subsequently declared war on Germany and ranged themselves with the Allies, as demonstrated by electoral experience, for example, in Finland, where the election was held without outside interference and yielded positive results.

Your comments on Belgium and Poland as war theatres and communication corridors are perfectly justified. As regards Poland, it is her being a neighbour of the Soviet Union that makes it essential for a future Polish Government to seek in practice friendly relations between Poland and the U.S.S.R., which is also in the interests of the other freedom-loving nations. This circumstance, too, speaks for the Yugoslav precedent. The United Nations are interested in constant and durable friendship between the U.S.S.R. and Poland. Hence we cannot acquiesce in the attempts that are being made to involve in the forming of a future Polish Government people who, to quote you, "are not fundamentally anti-Russian," or to bar from participation only those who, in your view, are "extreme people unfriendly to Russia." Neither one nor the other can satisfy us. We insist, and shall continue to insist, that only people who have demonstrated by deeds their friendly attitude to the Soviet Union, who are willing honestly and sincerely to cooperate with the Soviet state, should be consulted on the formation of a future Polish Government.

3. I must deal specially with paragraph 11 of your message concerning the difficulties arising from rumours about the arrest of 15 Poles, about deportations, etc.

I am able to inform you that the group of Poles mentioned by you comprises 16, not 15, persons. The group is headed by the well-known General Okulicki. The British information services maintain a deliberate silence, in view of his particular odiousness, about this Polish General, who, along with the 15 other Poles, has "disappeared." But we have no intention of being silent about the matter. This group of 16, led by General Okulicki, has been arrested by the military authorities of the Soviet front and is undergoing investigation in Moscow. General Okulicki's group, in the first place General Okulicki himself, is charged with preparing and carrying out subversive activities behind the lines of the Red Army, subversion which has taken a toll of over a hundred Red Army soldiers and officers; the group is also charged with keeping illegal radio-transmitters in the rear of our troops, which is prohibited by law. All, or part of them—depending on the outcome of the investigation—will be tried. That is how the Red Army is forced to protect its units and its rear-lines against saboteurs and those who create disorder.

The British information services are spreading rumours about the murder or shooting of Poles in Siedlce. The report is a fabrication from beginning to end and has, apparently, been concocted by Arciszewski's agents.

4. It appears from your message that you are unwilling to consider the Polish Provisional Government as a basis for a future Government of National Unity, or to accord it the place in that Government to which it is entitled. I must say frankly that this attitude precludes the possibility of an agreed decision on the Polish question. May 4, 1945

DOCUMENT 14

CORRESPONDENCE BETWEEN PRIME MINISTER CHURCHILL AND PRESIDENT TRUMAN CONCERNING THE IMPLICATIONS OF WESTERN WITHDRAWAL FROM CENTRAL GERMANY, MAY 11, 12, 14, 1945

When the war in Europe ended, the Western allies' troops found themselves deep within the zone of occupation previously assigned to the Russians. Churchill, fearful of Soviet designs and further Russian advances, suggested that care be taken to negotiate with the Soviets before any troops were withdrawn. In the second letter on this subject, he referred to "an iron curtain" which was being drawn by the Russians. Harry Truman, preoccupied with the war against Japan, gave an evasive reply, and the troops were withdrawn.

Foreign Relations of the United States: *The Conference of Berlin (The Potsdam Conference), 1945*, State Department Publication No. 7015 and 7163 (Washington, 1960), I, 6–9, 11.

TOP SECRET   LONDON, 11 May 1945.

Prime Minister to President Truman. Personal and top secret. Number 41.

Following is text of telegram referred to in my immediately preceding telegram.

1. I consider that the Polish deadlock can now probably only be resolved at a conference between the three heads of governments in some unshattered town in Germany, if such can be found. This should take place at latest at the beginning of July. I propose to telegraph a suggestion to President Truman about his visit here and the further indispensable meeting of the three major powers.

2. The Polish problem may be easier to settle when set in relation to the now numerous outstanding questions of the utmost gravity which require urgent settlement with the Russians. I fear terrible things have happened during the Russian advance through Germany to the Elbe. The proposed withdrawal of the United States Army to the occupational lines which were arranged with the Russians and Americans in Quebec and which were marked in yellow on the maps we studied there, would mean the tide of Russian domination sweeping forward 120 miles on a front of 300 or 400 miles. This would be an event which, if it occurred, would be one of the most melancholy in history. After it was over and the territory occupied by the Russians, Poland would be completely engulfed and buried deep in Russian-occupied lands. What would in fact be the Russian frontier would run from the North Cape in Norway along the Finnish-Swedish frontier, across the Baltic to a point just east of Lübeck along the at present agreed line of occupation and along the frontier between Bavaria to Czechoslovakia to the frontiers of Austria which is nominally to be in quadruple occupation, and half-way across that country to the Isonzo River behind which Tito and Russia will claim everything to the east. Thus the territories under Russian control would include the Baltic provinces, all of Germany to the occupational line, all Czechoslovakia, a large part of Austria, the whole of Yugoslavia, Hungary, Roumania, Bulgaria until Greece in her present tottering condition is reached. It would include all the great capitals of middle Europe including Berlin, Vienna, Budapest, Belgrade, Bucharest and Sofia. The position of Turkey and Constantinople will certainly come immediately into discussion.

3. This constitutes an event in the history of Europe to which there has been no parallel, and which has not been faced by the Allies in their long and hazardous struggle. The Russian demands on Germany for reparations alone will be such as to enable her to prolong the occupation almost indefinitely, at any rate for many years during which time Poland will sink with many other states into the vast zone of Russian-controlled Europe, not necessarily economically Sovietised but police-governed.

4. It is just about time that these formidable issues were examined between the principal powers as a whole. We have several powerful bargaining counters on our side, the use of which might make for a peaceful agreement. First, the Allies ought not to retreat from their present positions to the occupational line until we are satisfied about Poland and also about the temporary character of the Russian occupation of Germany, and the conditions to be established in the Russianised or Russian-controlled countries in the Danube valley particularly Hungary, Austria and Czechoslovakia and the Balkans. Secondly, we may be able to please them about the exits from the Black Sea and the Baltic as part of a general settlement. All these matters can only be settled before the United States armies in Europe are weakened. If they are not settled before the United States armies withdraw from Europe and the Western world folds up its war machines, there are no prospects of a satisfactory solution and very little of preventing a third world war. It is to this early and speedy showdown and settlement with Russia that we must now turn our hopes. Meanwhile I am against weakening our claim against Russia on behalf of Poland in any way. I think it should stand where it was put in the telegrams from the President and me.

TOP SECRET   LONDON, 12th May 1945.

Prime Minister to President Truman. Personal and top secret. Number 44.

1. I am profoundly concerned about the European situation as outlined in my number 41. I learn that half the American air force in Europe has already begun to move to the Pacific Theatre. The newspapers are full of the great movements of the American armies out of Europe. Our armies also are under previous arrangements likely to undergo a marked reduction. The Canadian Army will cer-

tainly leave. The French are weak and difficult to deal with. Anyone can see that in a very short space of time our armed power on the Continent will have vanished except for moderate forces to hold down Germany.

2. Meanwhile what is to happen about Russia? I have always worked for friendship with Russia, but like you, I feel deep anxiety because of their misinterpretation of the Yalta decisions, their attitude towards Poland, their overwhelming influence in the Balkans excepting Greece, the difficulties they make about Vienna, the combination of Russian power and the territories under their control or occupied, coupled with the Communist technique in so many other countries, and above all their power to maintain very large armies in the field for a long time. What will be the position in a year or two, when the British and American armies have melted and the French has not yet been formed on any major scale, when we may have a handful of divisions mostly French, and when Russia may choose to keep two or three hundred on active service?

3. An iron curtain is drawn down upon their front. We do not know what is going on behind. There seems little doubt that the whole of the regions east of the line Lübeck-Trieste-Corfu will soon be completely in their hands. To this must be added the further enormous area conquered by the American armies between Eisenach and [the] Elbe, which will I suppose in a few weeks be occupied, when the Americans retreat, by the Russian power. All kinds of arrangements will have to be made by General Eisenhower to prevent another immense flight of the German population westward as this enormous Muscovite advance into the centre of Europe takes place. And then the curtain will descend again to a very large extent if not entirely. Thus a broad band of many hundreds of miles of Russian-occupied territory will isolate us from Poland.

4. Meanwhile the attention of our peoples will be occupied in inflicting severities upon Germany, which is ruined and prostrate, and it would be open to the Russians in a very short time to advance if they chose to the waters of the North Sea and the Atlantic.

5. Surely it is vital now to come to an understanding with Russia, or see where we are with her, before we weaken our armies mortally or retire to the zones of occupation. This can only be done by a personal meeting. I should be most grateful for your opinion and advice. Of course we may take the view that Russia will behave im-

peccably and no doubt that offers the most convenient solution. To sum up, this issue of a settlement with Russia before our strength has gone seems to me to dwarf all others.

PRIME

President Truman to Prime Minister Churchill

[WASHINGTON,] 14 May 1945.

39. Your numbers 44 and 46.

Thank you for your estimate of the future situation in Europe as outlined in your No. 44. From the present point of view it is impossible to make a conjecture as to what the Soviet may do when Germany is under the small forces of occupation and the great part of such armies as we can maintain are fighting in the Orient against Japan.

I am in full agreement with you that an early tripartite meeting is necessary to come to an understanding with Russia.

A report from our Embassies in Moscow seems necessary before we can approach a decision on the time or place for the meeting.

I have talked with Mr. Eden today and I shall make every practicable effort to so arrange my affairs here as to permit an early meeting somewhere.

DOCUMENT 15

CORRESPONDENCE BETWEEN PRESIDENT TRUMAN AND MARSHAL STALIN CONCERNING WESTERN ENTRY INTO BERLIN AND AUSTRIAN OCCUPATION ZONES, AND IMPLEMENTATION OF AGREEMENT ON BERLIN, JUNE, 1945

When President Truman turned down a renewed request by Churchill on June 4 to reconsider the withdrawal of American troops in Germany, he also insisted that Stalin pull back Soviet troops from parts of Austria and implement agreements for the entry of Western forces into Berlin

Stalin Correspondence, II, 245–246, 247–248 (Truman–Stalin, June 15, 1945, and Stalin–Truman, June 16, 1945); Foreign Relations of the United States: *The Conference at Berlin*, I, 107, 135–136 (Truman–Stalin, June 18, 1945, Murphy–Secretary of State ad interim, June 30, 1945).

and Vienna. Stalin, asking for a slight delay, agreed on June 16, and detailed arrangements concerning access routes to Berlin were concluded between the commanders on the ground, as reported to Washington by Robert D. Murphy, the American Political Adviser in Germany.

Received on June 15, 1945

PERSONAL AND TOP SECRET FOR MARSHAL STALIN
FROM PRESIDENT TRUMAN

I propose, now that Germany's unconditional defeat has been announced and the Control Council for Germany has had its first meeting, that we should issue at once definite instructions which will get forces into their respective zones and will initiate orderly administration of the defeated territory. As to Germany, I am ready to have instructions issued to all American troops to begin withdrawal into their own zone on June 21 in accordance with arrangements between the respective commanders, including in these arrangements simultaneous movement of the national garrisons into Greater Berlin and provision of free access for United States forces by air, road and rail to Berlin from Frankfurt and Bremen.

The settlement of the Austrian problem I consider of equal urgency to the German matter. The redistribution of forces into occupation zones which have been agreed in principle by the European Advisory Commission, the movement of the national garrisons into Vienna and the establishment of the Allied Commission for Austria should take place simultaneously with these developments in Germany. I attach, therefore, utmost importance to settling the outstanding Austrian problems in order that the whole arrangement of German and Austrian affairs can be put into operation simultaneously. The recent visit of American, British and French missions to Vienna will, I hope, result in the European Advisory Commission being able without delay to take the necessary remaining decisions to this end.

I propose, if you agree with the foregoing, that our respective commanders be issued appropriate instructions at once.

PERSONAL AND SECRET FROM PREMIER J. V. STALIN
TO THE PRESIDENT, MR. H. TRUMAN

Your message about the withdrawal of Allied troops in Germany and Austria into their respective zones received.

Regretfully I must tell you that your proposal for beginning the withdrawal of U.S. troops into their zone and moving U.S. troops into Berlin on June 21 is meeting with difficulties, for Marshal Zhukov and other military commanders have been summoned to the Supreme Soviet session which opens in Moscow on June 19, and also to arrange and take part in a parade on June 24. Moreover, some of the districts of Berlin have not yet been cleared of mines, nor can the mine-clearing operations be finished until late June. Since Marshal Zhukov and the other Soviet military commanders will not be able to return to Germany before June 28–30, I should like the beginning of the withdrawal to be put off till July 1, when the commanders will be back at their posts and the mine-clearing finished.

As regards Austria, what I have said about summoning the Soviet commanders to Moscow and the time of their return to their posts applies to that country as well. It is essential, furthermore, that in the next few days the European Advisory Commission should complete its work on establishing the occupation zones in Austria and in Vienna. In view of the foregoing the stationing of the respective forces in the zones assigned to them in Austria should likewise be postponed till July 1.

Besides, in respect of both Germany and Austria we must establish occupation zones right away for the French troops.

We for our part shall take proper steps in Germany and Austria according to the plan set out above.
June 16, 1945

President Truman to Marshal Stalin

TOP SECRET   [WASHINGTON,] 18 June 1945.

PRIORITY

Number 297. Top secret and personal from the President for Marshal Stalin.

Your message of June 16 regarding Allied occupation of agreed zones in Germany and Austria is received.

I have issued instructions to the American commanders to begin the movement on July 1 as requested by you. It is assumed that American troops will be in Berlin at an earlier date in sufficient number to accomplish their duties in preparation for our conference.

TRUMAN

*The Political Adviser in Germany (Murphy) to the Secretary of State
ad interim*

SECRET   HOECHST, June 30, 1945—8 p. m.

US URGENT—NIACT . . .

For the Depts most secret information, following is the gist of
yesterday's conference at Berlin between Generals Clay and Weeks
and Marshal Zhukov.

Soviets desire as quick withdrawal as possible from remainder of
their zone starting July 1. Following is program which U.S. Command will endeavor to fulfill: July 1—Russians send in reconnaissance parties to twelve towns; July 2—reconnaissance parties to certain airfields; July 4—Allied withdrawl to be completed. There is to
be a gap of some three to five kilometres between Russian advanced
and Allied rear guards. Allied move into Berlin to start on last day
of withdrawal, with entry on following day.

.   .   .   .

Following is program for occupation of Berlin sectors: July 1—
ground reconnaissance; July 2—airfield reconnaissance; July 3—
main bodies troops start moving in and complete move in on July 4.

With respect to roads, *Autobahn* Hanau–Magdeburg–Berlin would
be used unrestrictedly by U.S. and British troops. Russians did not
agree for free use of Berlin–Frankfurt *Autobahn* and road agreement
is subject to reservation for consideration in Control Council or consideration by govts.

With respect to rail transport, Soviets are not at present converting
to Russian gauge railways west of Berlin. They agree to exclusive use
by the U.S. of standard gauge line Greene–Goettingen–Bebra and
unrestricted use by the Allies of line Goslar–Magdeburg–Berlin.

It was agreed that all road, rail and air traffic on authorized routes
would be free from border search or control by customs or military
authorities. Traffic would have to conform, however, to Russian police control in the normal way. Zhukov promised that all reasonable
requests for transport of U.S. and British troops essential for preparations for the conference would be met. Cable service between Berlin
and Frankfurt agreed upon.

With respect to air routes, Russians offered airlane of approximately twenty miles width from Berlin to Magdeburg and two lanes from Magdeburg to Frankfurt. For the conference Gatow Airfield would be controlled entirely on U.S.–British basis. Tempelhof in the U.S. zone would be available to the U.S. Soviets require one hour notification of each flight but acknowledgment of notification prior to flight not required.

After subsequent clearance with the Russians it is arranged that a token French force of one thousand will accompany U.S.–British forces into Berlin, and French reconnaissance party will proceed to Berlin tomorrow.

Press release is being issued announcing that withdrawal from Russian zone will start July 1.

MURPHY

DOCUMENT 16

ZONES OF OCCUPATION IN AUSTRIA: AGREEMENT BE-
TWEEN THE UNITED STATES, THE UNION OF SOVIET SO-
CIALIST REPUBLICS AND THE UNITED KINGDOM AND
THE PROVISIONAL GOVERNMENT OF THE FRENCH RE-
PUBLIC, JULY 9, 1945

As in Germany, zones of occupation were established in Austria by the summer of 1945. A general realignment of allied troops took place accordingly shortly afterward.

1. The Governments of the United States of America, the Union of Soviet Socialist Republics and the United Kingdom of Great Britain and Northern Ireland and the Provisional Government of the French Republic have agreed that the territory of Austria within her frontiers as they were on 31st December, 1937, will be occupied by armed forces of the United States of America, the Union of Soviet Socialist Republics, the United Kingdom and the French Republic.

2. For the purposes of occupation, Austria will be divided as follows into four zones, one of which will be allotted to each of the four Powers, and a special Vienna area which will be jointly occupied by armed forces of the four Powers:

North-Eastern (Soviet) Zone	The province of Lower Austria with the exception of the City of Vienna, that part of the province of Upper Austria situated on the left bank of the Danube, and the province of Burgenland which existed prior to the Decree of 1st October, 1938,[1] concerning boundary changes in Austria, will be occupied by armed forces of the Union of Soviet Socialist Republics.
North-Western (United States) Zone	The province of Salzburg and that part of the province of Upper Austria situated on the right bank of the Danube will be occupied by armed forces of the United States.
Western (French) Zone	The provinces of Tirol and Vorarlberg will be occupied by armed forces of the French Republic.
Southern (United Kingdom) Zone	The province of Carinthia, including Ost Tirol, and the province of Styria, except the area of the Burgenland as it existed before the Decree of 1st October, 1938, will be occupied by armed forces of the United Kingdom.

City of Vienna

The territory of the City of Vienna will be divided into the following parts . . . :—

The districts of Leopoldstadt, Brigittenau, Floridsdorf, Wieden and Favoriten will be occupied by armed forces of the Soviet Union;

The districts of Neubau, Josefstadt, Hernals, Alsergrund, Währing and Döbling will be occupied by armed forces of the United States of America:

The districts of Mariahilf, Penzing, Funfhaus (including the district of Rudolfsheim) and Ottakring will be occupied by armed forces of the French Republic;

The districts of Hietzing, Margareten, Meidling, Landstrasse and Simmering will be occupied by armed forces of the United Kingdom.

The district of Innere Stadt will be occupied by armed forces of the four Powers.

3. Boundaries between the zones of occupation, with the exception of the boundaries of the City of Vienna and of the province of Burgenland, will be those obtaining after the coming into effect of the Decree of 1st October, 1938, concerning boundary changes in Austria. The boundaries of the City of Vienna and of the province of Burgenland will be those which existed on 31st December, 1937.

4. An inter-Allied Governing Authority (Komendatura), consisting of four Commandants appointed by their respective Commanders-in-Chief, will be established to direct jointly the administration of the City of Vienna. . . .

7. The present Agreement will come into force as soon as it has been approved by the four Governments.[1] . . .

DOCUMENT 17

THE FRENCH ZONE OF OCCUPATION: AMENDING AGREEMENT ON ZONES OF OCCUPATION AND ADMINISTRATION OF THE "GREATER BERLIN" AREA, JULY 26, 1945

Upon President Roosevelt's insistence that France be treated as one of the great powers, Stalin reluctantly consented on condition that the French sector be carved out of the Western zones of occupation. This arrangement was belatedly carried out on July 26, 1945.

The Governments of the United States of America, the Union of Soviet Socialist Republics and the United Kingdom having, pursuant to the decision of the Crimea Conference announced on 12th Feb-

---

[1] Notices of approval dated as follows: by the United Kingdom July 12, 1945; by France July 16, 1945; by the Union of Soviet Socialist Republics July 21, 1945; and by the United States of America July 24, 1945.

Documents on Germany, 1944–1961, 20–23.

ruary, 1945, invited the Provisional Government of the French Republic to take part in the occupation of Germany,

> the Governments of the United States of America, the Union of Soviet Socialist Republics and the United Kingdom and the Provisional Government of the French Republic have agreed to amend and to supplement the Protocol of 12th September, 1944, between the Governments of the United States of America, the Union of Soviet Socialist Republics and the United Kingdom on the zones of occupation in Germany and the administration of "Greater Berlin,"

and have reached the following agreement:

1. In the Preamble of the Protocol of 12th September, 1944, add the words "and the Provisional Government of the French Republic" in the enumeration of the participating Governments.

2. In Article 1 of the above-mentioned Protocol, substitute "four" for "three" in the words "three zones," "three Powers" and "three Powers."

3. In the first paragraph of Article 2 of the above-mentioned Protocol, add "and the French Republic" in the enumeration of the participating Powers; substitute "four" for "three" in the words "three zones" and "three zones."

4. In place of the description of the North-Western Zone given in Article 2 of the above-mentioned Protocol, the description of the North-Western Zone will read as follows;

> *"North-Western (United Kingdom) Zone ...*
>
> "The territory of Germany situated to west of the line defined in the description of the Eastern (Soviet) Zone, and bounded on the south by a line drawn from the point where the frontier between the Prussian provinces of Hanover and Hessen-Nassau meets the western frontier of the Prussian province of Saxony; thence along the southern frontier of Hanover; thence along the south-eastern and south-western frontiers of the Prussian province of Westphalia and along the southern frontiers of the Prussian Regierungsbezirke of Köln and Aachen to the point where this frontier meets the Belgian-German frontier will be occupied by armed forces of the United Kingdom."

5. In place of the description of the South-Western Zone given in Article 2 of the above-mentioned Protocol, description of the South-Western Zone will read as follows:—

"South-Western (United States) Zone . . .

"The territory of Germany situated to the south and east of a line commencing at the junction of the frontiers of Saxony, Bavaria and Czechoslovakia and extending westward along the northern frontier of Bavaria to the junction of the frontiers of Hessen-Nassau, Thuringia and Bavaria; thence north and west along the eastern and northern frontiers of Hessen-Nassau to the point where the frontier of the district of Dill meets the frontier of the district of Oberwesterwald; thence along the western frontier of the district of Dill, the northwestern frontier of the district of Oberlahn, the northern and western frontiers of the district of Limburg-an-der-lahn, the north-western frontier of the district of Untertaunus and the northern frontier of the district of Rheingau; thence south and east along the western and southern frontiers of Hessen-Nassau to the point where the River Rhine leaves the southern frontier of Hessen-Nassau; thence southwards along the centre of the navigable channel of the River Rhine to the point where the latter leaves Hessen-Darmstadt; thence along the western frontier of Baden to the point where the frontier of the district of Karlsruhe meets the frontier of the district of Rastatt; thence southeast along the southern frontier of the district of Karlsruhe; thence north-east and south-east along the eastern frontier of Baden to the point where the frontier of Baden meets the frontier between the districts of Calw and Leonberg; thence south and east along the western frontier of the district of Leonberg, the western and southern frontiers of the district of Böblingen, the southern frontier of the district of Nürtingen and the southern frontier of the district of Göppingen to the point where the latter meets the Reichsautobahn between Stuttgart and Ulm; thence along the southern boundary of the Reichsautobahn to the point where the latter meets the western frontier of the district of Ulm; thence south along the western frontier of the district of Ulm to the point where the latter meets the western frontier of the State of Bavaria; thence south along the western frontier of Bavaria to the point where the frontier of the district of Kempten meets the frontier of the district of Lindau; thence south-west along the western frontier of the district of Kempten and the western frontier of the district of Sonthofen to the point where the latter meets the Austro-German frontier will be occupied by armed forces of the United States of America."

6. The following additional paragraph will be inserted in Article 2 of the above-mentioned Protocol, following the description of the South-Western Zone:—

"Western (French) Zone ...

"The territory of Germany, situated to the south and west of a line commencing at the junction of the frontiers of Belgium and of the Prussian Regierungsbezirke of Trier and Aachen and extending eastward along the northern frontier of the Prussian Regierungsbezirk of Trier; thence north, east and south along the western, northern and eastern frontier of the Prussian Regierungsbezirk of Koblenz to the point where the frontier of Koblenz meets the frontier of the district of Oberwesterwald; thence east, south and west along the northern, eastern and southern frontiers of the district of Oberwesterwald and along the eastern frontiers of the districts of Unterwesterwald, Unterlahn and Sankt Goarshausen to the point where the frontier of the district of Sankt Goarshausen meets the frontier of the Regierungsbezirk of Koblenz; thence south and east along the eastern frontier of Koblenz; and the northern frontier of Hessen-Darmstadt to the point where the River Rhine leaves the southern frontier of Hessen-Nassau; thence southwards along the centre of the navigable channel of the River Rhine to the point where the latter leaves Hessen-

---

This agreement was approved by the United States on July 29, 1945; the United Kingdom, August 2, 1945; France, August 7, 1945; and the Soviet Union, August 13, 1945.

Darmstadt; thence along the western frontier of Baden to the point where the frontier of the district of Karlsruhe meets the frontier of the district of Rastatt; thence south-east along the northern frontier of the district of Rastatt; thence north, east and south along the western, northern and eastern frontiers of the district of Claw; thence eastwards along the northern frontiers of the districts of Horb, Tübingen, Reutlingen and Münsingen to the point where the northern frontier of the district of Münsingen meets the Reichsautobahn between Stuttgart and Ulm; thence south-east along the southern boundary of the Reichsautobahn to the point where the latter meets the eastern frontier of the district of Münsingen; thence south-east along the north-eastern frontiers of the districts of Münsingen, Ehingen and Biberach; thence southwards along the eastern frontiers of the districts of Bieberach, Wagen and Lindau to the point where the eastern frontier of the district of Lindau meets the Austro-German frontier will be occupied by armed forces of the French Republic." . . .

DOCUMENT 18

THE BERLIN (POTSDAM) CONFERENCE JULY 17–AUGUST 1, 1945

The Potsdam Conference was the last of the great wartime meetings of the allies. Interrupted by the British general election, it began with Winston Churchill's representing the United Kingdom but ended only after he had been replaced by Clement Attlee. While the conference was in session, President Truman was informed of the successful detonation of an atom bomb at Los Alamos, New Mexico, and an ultimatum was issued to Japan to surrender. On the principal points at issue, the conferees were able to arrive only at vague general agreements. The Western powers accepted the Oder-Neisse line as a temporary frontier between Poland and Germany pending the conclusion of a peace treaty; they promised the Koenigsberg area to the Soviet Union, and they agreed to certain reparations percentages. No central government for Germany was set up,

Foreign Relations of the United States: *The Berlin Conference*, II, 1478–1498.

however, and a Council of Foreign Ministers was charged with the preparatory work for a peace settlement. The following text, dated August 1, 1945, consists of excerpts from the original manuscript annotated to show later changes. Some footnotes have been omitted.

PROTOCOL OF THE PROCEEDINGS OF THE BERLIN CONFERENCE[1]

The Berlin Conference of the Three Heads of Government of the U.S.S.R., U.S.A., and U.K., which took place from July 17 to August 1,[5] 1945, came to the following conclusions:

I. ESTABLISHMENT OF A COUNCIL OF FOREIGN MINISTERS

[6] The Conference reached the following agreement for the establishment of a Council of Foreign Ministers to do the necessary preparatory work for the peace settlements:

"(1) There shall be established a Council composed of the Foreign Ministers of the United Kingdom, the Union of Soviet Socialist Republics, China, France and the United States. . . .

(3) (i) As its immediate important task, the Council shall be authorized to draw up, with a view to their submission to the United Nations, treaties of peace with Italy, Rumania, Bulgaria, Hungary and Finland, and to propose settlements of territorial questions outstanding on the termination of the war in Europe. The Council shall be utilized for the preparation of a peace settlement for Germany to be accepted by the Government of Germany when a government adequate for the purpose is established. . . .

---

[1] Except that variations in punctuation, spelling, and capitalization which occurred in Stage 3, and minor variations in Stage 3 which were obviously the result of typographical errors, have not been annotated.

In the footnotes which follow, an asterisk (*) indicates that the United States text, as changed, is in harmony with the text published by the British Government in 1947. A dagger (†) indicates that the United States text, as changed, is in harmony with the Russian text published by the Soviet Government in 1955. There remain, however, both editorial and substantive differences between the United States, British, and Soviet texts. Attention is called to the principal remaining substantive differences in the footnotes which follow.

[5] Changed in Stage 3 to "August 2."*†

[6] "A." introduced at the beginning of this paragraph in Stage 2.*†

II. THE PRINCIPLES TO GOVERN THE TREATMENT OF GERMANY IN THE INITIAL CONTROL PERIOD[15a]

A. *Political Principles.*

1. In accordance with the Agreement on Control Machinery in Germany,[16] supreme authority in Germany is exercised, on instructions from their respective Governments, by the Commanders-in-Chief of the armed forces of the United States of America, the United Kingdom, the Union of Soviet Socialist Republics, and the French Republic, each in his own zone of occupation, and also jointly, in matters affecting Germany as a whole, in their capacity as members of the Control Council.

2. So far as is practicable, there shall be uniformity of treatment of the German population throughout Germany.

3. The purposes of the occupation of Germany by which the Control Council shall be guided are:

(1) [17] The complete disarmament and demilitarization of Germany and the elimination or control of all German industry that could be used for military production. . . .

9. The administration of affairs[20] in Germany should be directed towards the decentralization of the political structure and the development of local responsibility.[20a] To this end:—

(i) local self-government shall be restored throughout Germany on democratic principles and in particular through elective councils as rapidly as is consistent with military security and the purposes of military occupation;

(ii) all democratic political parties with rights of assembly and of public discussion shall be allowed and encouraged throughout Germany;

[15a] The Soviet text, which contains the words "Political and Economic Principles" in this heading, also contains the following introductory statement following the heading: "The following political and economic principles for the treatment of Germany were adopted:".

[16] Signed at London, November 14, 1944, as amended by a further agreement signed at London, May 1, 1945.

[17] Corrected in Stage 3 to "(i)."*†

[20] The words "of affairs" deleted in Stage 3.*†

[20a] The Soviet text reads, in literal translation, "the development of a sense of responsibility."

(iii) representative and elective principles shall be introduced into regional, provincial and state (Land) administration as rapidly as may be justified by the successful application of these principles in local self-government;

(iv) for the time being, no central German Government shall be established. Notwithstanding this, however, certain essential central German administrative departments, headed by State Secretaries, shall be established, particularly in the fields of finance, transport, communications, foreign trade and industry. Such departments will act under the direction of the Control Council.

10. Subject to the necessity for maintaining military security, freedom of speech, press and religion shall be permitted, and religious institutions shall be respected. Subject likewise to the maintenance of military security, the formation of free trade unions shall be permitted. . . .

14. During the period of occupation Germany shall be treated as a single economic unit. . . .

III. GERMAN REPARATION[30]

1. Reparation claims of[31] U.S.S.R. shall be met by removals from the zone of Germany occupied by the U.S.S.R., and from appropriate German external assets.

2. The U.S.S.R. undertakes to settle the reparation claims of Poland from its own share of reparations.

3. The reparations[32] claims of the United States, the United Kingdom and other countries entitled to reparations shall be met from the Western Zones and from appropriate German external assets.

4. In addition to the reparations to be taken by the U.S.S.R. from its own zone of occupation, the U.S.S.R. shall receive additionally from the Western Zones:

(*a*) 15 per cent of such usable and complete industrial capital equipment, in the first place from the metallurgical, chemical and machine manufacturing industries as is unnecessary for the German peace economy and should be removed from the Western Zones of

---

[30] Changed in Stage 3 to "Reparations From Germany."*†
[31] The word "the" introduced at this point in Stage 3.*†
[32] Changed in Stage 3 to "reparation."

Germany, in exchange for an equivalent value of food, coal, potash, zinc, timber, clay products, petroleum products, and such other commodities as may be agreed upon.

(*b*) 10 per cent of such industrial capital equipment as is unnecessary for the German peace economy and should be removed from the Western Zones, to be transferred to the Soviet Government on reparations account without payment or exchange of any kind in return.

Removals of equipment as provided in (*a*) and (*b*) above shall be made simultaneously. . . .

VI[42]

CITY OF KOENIGSBERG AND THE ADJACENT AREA

The Conference examined a proposal by the Soviet Government to the effect that pending the final determination of territorial questions at the peace settlement, the section of the western frontier of the Union of Soviet Socialist Republics which is adjacent to the Baltic Sea should pass from a point on the eastern shore of the Bay of Danzig to the east, north of Braunsberg–Goldap, to the meeting point of the frontiers of Lithuania, the Polish Republic and East Prussia.

The Conference has agreed in principle to the proposal of the Soviet Government concerning the ultimate transfer[42a] to the Soviet Union of the City of Koenigsberg and the area adjacent to it as described above subject to expert[43] examination of the actual frontier.

---

[42] Corrected in Stage 2 to "v."*† This correction is marked in Dunn's working copy of the Protocol, where the numbering of all the succeeding sections of the Protocol is likewise corrected. An undated working paper (file No. 740.00119 Potsdam/7–3045) which contains a numbered list of the proposed sections of the Protocol indicates that at one stage it was expected that section v of the Protocol would deal with the Ruhr. When the Heads of Government decided on August 1 that the Protocol would not contain a section on the Ruhr, this decision should have precipitated a renumbering of section vi (on the city of Königsberg and the adjacent area) to section v, and an appropriate renumbering of all succeeding sections of the Protocol. As noted above, this renumbering was carried out in Dunn's working copy of the Protocol, but the correct numbering was not entered on the United States original of the Protocol until Stage 2, as defined above.

[42a] The Soviet text reads, in literal translation, "concerning the transfer."

[43] Corrected by hand in Stage 1 from "exper."

The President of the United States and the British Prime Minister have declared that they will support the proposal of the Conference at the forthcoming peace settlement.

VII[44]

WAR CRIMES[45]

The Three Governments have taken note of the discussions which have been proceeding in recent weeks in London between British, United States, Soviet and French representatives with a view to reaching agreement on the methods of trial of those major war criminals whose crimes under the Moscow Declaration of October, 1943 have no particular geographical localisation. The Three Governments re-affirm their intention to bring these criminals to swift and sure justice. They hope that the negotiations in London will result in speedy agreement being reached for this purpose, and they regard it as a matter of great importance that the trial of these major criminals should begin at the earliest possible date. The first list of defendants will be published before 1st September.[48]

VIII[49]

AUSTRIA

The Conference examined a proposal by the Soviet Government on the extension of the authority of the Austrian Provisional Government to all of Austria.

The three Governments agreed that they were prepared to examine this question after the entry of the British and American forces into the city of Vienna.

It was agreed that reparations should not be exacted from Austria.

---

[44] Corrected in Stage 2 to "VI."*†
[45] Changed in Stage 2 to "War Criminals."*†
[48] For the list referred to, which was made public on August 29, 1945, see Department of State *Bulletin*, vol. XIII, p. 301.
[49] Corrected in Stage 2 to "VII."*†

IX[50]

POLAND

A. *Declaration*[50a]

We have taken note with pleasure of the agreement reached among representative Poles from Poland and abroad which has made possible the formation, in accordance with the decisions reached at the Crimea Conference, of a Polish Provisional Government of National Unity recognised by the Three Powers. The establishment by the British and United States Governments of diplomatic relations with the Polish Provisional Government[52] has resulted in the withdrawal of their recognition from the former Polish Government in London,[53] which no longer exists. . . .

The Three Powers are anxious to assist the Polish Provisional Government[56] in facilitating the return to Poland as soon as practicable of all Poles abroad who wish to go, including members of the Polish armed forces and the merchant marine. They expect that those Poles who return home shall be accorded personal rights[57] and property rights on the same basis as all Polish citizens.

The Three Powers note that the Polish Provisional Government[56] in accordance with the decisions of the Crimea Conference has agreed to the holding of free and unfettered elections as soon as possible on the basis of universal suffrage and secret ballot in which all democratic and anti-Nazi parties shall have the right to take part and to put forward candidates; and that representatives of the Allied Press shall enjoy full freedom to report to the world upon developments in Poland before and during the elections.

---

[50] Corrected in Stage 2 to "VIII."*†

[50a] In the Soviet text this heading reads, in literal translation, "A. Declaration on the Polish Question," and the following introductory statement follows the heading: "The Conference has adopted the following declaration on the Polish question:"

[52] The words "of National Unity" introduced at this point in Stage 3.*

[53] Concerning United States recognition of the Polish Provisional Government of National Unity, see vol. I, document No. 501.

[56] The words "of National Unity" introduced at this point in Stage 3.*†

[57] The word "rights" deleted in Stage 3.*† This change was marked in Dunn's handwriting in Dunn's working copy of the Protocol.

B. *Western Frontier of Poland.*

In conformity with the agreement on Poland reached at the Crimea Conference the three Heads of Government have sought the opinion of the Polish Provisional Government of National Unity in regard to the accession of territory in the north and west which Poland should receive. The President of the National Council of Poland[58] and members of the Polish Provisional Government of National Unity have been received at the Conference and have fully presented their views. The three Heads of Government reaffirm their opinion that the final delimitation of the western frontier of Poland should await the peace settlement.

The three Heads of Government agree that, pending the final determination of Poland's western frontier, the former German territories east of a line running from the Baltic Sea immediately west [of][60] Swinemunde, and thence along the Oder River to the confluence of the western Neisse River and along the western Neisse to the Czechoslovak frontier, including that portion of East Prussia not placed under the administration of the Union of Soviet Socialist Republics in accordance with the understanding reached at this conference and including the area of the former free city of Danzig, shall be under the administration of the Polish State and for such purposes should not be considered as part of the Soviet zone of occupation in Germany. . . .

DOCUMENT 19

MINUTES OF MEETING OF CONTROL COUNCIL APPROVING ESTABLISHMENT OF AIR CORRIDORS TO BERLIN, NOVEMBER 30, 1945

Because the Western forces in Berlin were cut off from their sources of supply by over one hundred miles of intervening Soviet occupied territory, it became important to establish formal rights of access to the city in

---

[58] Bolesław Bierut.
[60] The words "immediately west" substituted for "through" in Stage 1.*† The word "of" introduced in Stage 2.*† The words "immediately west of" appear in Dunn's handwriting as an interlineation in Dunn's working copy of the Protocol. *Documents on Germany, 1944–1961*, 48–49.

accordance with the agreements made between Russia and the West. The meeting of the Allied Control Council of November 30, 1945, dealt with this subject and resulted in Marshal Zhukhov's acceptance of previous arrangements.

THERE WERE PRESENT:

Marshal of the Soviet Union [Zhukov] (Chairman)
General MCNARNEY
Field Marshal MONTGOMERY
Lt. General KOENIG

110. *Proposed Air Routes for Inter-Zonal Flights.*

The Meeting had before them CONL/P(45)63.

Marshal ZHUKOV recalled that the Coordinating Committee had approved the establishing of three air corridors, namely, Berlin-Hamburg, Berlin-Buckeburg and Berlin-Frankfurt-on-Main.

Field Marshal MONTGOMERY expressed the hope that in due course the question of establishing the remaining air corridors would be settled satisfactorily.

General KOENIG approved the paper in principle and shared the opinion of Field Marshal MONTGOMERY.

Marshal ZHUKOV expressed himself confident that in due course the other air corridors would be opened. He added that he would like to make a proposal on this paper. He assumed that his colleagues would give the Soviet military authorities the right to fly along these air corridors into the Western zones and would consent to put at their disposal appropriate airfields for landing Soviet aircraft, or at least allow Soviet ground staffs on terminal and intermediate airfields along the proposed air corridors to facilitate the servicing of Soviet aircraft. The reason which Marshal ZHUKOV gave for the necessity of establishing Soviet airfields in the Western zones was the work of dismantling plants for deliveries on account of reparations when it comes to sending Soviet experts to organise that work.

Field Marshal MONTGOMERY stated that in his zone he would afford every facility for Soviet aircraft.

Marshal ZHUKOV said that he would like to clarify his declaration: namely, he proposed that appropriate airfields should be placed at the disposal of the Soviet authorities in the Western zones, or that permission should be given for Soviet ground crews for the servicing of Soviet aircraft to be stationed at these airfields.

Field Marshal MONTGOMERY proposed to refer the proposal made by the head of the Soviet delegation to the Air Directorate for examination. He asked whether his understanding was correct that the question of the three air corridors from the Western zones to Berlin was settled and that the organisation of these air corridors could be started immediately, without awaiting the results of the examination of the Soviet proposal.

Marshal ZHUKOV observed that he considered the paper accepted and expressed the hope that the proposal of the Soviet delegation on placing airfields in the Western zones at the disposal of the Soviet authorities would meet with full sympathy on the part of his colleagues.

The Meeting

(110)(a) approved the establishment of three air corridors from Berlin to the Western zones as defined in CONL/P(45)63

(b) agreed to refer the proposal of the Soviet delegation on the placing of airfields at the disposal of the Soviet authorities or the setting up of Soviet ground crews in the Western zones to the Air Directorate for study.

THREE

The Cold War in Europe, 1945-1950

With the surrender of Japan on September 2, 1945, World War II came to a close. But if the collapse of Germany had subjected allied cooperation to a severe strain, the end of the war in the Pacific virtually terminated it. No longer confronted with a common enemy, the wartime partners were unable to overcome their differences, and the Cold War began in earnest. The Soviets tightened their grip upon Eastern Europe so ruthlessly that Winston Churchill publicly deplored the "iron curtain" which he had mentioned privately earlier; constant recriminations became the order of the day, and deep disillusionment set in in the West. Militarily speaking, the United States was in an advantageous position because of its monopoly of the atom bomb, a secret it offered to share with the rest of the world under the conditions of the Baruch plan. The Soviets, in a counterproposal designed to nullify America's strategic advantage, refused, and a nuclear deadlock became part of the East-West struggle.

At this juncture, the United States felt constrained to counter Soviet expansion in some manner. In September, 1946, Secretary of State James F. Byrnes told the Germans their country was to be rehabilitated; in the spring of 1947, the Truman administration undertook to "contain" the Communist threat. The Truman Doctrine and the Marshall Plan marked the beginning of this endeavor—a policy which seemed eminently justified when the Communists executed the leader of the Bulgarian opposition, did away with the last vestiges of democracy in Hungary and Czechoslovakia, and blockaded Berlin. The successful airlift, the launching of NATO, the establishment of the Federal Republic in West Germany, and the inauguration of the Point Four program were further steps to bolster the West. Communist expansion was contained along the line of Soviet occupation, and although the Russians established a satellite in East Germany, they were unable to penetrate the heart of industrial Europe. The West had met the challenge.

DOCUMENT 20

CHURCHILL'S "IRON CURTAIN" SPEECH AT WESTMINSTER COLLEGE, FULTON, MISSOURI, MARCH 5, 1946

The postwar frustrations felt by many Western observers were given a classic expression by Winston Churchill in his speech at Westminster College, Fulton, Missouri, on March 5, 1946, in the presence of President Truman. The term "iron curtain," by which he characterized the border with the Communist-controlled countries in Europe, was soon in general use.

I am glad to come to Westminster College this afternoon and am complimented that you should give me a degree. The name Westminster is somehow familiar to me. I seem to have heard of it before. Indeed it was at Westminster that I received a very large part of my education in politics, dialectic, rhetoric and one or two other things. . . .

The United States stands at this time at the pinnacle of world power. It is a solemn moment for the American democracy. With primacy in power is also joined an awe-inspiring accountability to the future. As you look around you, you must feel not only the sense of duty done but also feel anxiety lest you fall below the level of achievement. Opportunity is here now, clear and shining, for both our countries. To reject it or ignore it or fritter it away will bring upon us all the long reproaches of the aftertime. It is necessary that constancy of mind, persistency of purpose and the grand simplicity of decision shall guide and rule the conduct of the English-speaking peoples in peace as they did in war. We must and I believe we shall prove ourselves equal to this severe requirement.

When American military men approach some serious situation they are wont to write at the head of their directive the words, "over-all strategic concept." There is wisdom in this as it leads to clarity of thought. What, then, is the over-all strategic concept which we should inscribe today? It is nothing less than the safety and welfare, the freedom and progress of all the homes and families of all the men and women in all the lands. And here I speak particularly of the myriad cottage or apartment homes, where the wage earner strives amid the accidents and difficulties of life, to guard his wife and children from privation and bring the family up in the fear of the Lord or upon ethical conceptions which often play their potent part.

To give security to these countless homes they must be shielded from the two gaunt marauders—war and tyranny. We all know the frightful disturbance in which the ordinary family is plunged when the curse of war swoops down upon the bread winner and those for whom he works and contrives. The awful ruin of Europe, with all its vanished glories, and of large parts of Asia, glares in our eyes. When the designs of wicked men or the aggressive urge of mighty states dissolve, over large areas, the frame of civilized society, humble folk are confronted with difficulties with which they cannot cope. For them all is distorted, broken or even ground to pulp.

When I stand here this quiet afternoon I shudder to visualize what is actually happening to millions now and what is going to happen in this period when famine stalks the earth. None can compute what has been called "the unestimated sum of human pain." Our supreme task and duty is to guard the homes of the common people from the horrors and miseries of another war. We are all agreed on that.

Our American military colleagues, after having proclaimed the "over-all strategic concept" and computed all available resources, always proceed to the next stop, namely the method. Here again there is widespread agreement. A world organization has already been erected for the prime purpose of preventing war. United Nations Organization, the successor of the League of Nations, with the decisive addition of the United States and all that that means, is already at work. We must make sure that its work is fruitful, that it is a reality and not a sham, that it is a force for action and not merely a frothing of words, that it is a true temple of peace in which the shields of many nations can some day be hung and not merely a cockpit in a tower of Babel. Before we cast away the solid assurances of national armaments for self-preservation, we must be certain that our temple is built not upon shifting sands or quagmires, but upon the rock. Any one with his eyes open can see that our path will be difficult and also long, but if we persevere together as we did in the two world wars—though not, alas, in the interval between them—I cannot doubt that we shall achieve our common purpose in the end.

I have, however, a definite and practical proposal to make for action. Courts and magistrates cannot function without sheriffs and constables. The United Nations Organization must immediately begin to be equipped with an international armed force. In such a matter we can only go step by step; but we must begin now. I propose that each of the powers and states should be invited to dedicate a certain number of air squadrons to the service of the world organization. These squadrons would be trained and prepared in their own countries but would move around in rotation from one country to another. They would wear the uniform of their own countries with different badges. They would not be required to act against their own nation but in other respects they would be directed by the world organization. This might be started on a modest scale and grow as confidence grew. I wished to see this done after the first world war and trust it may be done forthwith.

It would nevertheless be wrong and imprudent to intrust the secret knowledge of experience of the atomic bomb, which the United States, Great Britain and Canada now share, to the world organization, while it is still in its infancy. It would be criminal madness to cast it adrift in this still agitated and ununited world. No one in any country has slept less well in their beds because this knowledge and the method and the raw materials to apply it are at present largely retained in American hands. I do not believe we should all have slept so soundly had the positions been reversed and some Communist or neo-Fascist state monopolized, for the time being, these dread agencies. The fear of them alone might easily have been used to enforce totalitarian systems upon the free democratic world, with consequences appalling to the human imagination. God has willed that this shall not be, and we have at least a breathing space before this peril has to be encountered, and even then, if no effort is spared, we should still possess so formidable superiority as to impose effective deterrents upon its employment or threat of employment by others. Ultimately, when the essential brotherhood of man is truly embodied and expressed in a world organization, these powers may be confided to it.

I now come to the second danger which threatens the cottage home and ordinary people, namely tyranny. We cannot be blind to the fact that the liberties enjoyed by individual citizens throughout the British Empire are not valid in a considerable number of countries, some of which are very powerful. In these states, control is enforced upon the common people by various kinds of all-embracing police governments, to a degree which is overwhelming and contrary to every principle of democracy. The power of the state is exercised without restraint, either by dictators or by compact oligarchies operating through a privileged party and a political police. It is not our duty at this time, when difficulties are so numerous, to interfere forcibly in the internal affairs of countries whom we have not conquered in war, but we must never cease to proclaim in fearless tones the great principles of freedom and the rights of man, which are the joint inheritance of the English-speaking world and which, through Magna Carta, the Bill of Rights, the habeas corpus, trial by jury and the English common law, find their most famous expression in the Declaration of Independence.

All this means that the people of any country have the right and should have the power by constitutional action, by free, unfettered elections, with secret ballot, to choose or change the character or form of government under which they dwell, that freedom of speech and thought should reign, that courts of justice independent of the executive, unbiased by any party, should administer laws which have received the broad assent of large majorities or are consecrated by time and custom. Here are the title deeds of freedom, which should lie in every cottage home. Here is the message of the British and American peoples to mankind. Let us preach what we practice and practice what we preach.

I have now stated the two great dangers which menace the homes of the people. I have not yet spoken of poverty and privation which are in many cases the prevailing anxiety. But if the dangers of war and tyranny are removed, there is no doubt that science and co-operation can bring in the next few years—certainly in the next few decades—to the world, newly taught in the hard school of war, an expansion of material well being beyond anything that has yet occurred in human experience. Now, at this sad, breathless moment, we are plunged in the hunger and distress which are the aftermath of our stupendous struggle; but this will pass and may pass quickly, and there is no reason except human folly or subhuman crime which should deny to all the nations the inauguration and enjoyment of an age of plenty. I have often used words which I learned fifty years ago from a great Irish-American orator, Mr. Bourke Cockran, "There is enough for all. The earth is a generous mother; she will provide in plentiful abundance food for all her children if they will but cultivate her soil in justice and in peace." So far we are evidently in full agreement.

Now, while still pursuing the method of realizing our over-all strategic concept, I come to the crux of what I have traveled here to say. Neither the sure prevention of war, nor the continuous rise of world organization will be gained without what I have called the fraternal association of the English-speaking peoples. This means a special relationship between the British Commonwealth and Empire and the United States. This is no time for generalities. I will venture to be precise. Fraternal association requires not only the growing friendship and mutual understanding between our two vast but kindred systems of society but the continuance of the intimate relationships between our military advisers, leading to common study of potential dangers, similarity of weapons and manuals of instruction and interchange of officers and cadets at colleges. It should carry with it the continuance of the present facilities for mutual security by the joint use of all naval and air-force bases in the possession of either country all over the world. This would perhaps double the mobility of the American Navy and Air Force. It would greatly expand that of the British Empire forces and it might well lead, if and as the world calms down, to important financial savings. Already we use together a large number of islands; many more will be intrusted to our joint care in the near future. The United States already has a permanent defense agreement with the Dominion of Canada, which is so devotedly attached to the British Commonwealth and Empire. This agreement is more effective than many of those which have often been made under formal alliances. This principle should be extended to all the British Common-wealths with full reciprocity. Thus, whatever happens, and thus only we shall be secure ourselves and able to work together for the high and simple causes that are dear to us and bode no ill to any. Eventually there may come the principle of common citizenship, but that we may be content to leave to destiny, whose outstretched arm so many of us can clearly see. . . .

A shadow has fallen upon the scenes so lately lighted by the Allied victory. Nobody knows what Soviet Russia and its Communist international organization intends to do in the immediate future, or what are the limits, if any, to their expansive and proselytizing tendencies. I have a strong admiration and regard for the valiant Russian people and for my war-time comrade, Marshal Stalin. There is sympathy and good will in Britain—and I doubt not here also—toward the peoples of all the Russias and a resolve to persevere through many differences and rebuffs in establishing lasting friendships. We understand the Russians need to be secure on her western frontiers from all renewal of German aggression. We welcome her to her rightful place among the leading nations of the world. Above all we welcome constant, frequent and growing contacts between the Russian people and our own people on both sides of the Atlantic. It is my duty, however, to place before you certain facts about the present position in Europe—I am sure I do not wish to, but it is my duty, I feel, to present them to you.

From Stettin in the Baltic to Triest in the Adriatic, an iron curtain has descended across the Continent. Behind that line lie all the capitals of the ancient states of central and eastern Europe. Warsaw, Berlin, Prague, Vienna, Budapest, Belgrade, Bucharest and Sofia, all these famous cities and the populations around them lie in the Soviet sphere and all are subject in one form or another, not only to Soviet influence but to a very high and increasing measure of control from Moscow. Athens alone, with its immortal glories, is free to decide its future at an election under British, American and French observation. The Russian-dominated Polish government has been encouraged to make enormous and wrongful inroads upon Germany, and mass expulsions of millions of Germans on a scale grievous and undreamed of are now taking place. The Communist parties, which were very small in all these eastern states of Europe, have been raised to pre-eminence and power far beyond their numbers and are seeking everywhere to obtain totalitarian control. Police governments are prevailing in nearly every case, and so far, except in Czechoslovakia, there is no true democracy. Turkey and Persia are both profoundly alarmed and disturbed at the claims which are made upon them and at the pressure being exerted by the Moscow government. An attempt is being made by the Russians in Berlin to build up a quasi-Communist party in their zone of occupied Germany by showing special favors to groups of Left-Wing German leaders. At the end of the fighting last June, the American and British armies withdrew westward, in accordance with an earlier agreement, to a depth at some points 150 miles on a front of nearly 400 miles to allow the Russians to occupy this vast expanse of territory which the western democracies had conquered. If now the Soviet government tries, by separate action, to build up a pro-Communist Germany in their areas this will cause new serious difficulties in the British and American zones, and will give the defeated Germans the power of putting themselves up to auction between the Soviets and western democracies. Whatever conclusions may be drawn from these facts—and facts they are—this is certainly not the liberated Europe we fought to build up. Nor is it one which contains the essentials of permanent peace.

The safety of the world, ladies and gentlemen, requires a new unity in Europe from which no nation should be permanently outcast.

It is impossible not to comprehend—twice we have seen them drawn by irresistible forces in time to secure the victory but only after frightful slaughter and devastation have occurred. Twice the United States has had to send millions of its young men to fight a war, but now war can find any nation between dusk and dawn. Surely we should work within the structure of the United Nations and in accordance with our charter. That is an open course of policy.

In front of the iron curtain which lies across Europe are other causes for anxiety. In Italy the Communist party is seriously hampered by having to support the Communist trained Marshal Tito's claims to former Italian territory at the head of the Adriatic. Nevertheless the future of Italy hangs in the balance. Again one cannot imagine a regenerated Europe without a strong France. All my public life I have worked for a strong France and I never lost faith in her destiny, even in the darkest hours. I will not lose faith now. However, in a great number of countries, far from the Russian frontiers and throughout the world, Communist fifth columns are established and work in complete unity and absolute obedience to the directions they receive from the Communist center. Except in the British Commonwealth and in this United States, where Communism is in its infancy, the Communist parties or fifth columns constitute a growing challenge and peril to Christian civilization. These are somber facts for any one to have to recite on the morrow of a victory gained by so much splendid comradeship in arms and in the cause of freedom and democracy, and we should be most unwise not to face them squarely while time remains.

The outlook is also anxious in the Far East and especially in Manchuria. The agreement which was made at Yalta, to which I was a party, was extremely favorable to Soviet Russia, but it was made at a time when no one could say that the German war might not extend all through the summer and autumn of 1945 and when the Japanese war was expected to last for a further eighteen months from the end of the German war. In this country you are all so well informed about the Far East, and such devoted friends of China, that I do not need to expatiate on the situation there.

I have felt bound to portray the shadow which, alike in the West and in the East, falls upon the world. I was a minister at the time of the Versailles treaty and a close friend of Mr. Lloyd George. I did not myself agree with many things that were done, but I have a very vague impression in my mind of that situation, and I find it painful to contrast it with that which prevails now. In those days there were high hopes and unbounded confidence that the wars were over, and that the League of Nations would become all-powerful. I do not see or feel the same confidence or even the same hopes in the haggard world at this time.

On the other hand I repulse the idea that a new war is inevitable; still more that it is imminent. It is because I am so sure that our fortunes are in our own hands and that we hold the power to save the future, that I feel the duty to speak out now that I have an occasion to do so. I do not believe that Soviet Russia desires war. What they desire is the fruits of war and the indefinite expansion of their power and doctrines. But what we have to consider here today while time remains, is the permanent prevention of war and the establishment of conditions of freedom and democracy as rapidly as possible in all countries. Our difficulties and dangers will not be removed by closing our eyes to them. They will not be removed by mere waiting to see what happens; nor will they be relieved by a policy of appeasement. What is needed is a settlement and the longer this is delayed the more difficult it will be and the greater our dangers will become. From what I have seen of our Russian friends and allies during the war, I am convinced that there is nothing they admire so much as strength, and there is nothing for which they have less respect than for military weakness. For that reason the old doctrine of a balance of power is unsound. We cannot afford, if we can help it, to work on narrow margins, offering temptations to a trial of strength. If the western democracies stand together in strict adherence to the principles of the United Nations Charter, their influence for furthering these principles will be immense and no one is likely to molest them. If, however, they become divided or falter in their duty, and if these all-important years are allowed to slip away, then indeed catastrophe may overwhelm us all.

Last time I saw it all coming, and cried aloud to my fellow countrymen and to the world, but no one paid any attention. Up till the year 1933 or even 1935, Germany might have been saved from the awful fate which has overtaken her and we might all have been spared the miseries Hitler let loose upon mankind. There never was a war in all history easier to prevent by timely action than the one which has just desolated such great areas of the globe. It could have been prevented without the firing of a single shot, and Germany might be powerful, prosperous and honored today, but no one would listen and one by one we were all sucked into the awful whirlpool. We surely must not let that happen again. This can only be achieved by reaching now, in 1946, a good understanding on all points with Russia under the general authority of the United Nations Organization and by the maintenance of that good understanding through many peaceful years, by the world instrument, supported by the whole strength of the English-speaking world and all its connections.

Let no man underrate the abiding power of the British Empire and Commonwealth. Because you see the forty-six millions in our island harassed about their food supply, of which they grew only one half, even in war time, or because we have difficulty in restarting our industries and export trade after six years of passionate war effort, do not suppose that we shall not come through these dark years of privation as we have come through the glorious years of agony, or that half a century from now you will not see seventy or eighty millions of Britons spread about the world and united in defense of our traditions, our way of life and of the world causes we and you espouse. If the population of the English-speaking commonwealth be added to that of the United States, with all that such cooperation implies in the air, on the sea and in science and industry, there will be no quivering, precarious balance of power to offer its temptation to ambition or adventure. On the contrary, there will be an overwhelming assurance of security. If we adhere faithfully to the charter of the United Nations and walk forward in sedate and sober strength, seeking no one's land or treasure, or seeking to lay no arbitrary control on the thoughts of men, if all British moral and material forces and convictions are joined with your own in fraternal association, the highroads of the future will be clear, not only for us but for all, not only for our time but for a century to come.

DOCUMENT 21

THE BARUCH PLAN FOR THE INTERNATIONAL CONTROL OF ATOMIC ENERGY AND SOVIET COUNTERPROPOSAL, JUNE 14, 19, 1946

Although, in 1946, the United States had a monopoly on nuclear power, it was willing to share its secrets with other powers under certain safeguards. On June 14, 1946, Bernard M. Baruch, the American Representative to the Atomic Energy Commission of the United Nations established by the General Assembly in January, 1946, proposed a plan of international control which included inspection of atomic sites and the elimination of the veto. Unwilling to cooperate on these terms, the Soviet Union, through its representative, Andrei A. Gromyko, made a counterproposal which simply called for the destruction of existing nuclear piles. Nothing came of either plan, and the Soviet Union developed its own atomic weapons a few years later.

Decade, 1079–1093.

Statement by Bernard M. Baruch, United States Representative to the Atomic Energy Commission, June 14, 1946

MY FELLOW MEMBERS OF THE UNITED NATIONS ATOMIC ENERGY COMMISSION, and
MY FELLOW CITIZENS OF THE WORLD:

We are here to make a choice between the quick and the dead. That is our business.

Behind the black portent of the new atomic age lies a hope which, seized upon with faith, can work our salvation. If we fail, then we have damned every man to be the slave of Fear. Let us not deceive ourselves: We must elect World Peace or World Destruction.

Science has torn from nature a secret so vast in its potentialities that our minds cower from the terror it creates. Yet terror is not enough to inhibit the use of the atomic bomb. The terror created by weapons has never stopped man from employing them. For each new weapon a defense has been produced, in time. But now we face a condition in which adequate defense does not exist.

Science, which gave us this dread power, shows that it *can* be made a giant help to humanity, but science does *not* show us how to prevent its baleful use. So we have been appointed to obviate that peril by finding a meeting of the minds and the hearts of our peoples. Only in the will of mankind lies the answer.

It is to express this will and make it effective that we have been assembled. We must provide the mechanism to assure that atomic energy is used for peaceful purposes and preclude its use in war. To that end, we must provide immediate, swift, and sure punishment of those who violate the agreements that are reached by the nations. Penalization is essential if peace is to be more than a feverish interlude between wars. And, too, the United Nations can prescribe individual responsibility and punishment on the principles applied at Nürnberg by the Union of Soviet Socialist Republics, The United Kingdom, France, and the United States—a formula certain to benefit the world's future.

In this crisis, we represent not only our governments but, in a larger way, we represent the peoples of the world. We must remember that the peoples do not belong to the governments but that the governments belong to the peoples. We must answer their demands; we must answer the world's longing for peace and security.

In that desire the United States shares ardently and hopefully. The search of science for the absolute weapon has reached fruition in this country. But she stands ready to proscribe and destroy this instrument—to lift its use from death to life—if the world will join in a pact to that end.

In our success lies the promise of a new life, freed from the heart-stopping fears that now beset the world. The beginning of victory for the great ideals for which millions have bled and died lies in building a workable plan. Now we approach fulfilment of the aspirations of mankind. At the end of the road lies the fairer, better, surer life we crave and mean to have. . . .

The United States proposes the creation of an International Atomic Development Authority, to which should be entrusted all phases of the development and use of atomic energy, starting with the raw material and including—

1. Managerial control or ownership of all atomic-energy activities potentially dangerous to world security.

2. Power to control, inspect, and license all other atomic activities.

3. The duty of fostering the beneficial uses of atomic energy.

4. Research and development responsibilities of an affirmative character intended to put the Authority in the forefront of atomic knowledge and thus to enable it to comprehend, and therefore to detect, misuse of atomic energy. To be effective, the Authority must itself be the world's leader in the field of atomic knowledge and development and thus supplement its legal authority with the great power inherent in possession of leadership in knowledge.

I offer this as a basis for beginning our discussion.

But I think the peoples we serve would not believe—and without faith nothing counts—that a treaty, merely outlawing possession or use of the atomic bomb, constitutes effective fulfilment of the instructions to this Commission. Previous failures have been recorded in trying the method of simple renunciation, unsupported by effective guaranties of security and armament limitation. No one would have faith in that approach alone.

Now, if ever, is the time to act for the common good. Public opinion supports a world movement toward security. If I read the signs aright, the peoples want a program not composed merely of pious thoughts but of enforceable sanctions—an international law with teeth in it.

We of this nation, desirous of helping to bring peace to the world and realizing the heavy obligations upon us arising from our possession of the means of producing the bomb and from the fact that it is part of our armament, are prepared to make our full contribution toward effective control of atomic energy.

When an adequate system for control of atomic energy, including the renunciation of the bomb as a weapon, has been agreed upon and put into effective operation and condign punishments set up for violations of the rules of control which are to be stigmatized as international crimes, we propose that—

1. Manufacture of atomic bombs shall stop;
2. Existing bombs shall be disposed of pursuant to the terms of the treaty, and
3. The Authority shall be in possession of full information as to the know-how for the production of atomic energy.

Let me repeat, so as to avoid misunderstanding: my country is ready to make its full contribution toward the end we seek, subject, of course, to our constitutional processes, and to an adequate system of control becoming fully effective, as we finally work it out.

Now as to violations: in the agreement, penalties of as serious a nature as the nations may wish and as immediate and certain in their execution as possible, should be fixed for:

1. Illegal possession or use of an atomic bomb;
2. Illegal possession, or separation, of atomic material suitable for use in an atomic bomb;
3. Seizure of any plant or other property belonging to or licensed by the Authority;
4. Wilful interference with the activities of the Authority;
5. Creation or operation of dangerous projects in a manner contrary to, or in the absence of, a license granted by the international control body.

It would be a deception, to which I am unwilling to lend myself, were I not to say to you and to our peoples, that the matter of punishment lies at the very heart of our present security system. It might as well be admitted, here and now, that the subject goes straight to the veto power contained in the Charter of the United Nations so far as it relates to the field of atomic energy. The Charter permits penalization only by concurrence of each of the five great powers—Union of Soviet Socialist Republics, the United Kingdom, China, France and the United States.

I want to make very plain that I am concerned here with the veto power only as it affects this particular problem. There must be no veto to protect those who violate their solemn agreements not to develop or use atomic energy for destructive purposes.

The bomb does not wait upon debate. To delay may be to die. The time between violation and preventive action or punishment would be all too short for extended discussion as to the course to be followed.

As matters now stand several years may be necessary for another country to produce a bomb, *de novo*. However, once the basic information is generally known, and the Authority has established producing plants for peaceful purposes in the several countries, an illegal seizure of such a plant might permit a malevolent nation to produce a bomb in 12 months, and if preceded by secret preparation and necessary facilities perhaps even in a much shorter time. The time required—the advance warning given of the possible use of a bomb—can only be generally estimated but obviously will depend upon many factors, including the success with which the Authority has been able to introduce elements of safety in the design of its plants and the degree to which illegal and secret preparation for the military use of atomic energy will have been eliminated. Presumably no nation would think of starting a war with only one bomb.

This shows how imperative speed is in detecting and penalizing violations.

The process of prevention and penalization—a problem of profound statecraft—is, as I read it, implicit in the Moscow statement, signed by the Union of Soviet Socialist Republics, the United States, and the United Kingdom a few months ago.

But before a country is ready to relinquish any winning weapons it must have more than words to reassure it. It must have a guarantee of safety, not only against the offenders in the atomic area but against the illegal users of other weapons—bacteriological, biological, gas—perhaps—why not?—against war itself.

In the elimination of war lies our solution, for only then will nations cease to compete with one another in the production and use of dread "secret" weapons which are evaluated solely by their capacity to kill. This devilish program takes us back not merely to the Dark Ages, but from cosmos to chaos. If we succeed in finding a suitable way to control atomic weapons, it is reasonable to hope that we may also preclude the use of other weapons adaptable to mass destruction. When a man learns to say "A" he can, if he chooses, learn the rest of the alphabet, too.

Let this be anchored in our minds:

Peace is never long preserved by weight of metal or by an armament race. Peace can be made tranquil and secure only by understanding and agreement fortified by sanctions. We must embrace international cooperation or international disintegration.

Science has taught us how to put the atom to work. But to make it work for good instead of for evil lies in the domain dealing with the principles of human duty. We are now facing a problem more of ethics than of physics.

The solution will require apparent sacrifice in pride and in position, but better pain as the price of peace than death as the price of war. . . .

Let us keep in mind the exhortation of Abraham Lincoln, whose words, uttered at a moment of shattering national peril, form a complete text for our deliberation. I quote, paraphrasing slightly:

"We cannot escape history. We of this meeting will be remembered in spite of ourselves. No personal significance or insignificance can spare one or another of us. The fiery trial through which we are passing will light us down in honor or dishonor to the latest generation.

"We say we are for Peace. The world will not forget that we say this. We know how to save Peace. The world knows that we do. We, even we here, hold the power and have the responsibility.

"We shall nobly save, or meanly lose, the last, best hope of earth. The way is plain, peaceful, generous, just—a way which, if followed, the world will forever applaud."

My thanks for your attention.

Statement by Andrei A. Gromyko, U.S.S.R. Representative to the Atomic Energy Commission, June 19, 1946

MR. GROMYKO (Soviet Union) (*translated from Russian*). . . .

As one of the primary measures for the fulfillment of the resolution of the General Assembly of 24 January 1946, the Soviet delegation proposes that consideration be given to the question of concluding an international convention prohibiting the production and employment of weapons based on the use of atomic energy for the purpose of mass destruction. The object of such a convention should be the prohibition of the production and employment of atomic weapons, the destruction of existing stocks of atomic weapons and the condemnation of all activities undertaken in violation of this convention. The elaboration and conclusion of a convention of this kind would be, in the opinion of the Soviet delegation, only one of the primary measures to be taken to prevent the use of atomic energy to the detriment of mankind. This act should be followed by other measures aiming at the establishment of methods to ensure the strict observance of the terms and obligations contained in the above-mentioned convention, the establishment of a system of control over the observance of the convention and the taking of decisions regarding the sanctions to be applied against the unlawful use of atomic energy. The public opinion of the whole civilized world has already rightly condemned the use in warfare of asphyxiating, poisonous and other similar gases, as well as all similar liquids and substances, and likewise bacteriological means, by concluding corresponding agreements for the prohibition of their use.

In view of this, the necessity of concluding a convention prohibiting the production and employment of atomic weapons is even more obvious. Such a convention would correspond in an even greater degree to the aspirations of the peoples of the whole world.

The conclusion of such a convention and the elaboration of a system of measures providing for the strict fulfillment of its terms, the establishment of control over the observance of the obligations imposed by the convention, and the establishment of sanctions to be applied against violators of the convention will, in the opinion of the Soviet delegation, be a serious step forward on the way towards the fulfillment of the tasks that lie before the Atomic Energy Commission, and fully corresponds to the aspirations and conscience of the whole of progressive humanity.

The necessity for the States to assume the obligation not to produce or employ atomic weapons is also dictated by the fact that the character of this weapon is such that its employment brings untold misery above all to the peaceful population. The results of its employment are incompatible with the generally accepted standards and ideas riveted in the consciousness of humanity in the course of many centuries to the effect that the rules of warfare must not allow the extermination of innocent civilian populations.

The situation existing at the present time, which has been brought about by the discovery of the means of applying atomic energy and using them for the production of atomic weapons, precludes the possibility of normal scientific co-operation between the States of the world. At the very basis of the present situation, which is characterized by the absence of any limitation in regard to the production and employment of atomic weapons, there are reasons which can only increase the suspicion of some countries in regard to others and give rise to political instability. It is clear that the continuation of such a situation is likely to bring only negative results in regard to peace.

Moreover, the continuation of the present situation means that the latest scientific attainments in this field will not be a basis for joint scientific efforts among the countries for the object of discovering ways of using atomic energy for peaceful purposes. Hence there follows only one correct conclusion, namely, the necessity of an exchange of scientific information between countries and the necessity of joint scientific efforts directed toward a broadening of the possibilities of the use of atomic energy only in the interests of promoting the material welfare of the peoples and developing science and culture. The success of the work of the Commission will be determined in a large measure by the extent to which it succeeds in solving this important task.

The proposal for a wide exchange of scientific information is timely because such a scientific discovery, as the discovery of methods of using atomic energy, cannot remain for an indefinite time the property of only one country or small group of countries. It is bound to become the property of a number of countries. This confirms the necessity of a wide exchange of scientific information on the problem in question, and the necessity of drawing up corresponding measures in this field, including measures of organization.

I have stated the general considerations regarding the tasks and the character of the activities of the Atomic Energy Commission. In order to develop these general statements, on the instructions of my Government, I will place before the Commission for consideration two concrete proposals which, in the opinion of the Soviet Government, may constitute a basis for the adoption by the Commission of recommendations to the Security Council and play an important role in the strengthening of peace. These proposals are as follows:

(1) concerning the conclusion of an international convention prohibiting the production and employment of weapons based on the use of atomic energy for the purpose of mass destruction.

(2) concerning the organization of the work of the Atomic Energy Commission. . . .

DOCUMENT 22

STUTTGART ADDRESS BY SECRETARY OF STATE BYRNES, SEPTEMBER 6, 1946

Just as a hostile Germany had been the main contributor to allied unity during the war, so a defeated Germany became one of the main stumbling blocks to East–West agreement afterward. Soviet refusal to countenance an all-German approach to economic and other problems led the Western powers to seek new ways of solving the German question. On September 6, 1946, Secretary of State James F. Byrnes outlined a new approach at Stuttgart.

I have come to Germany to learn at firsthand the problems involved in the reconstruction of Germany and to discuss with our representatives the views of the United States Government as to some of the problems confronting us. . . .

German militarism and Nazism have devastated twice in our generation the lands of Germany's neighbors. It is fair and just that Germany should do her part to repair that devastation. Most of the victims of Nazi aggression were before the war less well off than Germany. They should not be expected by Germany to bear, unaided, the major costs of Nazi aggression.

Documents on Germany, 1944–1961, 55–62.

The United States, therefore, is prepared to carry out fully the principles outlined in the Potsdam Agreement on demilitarization and reparations. However, there should be changes in the levels of industry agreed upon by the Allied Control Commission if Germany is not to be administered as an economic unit as the Potsdam Agreement contemplates and requires. . . .

The carrying out of the Potsdam Agreement has, however, been obstructed by the failure of the Allied Control Council to take the necessary steps to enable the German economy to function as an economic unit. Essential central German administrative departments have not been established, although they are expressly required by the Potsdam Agreement. . . .

~ The United States is firmly of the belief that Germany should be administered as an economic unit and that zonal barriers should be completely obliterated so far as the economic life and activity in Germany are concerned.

The conditions which now exist in Germany make it impossible for industrial production to reach the levels which the occupying powers agreed were essential for a minimum German peacetime economy. Obviously, if the agreed levels of industry are to be reached, we cannot continue to restrict the free exchange of commodities, persons, and ideas throughout Germany. The barriers between the four zones of Germany are far more difficult to surmount than those between normal independent states.

The time has come when the zonal boundaries should be regarded as defining only the areas to be occupied for security purposes by the armed forces of the occupying powers and not as self-contained economic or political units.

That was the course of development envisaged by the Potsdam Agreement, and that is the course of development which the American Government intends to follow to the full limit of its authority. It has formally announced that it is its intention to unify the economy of its own zone with any or all of the other zones willing to participate in the unification.

So far only the British Government has agreed to let its zone participate. We deeply appreciate their cooperation. Of course, this policy of unification is not intended to exclude the governments not now willing to join. The unification will be open to them at any time they wish to join.

We favor the economic unification of Germany. If complete unification cannot be secured, we shall do everything in our power to secure the maximum possible unification.

Important as the economic unification is for the recovery of Germany and of Europe, the German people must recognize that the basic cause of their suffering and distress is the war which the Nazi dictatorship brought upon the world.

But just because suffering and distress in Germany are inevitable, the American Government is unwilling to accept responsibility for the needless aggravation of economic distress that is caused by the failure of the Allied Control Council to agree to give the German people a chance to solve some of their most urgent economic problems.

So far as many vital questions are concerned, the Control Council is neither governing Germany nor allowing Germany to govern itself.

A common financial policy is essential for the successful rehabilitation of Germany. Runaway inflation accompanied by economic paralysis is almost certain to develop unless there is a common financial policy directed to the control of inflation. A program of drastic fiscal reform to reduce currency and monetary claims, to revise the debt structure, and to place Germany on a sound financial basis is urgently required.

The United States has worked hard to develop such a program, but fully coordinated measures must be accepted and applied uniformly to all zones if ruinous inflation is to be prevented. A central agency of finance is obviously necessary to carry out any such program effectively.

It is also essential that transportation, communications, and postal services should be organized throughout Germany without regard to zonal barriers. The nation-wide organization of these public services was contemplated by the Potsdam Agreement. Twelve months have passed and nothing has been done.

Germany needs all the food she can produce. Before the war she could not produce enough food for her population. The area of Germany has been reduced. The population in Silesia, for instance, has been forced back into a restricted Germany. Armies of occupation and displaced persons increase demands while the lack of farm machinery and fertilizer reduces supplies. To secure the greatest possible production of food and the most effective use and distribution of the food that can be produced, a central administrative department for agriculture should be set up and allowed to function without delay.

Similarly, there is urgent need for the setting up of a central German administrative agency for industry and foreign trade. While Germany must be prepared to share her coal and steel with the liberated countries of Europe dependent upon those supplies, Germany must be enabled to use her skills and her energies to increase her industrial production and to organize the most effective use of her raw materials.

Germany must be given a chance to export goods in order to import enough to make her economy self-sustaining. Germany is a part of Europe, and recovery in Europe, and particularly in the states adjoining Germany, will be slow indeed if Germany with her great resources of iron and coal is turned into a poorhouse. . . .

But it never was the intention of the American Government to deny to the German people the right to manage their own internal affairs as soon as they were able to do so in a democratic way with genuine respect for human rights and fundamental freedoms. . . .

The Potsdam Agreement did not provide that there should never be a central German government; it merely provided that for the time being there should be no central German government. Certainly this only meant that no central government should be established until some sort of democracy was rooted in the soil of Germany and some sense of local responsibility developed.

The Potsdam Agreement wisely provided that administration of the affairs of Germany should be directed toward decentralization of the political structure and the development of local responsibility. This was not intended to prevent progress toward a central government with the powers necessary to deal with matters which would be dealt with on a nation-wide basis. But it was intended to prevent the establishment of a strong central government dominating the German people instead of being responsible to their democratic will.

It is the view of the American Government that the German people throughout Germany, under proper safeguards, should now be given the primary responsibility for the running of their own affairs.

More than a year has passed since hostilities ceased. The millions of German people should not be forced to live in doubt as to their fate. It is the view of the American Government that the Allies should, without delay, make clear to the German people the essential terms of the peace settlement which they expect the German people to accept and observe. It is our view that the German people should now be permitted and helped to make the necessary preparations for setting up of a democratic German government which can accept and observe these terms. . . .

The United States favors the early establishment of a provisional German government for Germany. Progress has been made in the American zone in developing local and state self-government in Germany, and the American Government believes similar progress is possible in all zones.

It is the view of the American Government that the provisional government should not be handpicked by other governments. It should be a German national council composed of the democratically responsible minister presidents or other chief officials of the several states or provinces which have been established in each of the four zones.

Subject to the reserved authority of the Allied Control Council, the German National Council should be responsible for the proper functioning of the central administrative agencies. Those agencies should have adequate power to assure the administration of Germany as an economic unit, as was contemplated by the Potsdam Agreement.

The German National Council should also be charged with the preparation of a draft of a federal constitution for Germany which, among other things, should insure the democratic character of the new Germany and the human rights and fundamental freedoms of all its inhabitants.

After approval in principle by the Allied Control Council, the proposed constitution should be submitted to an elected convention for final drafting and then submitted to the German people for ratification.

While we shall insist that Germany observe the principles of peace, good-neighborliness, and humanity, we do not want Germany to become the satellite of any power or powers or to live under a dictatorship, foreign or domestic. The American people hope to see peaceful democratic Germans become and remain free and independent. . . .

The heads of government agreed to support at the peace settlement the proposal of the Soviet Government concerning the ultimate transfer to the Soviet Union of the city of Königsberg and the area adjacent to it. Unless the Soviet Government changes its views on the subject we will certainly stand by our agreement.

With regard to Silesia and other eastern German areas, the assignment of this territory to Poland by Russia for administrative purposes had taken place before the Potsdam meeting. The heads of government agreed that, pending the final determination of Poland's western frontier, Silesia and other eastern German areas should be under the administration of the Polish state and for such purposes should not be considered as a part of the Soviet zone of occupation in Germany. However, as the Protocol of the Potsdam Conference makes clear, the heads of government did not agree to support at the peace settlement the cession of this particular area.

The Soviets and the Poles suffered greatly at the hands of Hitler's invading armies. As a result of the agreement at Yalta, Poland ceded to the Soviet Union territory east of the Curzon Line. Because of this, Poland asked for revision of her northern and western frontiers. The United States will support a revision of these frontiers in Poland's favor. However, the extent of the area to be ceded to Poland must be determined when the final settlement is agreed upon.

The United States does not feel that it can deny to France, which has been invaded three times by Germany in 70 years, its claim to the Saar territory, whose economy has long been closely linked with France. Of course, if the Saar territory is integrated with France she should readjust her reparation claims against Germany.

Except as here indicated, the United States will not support any encroachment on territory which is indisputably German or any division of Germany which is not genuinely desired by the people concerned. So far as the United States is aware the people of the Ruhr and the Rhineland desire to remain united with the rest of Germany. And the United States is not going to oppose their desire.

While the people of the Ruhr were the last to succumb to Nazism, without the resources of the Ruhr Nazism could never have threatened the world. Never again must those resources be used for destructive purposes. They must be used to rebuild a free, peaceful Germany and a free, peaceful Europe.

The United States will favor such control over the whole of Germany, including the Ruhr and the Rhineland, as may be necessary for security purposes. It will help to enforce those controls. But it will not favor any controls that would subject the Ruhr and the Rhineland to political domination or manipulation of outside powers.

The German people are now feeling the devastating effects of the war which Hitler and his minions brought upon the world. Other people felt those devastating effects long before they were brought home to the people of Germany.

The German people must realize that it was Hitler and his minions who tortured and exterminated innocent men, women, and children and sought with German arms to dominate and degrade the world. It was the massed, angered forces of humanity which had to fight their way into Germany to give the world the hope of freedom and peace.

The American people who fought for freedom have no desire to enslave the German people. The freedom Americans believe in and fought for is a freedom which must be shared with all willing to respect the freedom of others.

The United States has returned to Germany practically all prisoners of war that were in the United States. We are taking prompt steps to return German prisoners of war in our custody in other parts of the world.

The United States cannot relieve Germany from the hardships inflicted upon her by the war her leaders started. But the United States has no desire to increase those hardships or to deny the German people an opportunity to work their way out of those hardships so long as they respect human freedom and follow the paths of peace.

The American people want to return the government of Germany to the German people. The American people want to help the German people to win their way back to an honorable place among the free and peace-loving nations of the world.

DOCUMENT 23

THE TRUMAN DOCTRINE: MESSAGE OF THE PRESIDENT TO CONGRESS, MARCH 12, 1947

When Great Britain, early in 1947, informed the United States that she could no longer support the struggle of the Greek government against Communist insurrectionists, President Truman went before Congress and

Decade, 1253–1257.

asked that the United States shoulder the burden in Greece and Turkey, which was similarly threatened. Congress voted the funds on May 15, 1947, and on May 22 the bill became law.

MR. PRESIDENT, MR. SPEAKER, MEMBERS OF THE CONGRESS OF THE UNITED STATES:

The gravity of the situation which confronts the world today necessitates my appearance before a joint session of the Congress.

The foreign policy and the national security of this country are involved.

One aspect of the present situation, which I wish to present to you at this time for your consideration and decision, concerns Greece and Turkey.

The United States has received from the Greek Government an urgent appeal for financial and economic assistance. Preliminary reports from the American Economic Mission now in Greece and reports from the American Ambassador in Greece corroborate the statement of the Greek Government that assistance is imperative if Greece is to survive as a free nation.

I do not believe that the American people and the Congress wish to turn a deaf ear to the appeal of the Greek Government.

Greece is not a rich country. Lack of sufficient natural resources has always forced the Greek people to work hard to make both ends meet. Since 1940 this industrious and peace-loving country has suffered invasion, four years of cruel enemy occupation, and bitter internal strife.

When forces of liberation entered Greece they found that the retreating Germans had destroyed virtually all the railways, roads, port facilities, communications, and merchant marine. More than a thousand villages had been burned. Eighty-five percent of the children were tubercular. Livestock, poultry, and draft animals had almost disappeared. Inflation had wiped out practically all savings.

As a result of these tragic conditions, a militant minority, exploiting human want and misery, was able to create political chaos which, until now, has made economic recovery impossible.

Greece is today without funds to finance the importation of those goods which are essential to bare subsistence. Under these circumstances the people of Greece cannot make progress in solving their problems of reconstruction. Greece is in desperate need of financial and economic assistance to enable it to resume purchases of food, clothing, fuel, and seeds. These are indispensable for the subsistence of its people and are obtainable only from abroad. Greece must have help to import the goods necessary to restore internal order and security so essential for economic and political recovery.

The Greek Government has also asked for the assistance of experienced American administrators, economists, and technicians to insure that the financial and other aid given to Greece shall be used effectively in creating a stable and self-sustaining economy and in improving its public administration.

The very existence of the Greek state is today threatened by the terrorist activities of several thousand armed men, led by Communists, who defy the Government's authority at a number of points, particularly along the northern boundaries. A commission appointed by the United Nations Security Council is at present investigating disturbed conditions in northern Greece and alleged border violations along the frontier between Greece on the one hand and Albania, Bulgaria, and Yugoslavia on the other.

Meanwhile, the Greek Government is unable to cope with the situation. The Greek Army is small and poorly equipped. It needs supplies and equipment if it is to restore authority to the Government throughout Greek territory.

Greece must have assistance if it is to become a self-supporting and self-respecting democracy.

The United States must supply that assistance. We have already extended to Greece certain types of relief and economic aid, but these are inadequate.

There is no other country to which democratic Greece can turn.

No other nation is willing and able to provide the necessary support for a democratic Greek Government.

The British Government, which has been helping Greece, can give no further financial or economic aid after March 31. Great Britain finds itself under the necessity of reducing or liquidating its commitments in several parts of the world, including Greece.

We have considered how the United Nations might assist in this crisis. But the situation is an urgent one requiring immediate action, and the United Nations and its related organizations are not in a position to extend help of the kind that is required.

It is important to note that the Greek Government has asked for our aid in utilizing effectively the financial and other assistance we may give to Greece, and in improving its public administration. It is of the utmost importance that we supervise the use of any funds made available to Greece, in such a manner that each dollar spent will count toward making Greece self-supporting, and will help to build an economy in which a healthy democracy can flourish.

No government is perfect. One of the chief virtues of a democracy, however, is that its defects are always visible and under democratic processes can be pointed out and corrected. The Government of Greece is not perfect. Nevertheless it represents 85 percent of the members of the Greek Parliament who were chosen in an election last year. Foreign observers, including 692 Americans, considered this election to be a fair expression of the views of the Greek people.

The Greek Government has been operating in an atmosphere of chaos and extremism. It has made mistakes. The extension of aid by this country does not mean that the United States condones everything that the Greek Government has done or will do. We have condemned in the past, and we condemn now, extremist measures of the right or the left. We have in the past advised tolerance, and we advise tolerance now.

Greece's neighbor, Turkey, also deserves our attention.

The future of Turkey as an independent and economically sound state is clearly no less important to the freedom-loving peoples of the world than the future of Greece. The circumstances in which Turkey finds itself today are considerably different from those of Greece. Turkey has been spared the disasters that have beset Greece. And during the war the United States and Great Britain furnished Turkey with material aid.

Nevertheless, Turkey now needs our support.

Since the war Turkey has sought additional financial assistance from Great Britain and the United States for the purpose of effecting that modernization necessary for the maintenance of its national integrity.

That integrity is essential to the preservation of order in the Middle East.

The British Government has informed us that, owing to its own difficulties, it can no longer extend financial or economic aid to Turkey.

As in the case of Greece, if Turkey is to have the assistance it needs, the United States must supply it. We are the only country able to provide that help.

I am fully aware of the broad implications involved if the United States extends assistance to Greece and Turkey, and I shall discuss these implications with you at this time.

One of the primary objectives of the foreign policy of the United States is the creation of conditions in which we and other nations will be able to work out a way of life free from coercion. This was a fundamental issue in the war with Germany and Japan. Our victory was won over countries which sought to impose their will, and their way of life, upon other nations.

To insure the peaceful development of nations, free from coercion, the United States has taken a leading part in establishing the United Nations. The United Nations is designed to make possible lasting freedom and independence for all its members. We shall not realize our objectives, however, unless we are willing to help free peoples to maintain their free institutions and their national integrity against aggressive movements that seek to impose upon them totalitarian regimes. This is no more than a frank recognition that totalitarian regimes imposed upon free peoples, by direct or indirect aggression, undermine the foundations of international peace and hence the security of the United States.

The peoples of a number of countries of the world have recently had totalitarian regimes forced upon them against their will. The Government of the United States has made frequent protests against coercion and intimidation, in violation of the Yalta agreement, in Poland, Rumania, and Bulgaria. I must also state that in a number of other countries there have been similar developments.

At the present moment in world history nearly every nation must choose between alternative ways of life. The choice is too often not a free one.

One way of life is based upon the will of the majority, and is distinguished by free institutions, representative government, free elections, guaranties, of individual liberty, freedom of speech and religion, and freedom from political oppression.

The second way of life is based upon the will of a minority forcibly imposed upon the majority. It relies upon terror and oppression, a controlled press and radio, fixed elections, and the suppression of personal freedoms.

I believe that it must be the policy of the United States to support free peoples who are resisting attempted subjugation by armed minorities or by outside pressures.

I believe that we must assist free peoples to work out their own destinies in their own way.

I believe that our help should be primarily through economic and financial aid which is essential to economic stability and orderly political processes.

The world is not static, and the *status quo* is not sacred. But we cannot allow changes in the *status quo* in violation of the Charter of the United Nations by such methods as coercion, or by such subterfuges as political infiltration. In helping free and independent nations to maintain their freedom, the United States will be giving effect to the principles of the Charter of the United Nations.

It is necessary only to glance at a map to realize that the survival and integrity of the Greek nation are of grave importance in a much wider situation. If Greece should fall under the control of an armed minority, the effect upon its neighbor, Turkey, would be immediate and serious. Confusion and disorder might well spread throughout the entire Middle East.

Moreover, the disappearance of Greece as an independent state would have a profound effect upon those countries in Europe whose peoples are struggling against great difficulties to maintain their freedoms and their independence while they repair the damages of war.

It would be an unspeakable tragedy if these countries, which have struggled so long against overwhelming odds, should lose that victory for which they sacrificed so much. Collapse of free institutions and loss of independence would be disastrous not only for them but for the world. Discouragement and possibly failure would quickly be the lot of neighboring peoples striving to maintain their freedom and independence.

Should we fail to aid Greece and Turkey in this fateful hour, the effect will be far-reaching to the West as well as to the East.

We must take immediate and resolute action.

I therefore ask the Congress to provide authority for assistance to Greece and Turkey in the amount of $400,000,000 for the period ending June 30, 1948. In requesting these funds, I have taken into consideration the maximum amount of relief assistance which would be furnished to Greece out of the $350,000,000 which I recently requested that the Congress authorize for the prevention of starvation and suffering in countries devastated by the war.

In addition to funds, I ask the Congress to authorize the detail of American civilian and military personnel to Greece and Turkey, at the request of those countries, to assist in the tasks of reconstruction, and for the purpose of supervising the use of such financial and material assistance as may be furnished. I recommend that authority also be provided for the instruction and training of selected Greek and Turkish personnel.

Finally, I ask that the Congress provide authority which will permit the speediest and most effective use, in terms of needed commodities, supplies, and equipment, of such funds as may be authorized.

If further funds, or further authority, should be needed for purposes indicated in this message, I shall not hesitate to bring the situation before the Congress. On this subject the Executive and Legislative branches of the Government must work together.

This is a serious course upon which we embark.

I would not recommend it except that the alternative is much more serious.

The United States contributed $341,000,000,000 toward winning World War II. This is an investment in world freedom and world peace.

The assistance that I am recommending for Greece and Turkey amounts to little more than one-tenth of one percent of this investment. It is only common sense that we should safeguard this investment and make sure that it was not in vain.

The seeds of totalitarian regimes are nurtured by misery and want. They spread and grow in the evil soil of poverty and strife. They reach their full growth when the hope of a people for a better life has died.

We must keep that hope alive.

The free peoples of the world look to us for support in maintaining their freedoms.

If we falter in our leadership, we may endanger the peace of the world—and we shall surely endanger the welfare of our own Nation.

Great responsibilities have been placed upon us by the swift movement of events.

I am confident that the Congress will face these responsibilities squarely.

DOCUMENT 24

THE MARSHALL PLAN: REMARKS BY SECRETARY OF STATE GEORGE C. MARSHALL, JUNE 5, 1947, AT HARVARD UNIVERSITY

Believing that revolutionary unrest flourished wherever hunger and poverty prevailed, Secretary of State George C. Marshall, on June 5, 1947, at the Harvard commencement, proposed that the United States assist European nations to help themselves. A conference to discuss the idea was held in Paris in July, but ran into fierce Soviet opposition despite the fact that the Soviet Union had been included in the original proposals. Because of Russian hostility, it became easier to induce Congress to appropriate the necessary funds, and the legislation to carry out the Marshall Plan was passed late in March, 1948. President Truman signed the bill on April 3, 1948.

I need not tell you gentlemen that the world situation is very serious. That must be apparent to all intelligent people. I think one difficulty is that the problem is one of such enormous complexity that the very mass of facts presented to the public by press and radio make it exceedingly difficult for the man in the street to reach a clear appraisement of the situation. Furthermore, the people of this country are distant from the troubled areas of the earth and it is hard for them to comprehend the plight and consequent reactions of the long-suffering peoples, and the effect of those reactions on their governments in connection with our efforts to promote peace in the world.

In considering the requirements for the rehabilitation of Europe, the physical loss of life, the visible destruction of cities, factories, mines, and railroads was correctly estimated, but it has become obvious during recent months that this visible destruction was probably less serious than the dislocation of the entire fabric of European economy. For the past 10 years conditions have been highly abnormal. The feverish preparation for war and the more feverish maintenance of the war effort engulfed all aspects of national economies. Machinery has fallen into disrepair or is entirely obsolete. Under the arbitrary and destructive Nazi rule, virtually every possible enterprise was geared into the German war machine. Long-standing commer-

Decade, 1268–1270.

cial ties, private institutions, banks, insurance companies, and shipping companies disappeared, through loss of capital, absorption through nationalization, or by simple destruction. In many countries, confidence in the local currency has been severely shaken. The breakdown of the business structure of Europe during the war was complete. Recovery has been seriously retarded by the fact that two years after the close of hostilities a peace settlement with Germany and Austria has not been agreed upon. But even given a more prompt solution of these difficult problems, the rehabilitation of the economic structure of Europe quite evidently will require a much longer time and greater effort than had been foreseen.

There is a phase of this matter which is both interesting and serious. The farmer has always produced the foodstuffs to exchange with the city dweller for the other necessities of life. This division of labor is the basis of modern civilization. At the present time it is threatened with breakdown. The town and city industries are not producing adequate goods to exchange with the food-producing farmer. Raw materials and fuel are in short supply. Machinery is lacking or worn out. The farmer or the peasant cannot find the goods for sale which he desires to purchase. So the sale of his farm produce for money which he cannot use seems to him an unprofitable transaction. He, therefore, has withdrawn many fields from crop cultivation and is using them for grazing. He feeds more grain to stock and finds for himself and his family an ample supply of food, however short he may be on clothing and the other ordinary gadgets of civilization. Meanwhile people in the cities are short of food and fuel. So the governments are forced to use their foreign money and credits to procure these necessities abroad. This process exhausts funds which are urgently needed for reconstruction. Thus a very serious situation is rapidly developing which bodes no good for the world. The modern system of the division of labor upon which the exchange of products is based is in danger of breaking down.

The truth of the matter is that Europe's requirements for the next three or four years of foreign food and other essential products—principally from America—are so much greater than her present ability to pay that she must have substantial additional help or face economic, social, and political deterioration of a very grave character.

The remedy lies in breaking the vicious circle and restoring the confidence of the European people in the economic future of their own countries and of Europe as a whole. The manufacturer and the farmer throughout wide areas must be able and willing to exchange their products for currencies the continuing value of which is not open to question.

Aside from the demoralizing effect on the world at large and the possibilities of disturbances arising as a result of the desperation of the people concerned, the consequences to the economy of the United States should be apparent to all. It is logical that the United States should do whatever it is able to do to assist in the return of normal economic health in the world, without which there can be no political stability and no assured peace. Our policy is directed not against any country or doctrine but against hunger, poverty, desperation, and chaos. Its purpose should be the revival of a working economy in the world so as to permit the emergence of political and social conditions in which free institutions can exist. Such assistance, I am convinced, must not be on a piecemeal basis as various crises develop. Any assistance that this Government may render in the future should provide a cure rather than a mere palliative. Any government that is willing to assist in the task of recovery will find full cooperation, I am sure, on the part of the United States Government. Any government which maneuvers to block the recovery of other countries cannot expect help from us. Furthermore, governments, political parties, or groups which seek to perpetuate human misery in order to profit therefrom politically or otherwise will encounter the opposition of the United States.

It is already evident that, before the United States Government can proceed much further in its efforts to alleviate the situation and help start the European world on its way to recovery, there must be some agreement among the countries of Europe as to the requirements of the situation and the part those countries themselves will take in order to give proper effect to whatever action might be undertaken by this Government. It would be neither fitting nor efficacious for this Government to undertake to draw up unilaterally a program designed to place Europe on its feet economically. This is the business of the Europeans. The initiative, I think, must come from Europe. The role of this country should consist of friendly aid in the drafting of a European program and of later support of such a program so far as it may be practical for us to do so. The program should be a joint one, agreed to by a number, if not all, European nations.

An essential part of any successful action on the part of the United States is an understanding on the part of the people of America of the character of the problem and the remedies to be applied. Political passion and prejudice should have no part. With foresight, and a willingness on the part of our people to face up to the vast responsibility which history has clearly placed upon our country, the difficulties I have outlined can and will be overcome.

DOCUMENT 25

DEATH SENTENCE OF NIKOLA PETKOV: EXCHANGE OF NOTES BETWEEN THE UNITED STATES AND THE UNION OF SOVIET SOCIALIST REPUBLICS, AUGUST 23 AND 25, 1947, CONCERNING THE SENTENCING OF THE LEADER OF THE BULGARIAN OPPOSITION

The Soviet Union's refusal to abide by the Declaration on Liberated Europe was particularly evident in Bulgaria, where a purge took place after the Soviet take-over. When the leader of the opposition, Nikola Petkov, was sentenced to death, the United States strongly protested. The Soviet Union refused to intervene, and Petkov was executed in the fall of 1947.

NOTE FROM THE UNITED STATES TO THE U.S.S.R.,
AUGUST 23, 1947

My Government has instructed me to bring to your attention, as a matter of urgency, the importance which the United States Government and world public opinion attaches to the case of Mr. Nikola Petkov, the opposition leader in the Bulgarian Parliament who was recently sentenced to death in Bulgaria.

My Government has instructed me to inform you that it cannot accept the position taken by the Soviet Chairman of the Allied Control Commission in Bulgaria to the effect that it was not possible for the Commission to interfere in Mr. Petkov's case on the allegation that it is a purely internal Bulgarian affair. It is the firm belief of my

Government that the sentencing of death to the duly elected leader of the Bulgarian opposition is a most grave matter, which if carried out will jeopardize the establishment of a representative democratic government in Bulgaria. The establishment of such a representative democratic government in Bulgaria and other countries was the primary objective of the declaration on liberated Europe agreed to by the United States, United Kingdom and the Soviet Union at Yalta. Therefore, my Government is of the opinion that the Soviet Chairman of the Allied Control Commission disregarded the obligations assumed by the Soviet Government in the Yalta Agreement when he refused to consult with the United States and British representatives in Bulgaria in order to reach concerted policies in regard to the case of Nikola Petkov.

In view of the inability of the United States and United Kingdom representatives in Bulgaria to reach a concerted policy with their Soviet colleague in regard to this case, the world wide interest which this case has received, and particularly the obligations assumed by the United States, the United Kingdom and the Soviet Union in the declaration on liberated Europe, my Government requests that immediate consultations take place at a governmental level among the Three Yalta Powers in order that they may reach concerted policies in regard to the matter.

The United States representative in Sofia also has emphasized to the Bulgarian Government the importance which the United States Government attaches to this case and has informed the Bulgarian Government that pending agreement of the Three Powers the United States Government expects that the sentence passed on Mr. Petkov will not be executed. It is hoped that the Soviet Government will make similar representations to the Bulgarian Government.

I should appreciate receiving an urgent reply indicating the Soviet Government's consent to the Three Power consultations proposed by my Government.

SOVIET REPLY TO THE UNITED STATES, AUGUST 25, 1947

It is impossible to agree with the appraisal contained in your note of the acts of the Deputy President of the Allied Control Commission who refused consideration of the proposition brought up by Maj. Gen. Roberts and Col. Greene to the effect that the Bulgarian Government be directed to delay execution of the sentence in the matter of Nikola Petkov until such time as the ACC could consider the matter. Such a statement of the question is incorrect and inadmissible, since the Control Commission in Bulgaria has no right to review judicial matters decided by Bulgarian court or to give the Bulgarian Government any directives whatsoever in such matters. Such acts by the Control Commission would constitute interference in Bulgarian internal affairs and would be direct infringement of the state sovereignty of Bulgaria.

As regards the proposition of the Government of the United States of America which was contained in your note, immediately to begin governmental consultations between the three powers which took part in the Yalta Conference in order to work out concerted policy regarding the matter of Nikola Petkov, the Soviet Government, for the reasons set forth above, does not see any possibility of agreement with indicated proposal. The Soviet Government has an attitude of full respect and confidence toward the Bulgarian court set up by the Bulgarian people as a guardian of justice.

DOCUMENT 26

THE COUP D'ÉTAT IN PRAGUE: CORRESPONDENCE BETWEEN THE PRESIDIUM OF THE COMMUNIST PARTY AND THE PRESIDENT OF CZECHOSLOVAKIA, EDUARD BENEŠ, FEBRUARY 24 AND 25, 1948

Of all the Eastern European countries, Czechoslovakia had been the most democratic before the war. Her high standard of living and liberal tradition, however, did not prevent her from becoming a Soviet satellite in February, 1948, when the Communist party forced President Eduard Beneš to agree to a reorganization of the government on a pro-Communist basis. Shortly afterward, Foreign Minister Jan Masaryk was found dead outside of his office window. President Beneš resigned on June 7. These events served to strengthen Western convictions that strong steps were necessary to contain Communist expansion.

The Strategy and Tactics of World Communism, Supplement III, *The Coup d'État in Prague*, House of Representatives, Committee on Foreign Affairs, National and International Movements, Subcommittee No. 5, Report (Washington, 1948), 25–27.

LETTER FROM PRESIDENT BENEŠ TO PRESIDIUM OF THE COMMUNIST PARTY, FEBRUARY 24, 1948

You sent me a letter on February 21 in which you express your attitude on a solution of the crisis and ask me to agree with it. Allow me to formulate my own attitude.

I feel fully the great responsibility of this fateful hour on our national and state life. From the beginning of this crisis I have been thinking about the situation as it was forming itself, putting these affairs of ours in connection with world affairs.

I am trying to see clearly not only the present situation but also the causes that led to it and the results that a decision can have. I am aware of the powerful forces through which the situation is being formed.

In a calm, matter of fact, impassionate and objective judgment of the situation I feel, through the common will of various groups of our citizens which turn their attention to me, that the will is expressed to maintain the peace and order and discipline voluntarily accepted to achieve a progressive and really socialist life.

How to achieve this goal? You know my sincerely democratic creed. I cannot but stay faithful to that creed even at this moment because democracy, according to my belief, is the only reliable and durable basis for a decent and dignified human life.

I insist on parliamentary democracy and parliamentary government as it limits democracy. I state I know very well it is necessary to social and economic content. I built my political work on these principles and cannot—without betraying myself—act otherwise.

The present crisis of democracy here too cannot be overcome but through democratic and parliamentary means. I thus do not overlook your demands. I regard all our political parties associated in the National Front as bearers of political responsibility. We all accepted the principle of the National Front and this proved successful up to the recent time when the crisis began.

This crisis, however, in my opinion, does not deny the principle in itself. I am convinced that on this principle, even in the future, the necessary cooperation of all can be achieved. All disputes can be solved for the benefit of the national and common state of the Czechs and the Slovaks.

I therefore have been in negotiation with five political parties. I have listened to their views and some of them also have been put in writing. These are grave matters and I cannot ignore them.

Therefore, I again have to appeal to all to find a peaceful solution and new successful cooperation through parliamentary means and through the National Front.

That much for the formal side. As far as the personal side is concerned, it is clear to me, as I have said already, that the Prime Minister will be the chairman of the strongest party element, Gottwald.

Finally, on the factual side of this matter it is clear to me that socialism is a way of life desired by an overwhelming part of our nation. At the same time I believe that with socialism a certain measure of freedom and unity is possible and that these are vital principles to all in our national life.

Our nation has struggled for freedom almost throughout its history. History also has shown us where discord can lead.

I beg of you therefore to relive these facts and make them the starting point for our negotiations. Let us all together begin negotiations again for further durable cooperation and let us not allow prolongation of the split of the nation into two quarreling parts.

I believe that a reasonable agreement is possible because it is indispensable.

REPLY BY THE PRESIDIUM OF THE COMMUNIST PARTY TO LETTER OF PRESIDENT BENEŠ, FEBRUARY 25, 1948

The Presidium of the Central Committee of the Communist Party acknowledged your letter dated February 24 and states again that it cannot enter into negotiations with the present leadership of the National Socialist, People's and Slovak Democratic Parties because this would not conform to the interests of the unity of the people nor with the interests of further peaceful development of the republic.

Recent events indisputably proved that these three parties no longer represent the interests of the working people of the cities and countryside, that their leaders have betrayed the fundamental ideas of the people's democracy and National Front as they have been stated by the Kosice Government program and that they assumed the position of undermining the opposition.

This was shown again and again in the government, in the Constitutional National Assembly, in the press of these parties, and in actions that, with menacing levity, were organized by their central secretariats against the interests of the working people, against the security of the state, against the alliances of the republic, against state finance, against nationalized industry, against urgent agricultural reforms—in one word, against the whole constructive efforts of our people and against the very foundations, internal and external, of the security of the country.

These parties even got in touch with foreign circles hostile to our people's democratic order and our alliances, and in collaboration with these hostile foreign elements they attempted disruption of the present development of the republic.

This constantly increasing activity was crowned by an attempt to break up the government, an attempt that, as it was proved, should have been accompanied by actions aiming at a putsch.

Massive people's manifestations during the last few days clearly have shown our working people denounce, with complete unity and with indignation, the policy of these parties and ask the creation of a government in which all honest progressive patriots devoted to the republic and the people are represented.

Also among the members of the above-mentioned three parties an increasing amount of indignation can be seen. The members ask for a rebirth of their own parties and the National Front.

In conformity with this powerfully expressed will of the people, the Presidium of the Central Committee of the Communist Party approved the proposals of Premier Klement Gottwald according to which the government will be filled in with prominent representatives of all parties and also big nation-wide organizations.

We stress that a government filled in this way will present itself, with full agreement with the principles of parliamentary democracy, before the Constitutional National Assembly with its program and ask for its approval.

Being convinced that only such a highly constitutional and parliamentary process can guarantee the peaceful development of the republic and at the same time it corresponds to the ideas of a complete majority of the working people, the Presidium of the Central Committee hopes firmly after careful consideration that you will recognize the correctness of its conclusions and will agree with its proposals.

DOCUMENT 27

EXCHANGE OF NOTES CONCERNING THE BERLIN BLOCKADE, JULY 6 AND 14, 1948

When, as a result of Russia's failure to cooperate, the Western allies decided to re-establish a German government in their zones of occupation in Germany and announced a currency reform for West Berlin in June, 1948, the Soviet Union countered with a blockade of the city. The following documents consist of the American protest against the blockade and the Soviet reply.

Note From Secretary Marshall to Ambassador Panyushkin, July 6, 1948

EXCELLENCY: The United States Government wishes to call to the attention of the Soviet Government the extremely serious international situation which has been brought about by the actions of the Soviet Government in imposing restrictive measures on transport which amount now to a blockade against the sectors in Berlin occupied by the United States, United Kingdom and France. The United States Government regards these measures of blockade as a clear violation of existing agreements concerning the administration of Berlin by the four occupying powers.

The rights of the United States as a joint occupying power in Berlin derive from the total defeat and unconditional surrender of Germany. The international agreements undertaken in connection therewith by the Governments of the United States, United Kingdom, France and the Soviet Union defined the zones in Germany and the sectors in Berlin which are occupied by these powers. They established the quadripartite control of Berlin on a basis of friendly cooperation which the Government of the United States earnestly desires to continue to pursue.

These agreements implied the right of free access to Berlin. This

---

Decade, 934–936 (U. S. note of July 6, 1948); The Ministry of Foreign Affairs of the USSR, *The Soviet Union and the Berlin Question, Documents* (Moscow, 1948), 42–46 (Soviet note of July 14, 1948).

right has long been confirmed by usage. It was directly specified in a message sent by President Truman to Premier Stalin on June 14, 1945, which agreed to the withdrawal of United States forces to the zonal boundaries, provided satisfactory arrangements could be entered into between the military commanders, which would give access by rail, road and air to United States forces in Berlin. Premier Stalin replied on June 16 suggesting a change in date but no other alteration in the plan proposed by the President. Premier Stalin then gave assurances that all necessary measures would be taken in accordance with the plan. Correspondence in a similar sense took place between Premier Stalin and Mr. Churchill. In accordance with this understanding, the United States, whose armies had penetrated deep into Saxony and Thuringia, parts of the Soviet zone, withdrew its forces to its own area of occupation in Germany and took up its position in its own sector in Berlin. Thereupon the agreements in regard to the occupation of Germany and Berlin went into effect. The United States would not have so withdrawn its troops from a large area now occupied by the Soviet Union had there been any doubt whatsoever about the observance of its agreed right of free access to its sector of Berlin. The right of the United States to its position in Berlin thus stems from precisely the same source as the right of the Soviet Union. It is impossible to assert the latter and deny the former.

It clearly results from these undertakings that Berlin is not a part of the Soviet zone, but is an international zone of occupation. Commitments entered into in good faith by the zone commanders, and subsequently confirmed by the Allied Control Authority, as well as practices sanctioned by usage, guarantee the United States together with other powers, free access to Berlin for the purpose of fulfilling its responsibilities as an occupying power. The facts are plain. Their meaning is clear. Any other interpretation would offend all the rules of comity and reason.

In order that there should be no misunderstanding whatsoever on this point, the United States Government categorically asserts that it is in occupation of its sector in Berlin with free access thereto as a matter of established right deriving from the defeat and surrender of Germany and confirmed by formal agreements among the principal Allies. It further declares that it will not be induced by threats, pressures or other actions to abandon these rights. It is hoped that the Soviet Government entertains no doubts whatsoever on this point.

This Government now shares with the Governments of France and the United Kingdom the responsibility initially undertaken at Soviet request on July 7, 1945, for the physical well-being of 2,400,000 persons in the western sectors of Berlin. Restrictions recently imposed by the Soviet authorities in Berlin have operated to prevent this Government and the Governments of the United Kingdom and of France from fulfilling that responsibility in an adequate manner.

The responsibility which this Government bears for the physical well-being and the safety of the German population in its sector of Berlin is outstandingly humanitarian in character. This population includes hundreds of thousands of women and children, whose health and safety are dependent on the continued use of adequate facilities for moving food, medical supplies and other items indispensable to the maintenance of human life in the western sectors of Berlin. The most elemental of these human rights which both our Governments are solemnly pledged to protect are thus placed in jeopardy by these restrictions. It is intolerable that any one of the occupying authorities should attempt to impose a blockade upon the people of Berlin.

The United States Government is therefore obliged to insist that in accordance with existing agreements the arrangements for the movement of freight and passenger traffic between the western zones and Berlin be fully restored. There can be no question of delay in the restoration of these essential services, since the needs of the civilian population in the Berlin area are imperative.

Holding these urgent views regarding its rights and obligations in the United States sector of Berlin, yet eager always to resolve controversies in the spirit of fair consideration for the viewpoints of all concerned, the Government of the United States declares that duress should not be invoked as a method of attempting to dispose of any disagreements which may exist between the Soviet Government and the Government of the United States in respect of any aspect of the Berlin situation.

Such disagreements if any should be settled by negotiation or by any of the other peaceful methods provided for in Article 33 of the Charter in keeping with our mutual pledges as copartners in the United Nations. For these reasons the Government of the United States is ready as a first step to participate in negotiations in Berlin among the four Allied Occupying Authorities for the settlement of any question in dispute arising out of the administration of the city of

Berlin. It is, however, a prerequisite that the lines of communication and the movement of persons and goods between the United Kingdom, the United States and the French sectors in Berlin and the Western Zones shall have been fully restored.

Accept [etc.]

G. C. MARSHALL

His Excellency
ALEXANDER S. PANYUSHKIN,
Ambassador of the Union of Soviet Socialist Republics.

Note of the Soviet Government to the Government of the United States of July 14, 1948[1]

1. The Soviet Government has acquainted itself with the note of the Government of the United States of America of July 6th last, in which the situation that has been created at the present time in Berlin is explained as a result of measures taken by the Soviet side. The Soviet Government cannot agree with this statement of the Government of the United States and considers that the situation which has been created in Berlin has arisen as a result of violation by the Governments of the United States, Great Britain and France of agreed decisions taken by the Four Powers in regard to Germany and Berlin, which (violation) has found its expression in the carrying out of a separate currency reform, in the introduction of a special currency for the western sectors of Berlin and in the policy of the dismemberment of Germany.

The Soviet Government repeatedly warned the Governments of the U.S.A., Great Britain and France in regard to the responsibility which they would take upon themselves in following along the path of the violation of agreed decisions previously adopted by the Four Powers in regard to Germany. The decisions adopted at the Yalta and Potsdam conferences and also the agreement of the Four Powers concerning the control machinery in Germany have as their aim the demilitarization and democratization of Germany, the undermining of the very basis of German militarism and the prevention of the revival of Germany as an aggressive Power and thereby the conversion of Germany into a peace-loving and democratic State. These

---

[1] Identical notes were sent to the Governments of Great Britain and France.

agreements envisage the obligation of Germany to pay reparations and thereby to make at least partial compensation for the damage to those countries which suffered from German aggression. In accordance with these agreements the Governments of the Four Powers took upon themselves the responsibility for the administration of Germany and bound themselves jointly to determine a statute for Germany or for any areas including Berlin which are part of German territory, and to conclude with Germany a peace treaty which should be signed by a Government of a democratic Germany adequate for that purpose.

These most important agreements of the Four Powers in regard to Germany have been violated by the Governments of the United States of America, Great Britain and France. Measures for the demilitarization of Germany have not been completed and such a very important centre of German war industry as the Ruhr region has been taken out from under the control of the Four Powers. The execution of the decision concerning reparations from the Western zones of occupation of Germany has been disrupted by the Governments of the U.S.A., Great Britain and France. By the separate actions of the Governments of the U.S.A., Great Britain and France the quadripartite control machinery in Germany has been destroyed and the Control Council as a result thereof has ceased its activity.

Following the London conference of the three Powers with the participation of the Benelux, measures have been undertaken by the Governments of the U.S.A., Great Britain and France aimed at the division and dismemberment of Germany, including preparations which are now in progress for the designation of a separate Government for the Western zones of Germany and the separate currency reform for the Western zones of Germany carried out on June 18, 1948.

Inasmuch as the situation created in Berlin as well as in all Germany is the direct result of the systematic violation by the Governments of the U.S.A., Great Britain and France of the decisions of the Potsdam Conference and also of the agreement of the Four Powers concerning the control machinery in Germany, the Soviet Government must reject as completely unfounded the declaration of the Government of the United States to the effect that the measures for the restriction of transport communications between Berlin and the Western zones of occupation of Germany introduced by the Soviet

Command to protect the economy of the Soviet zone from its disorganization are allegedly in violation of the existing agreements concerning the administration of Berlin.

2. The Government of the United States declares that it is occupying its sector in Berlin by right deriving from the defeat and surrender of Germany referring in this connection to agreement among the Four Powers in regard to Germany and Berlin. This merely confirms the fact that the exercise of the above-mentioned right in regard to Berlin is linked to the obligatory execution by the Powers occupying Germany of the quadripartite agreements concluded among themselves in regard to Germany as a whole. In accordance with these agreements, Berlin was envisaged as the seat of the supreme authority of the Four Powers occupying Germany, in which connection the agreement concerning the administration of Greater Berlin under the direction of the Control Council was reached.

Thus, the agreement concerning the quadripartite administration of Berlin is an inseparable component part of the agreement for the quadripartite administration of Germany as a whole. After the United States, Great Britain and France by their separate actions in the Western zones of Germany destroyed the system of quadripartite administration of Germany and had begun to set up a capital for a Government for Western Germany in Frankfurt-am-Main they thereby undermined as well the very legal basis which assured their right to participation in the administration of Berlin.

The Government of the United States in its Note points out that its right to stay in Berlin is based also on the fact that the United States withdrew its troops from certain areas of the Soviet zone of occupation into which they had entered during the period of military operations in Germany, and that, had it foreseen the situation which has been created in Berlin, it would not have withdrawn its forces from these areas. However, the Government of the United States is well aware that in removing its forces to the boundaries of the American zone established by agreement of the Four Powers concerning zones of occupation in Germany it was only carrying out the obligations which it had taken upon itself, the execution of which could alone give the right of the entry of the troops of the U.S.A. into Berlin.

A perusal of President Truman's letter to Premier Stalin of June 14, 1945, and of Premier Stalin's letter in reply of June 16, 1945, which are mentioned in the United States Government's Note, confirms the fact that thanks to the agreement then reached, the forces of the United States, Great Britain and France were given the opportunity to enter both the capital of Germany, Berlin, and the capital of Austria, Vienna, which, as is known, were taken only by the forces of the Soviet army. It is also known that the agreements referred to concerning the question of Berlin and also of Vienna were only a part of the agreements concerning Germany and Austria upon the fulfillment of which the Soviet Government continues to insist.

3. The Government of the United States declares that the temporary measures introduced by the Soviet Command for the restriction of transport communications between Berlin and the Western zones have created difficulties in supplying the Berlin population of the western sectors. It cannot, however, be denied that these difficulties were caused by the actions of the Governments of the U.S.A., Great Britain and France, and above all by their separate actions in the introduction of a new currency in the Western zones of Germany and special currency in the western sectors of Berlin.

Berlin lies in the centre of the Soviet zone and is a part of that zone. The interests of the Berlin population do not permit a situation in which in Berlin or only in the western sectors of Berlin there shall be introduced special currency which has no validity in the Soviet zone. Moreover, the carrying out of a separate monetary reform in the Western zones of Germany has placed Berlin and the whole Soviet zone of occupation as well in a position in which the entire mass of currency notes which were invalidated in the Western zones threatened to pour into Berlin and the Soviet zone of occupation of Germany.

The Soviet Command has been forced therefore to take urgent measures for the protection of the interests of the German population and also of the economy of the Soviet zone of occupation and the area of Greater Berlin. The danger of the disruption of the normal economic activity of the Soviet occupation zone and of Berlin has not been averted even at the present time inasmuch as the United States, Great Britain and France continue to maintain in Berlin their special currency.

At the same time, the Soviet Command has invariably manifested and is manifesting concern for the well-being of the Berlin population and for ensuring to them normal supply in all essentials and is striving for the speediest elimination of the difficulties which have arisen recently in this matter. In this connection, if the situation requires, the Soviet Government would not object to ensuring by its own means adequate supply for all Greater Berlin.

As regards the declaration of the Government of the United States that it will not be induced by threats, pressure or other actions to abandon its right to participation in the occupation of Berlin, the Soviet Government does not intend to enter into discussion of this declaration since it has no need for a policy of pressure, since by violation of the agreed decisions concerning the administration of Berlin the above-mentioned Governments themselves are reducing to naught their right to participation in the occupation of Berlin.

4. The Government of the United States in its Note of July 6, expresses the readiness to begin negotiations among the four Allied Occupying Authorities for consideration of the situation created in Berlin but passes by in silence the question of Germany as a whole.

The Soviet Government, while not objecting to negotiations, deems, however, it necessary to declare that it cannot link the inauguration of these negotiations with the fulfillment of any preliminary conditions, and that, in the second place, the quadripartite negotiations could be effective only in the event that they were not confined to the question of the administration of Berlin, since that question cannot be separated from the general question of quadripartite control in regard to Germany.

DOCUMENT 28

THE POINT FOUR PROGRAM: EXCERPT FROM PRESIDENT TRUMAN'S INAUGURAL ADDRESS, JANUARY 20, 1949

While the focal point in the struggle between the democracies and the Soviet bloc remained in highly developed areas in Europe, the United States did not neglect the problem of the underdeveloped nations elsewhere. In his inaugural address on January 20, 1949, President Harry S. Truman advocated a comprehensive program of technical assistance to countries that needed it, and Congress, in June, 1950, appropriated funds for the program.

Decade, 1366–1367.

Fourth, we must embark on a bold new program for making the benefits of our scientific advances and industrial progress available for the improvement and growth of underdeveloped areas.

More than half the people of the world are living in conditions approaching misery. Their food is inadequate. They are victims of disease. Their economic life is primitive and stagnant. Their poverty is a handicap and a threat both to them and to more prosperous areas.

For the first time in history, humanity possesses the knowledge and the skill to relieve the suffering of these people.

The United States is preeminent among nations in the development of industrial and scientific techniques. The material resources which we can afford to use for the assistance of other peoples are limited. But our imponderable resources in technical knowledge are constantly growing and are inexhaustible.

I believe that we should make available to peace-loving peoples the benefits of our store of technical knowledge in order to help them realize their aspirations for a better life. And, in cooperation with other nations, we should foster capital investment in areas needing development.

Our aim should be to help the free peoples of the world, through their own efforts, to produce more food, more clothing, more materials for housing, and more mechanical power to lighten their burdens.

We invite other countries to pool their technological resources in this undertaking. Their contributions will be warmly welcomed. This should be a cooperative enterprise in which all nations work together through the United Nations and its specialized agencies wherever practicable. It must be a world-wide effort for the achievement of peace, plenty, and freedom.

With the cooperation of business, private capital, agriculture, and labor in this country, this program can greatly increase the industrial activity in other nations and can raise substantially their standards of living.

Such new economic developments must be devised and controlled to benefit the peoples of the areas in which they are established. Guaranties to the investor must be balanced by guaranties in the interest of the people whose resources and whose labor go into these developments.

The old imperialism—exploitation for foreign profit—has no place in our plans. What we envisage is a program of development based on the concepts of democratic fair-dealing.

All countries, including our own, will greatly benefit from a constructive program for the better use of the world's human and natural resources. Experience shows that our commerce with other countries expands as they progress industrially and economically.

Greater production is the key to prosperity and peace. And the key to greater production is a wider and more vigorous application of modern scientific and technical knowledge.

Only by helping the least fortunate of its members to help themselves can the human family achieve the decent, satisfying life that is the right of all people.

Democracy alone can supply the vitalizing force to stir the peoples of the world into triumphant action, not only against their human oppressors, but also against their ancient enemies—hunger, misery, and despair.

DOCUMENT 29

THE NORTH ATLANTIC TREATY, APRIL 4, 1949

To counter Soviet pressure, the United States abandoned its traditional refusal to enter into entangling alliances. America became the mainstay of the North Atlantic Treaty Organization, a defensive military alliance including Belgium, Canada, Denmark, France, Iceland, Italy, Luxembourg, the Netherlands, Norway, Portugal and the United Kingdom. Eventually, Greece and Turkey also adhered to it.

The Parties to this Treaty reaffirm their faith in the purposes and principles of the Charter of the United Nations and their desire to live in peace with all peoples and all governments.

They are determined to safeguard the freedom, common heritage and civilization of their peoples, founded on the principles of democracy, individual liberty and the rule of law.

They seek to promote stability and well-being in the North Atlantic area.

Decade, 1328–1330.

They are resolved to unite their efforts for collective defense and for the preservation of peace and security.

They therefore agree to this North Atlantic Treaty:

ARTICLE 1

The Parties undertake, as set forth in the Charter of the United Nations, to settle any international disputes in which they may be involved by peaceful means in such a manner that international peace and security, and justice, are not endangered, and to refrain in their international relations from the threat or use of force in any manner inconsistent with the purposes of the United Nations.

ARTICLE 2

The Parties will contribute toward the further development of peaceful and friendly international relations by strengthening their free institutions, by bringing about a better understanding of the principles upon which these institutions are founded, and by promoting conditions of stability and well-being. They will seek to eliminate conflict in their international economic policies and will encourage economic collaboration between any or all of them.

ARTICLE 3

In order more effectively to achieve the objectives of this Treaty, the Parties, separately and jointly, by means of continuous and effective self-help and mutual aid, will maintain and develop their individual and collective capacity to resist armed attack.

ARTICLE 4

The Parties will consult together whenever, in the opinion of any of them, the territorial integrity, political independence or security of any of the Parties is threatened.

ARTICLE 5

The Parties agree that an armed attack against one or more of them in Europe or North America shall be considered an attack against them all; and consequently they agree that, if such an armed attack occurs, each of them, in exercise of the right of individual or collective self-defense recognized by Article 51 of the Charter of the

United Nations, will assist the Party or Parties so attacked by taking forthwith, individually and in concert with the other Parties, such action as it deems necessary, including the use of armed force, to restore and maintain the security of the North Atlantic area.

Any such armed attack and all measures taken as a result thereof shall immediately be reported to the Security Council. Such measures shall be terminated when the Security Council has taken the measures necessary to restore and maintain international peace and security.

ARTICLE 6

For the purpose of Article 5 an armed attack on one or more of the Parties is deemed to include an armed attack on the territory of any of the Parties in Europe or North America, on the Algerian departments of France, on the occupation forces of any Party in Europe, on the islands under the jurisdiction of any Party in the North Atlantic area north of the Tropic of Cancer or on the vessels or aircraft in this area of any of the Parties.

ARTICLE 7

This Treaty does not affect, and shall not be interpreted as affecting, in any way the rights and obligations under the Charter of the Parties which are members of the United Nations, or the primary responsibility of the Security Council for the maintenance of international peace and security.

ARTICLE 8

Each Party declares that none of the international engagements now in force between it and any other of the Parties or any third state is in conflict with the provisions of this Treaty, and undertakes not to enter into any international engagement in conflict with this Treaty.

ARTICLE 9

The Parties hereby establish a council, on which each of them shall be represented, to consider matters concerning the implementation of this Treaty. The council shall be so organized as to be able to meet promptly at any time. The council shall set up such subsidiary bodies as may be necessary; in particular it shall establish immediately a defense committee which shall recommend measures for the implementation of Articles 3 and 5.

ARTICLE 10

The Parties may, by unanimous agreement, invite any other European state in a position to further the principles of this Treaty and to contribute to the security of the North Atlantic area to accede to this Treaty. Any state so invited may become a party to the Treaty by depositing its instrument of accession with the Government of the United States of America. The Government of the United States of America will inform each of the Parties of the deposit of each such instrument of accession.

ARTICLE 11

This Treaty shall be ratified and its provisions carried out by the Parties in accordance with their respective constitutional processes. The instruments of ratification shall be deposited as soon as possible with the Government of the United States of America, which will notify all the other signatories of each deposit. The Treaty shall enter into force between the states which have ratified it as soon as the ratifications of the majority of the signatories, including the ratifications of Belgium, Canada, France, Luxembourg, the Netherlands, the United Kingdom and the United States, have been deposited and shall come into effect with respect to other states on the date of the deposit of their ratifications.

ARTICLE 12

After the Treaty has been in force for ten years, or at any time thereafter, the Parties shall, if any of them so requests, consult together for the purpose of reviewing the Treaty, having regard for the factors then affecting peace and security in the North Atlantic area, including the development of universal as well as regional arrangements under the Charter of the United Nations for the maintenance of international peace and security.

ARTICLE 13

After the Treaty has been in force for twenty years, any Party may cease to be a party one year after its notice of denunciation has been given to the Government of the United States of America, which will inform the Governments of the other Parties of the deposit of each notice of denunciation. . . .

DOCUMENT 30

END OF THE BERLIN BLOCKADE, MAY 4, 1949

The allied reaction to the Berlin blockade was an airlift to supply the 2,400,000 people in the Western sectors of the city. This operation was so successful that in May, 1949, the Soviets yielded and abandoned their policy of blockading the city. A Foreign Ministers' conference was called, but the Berlin question remained a major issue between East and West.

Four-Power Communiqué, on Agreement on Lifting the Berlin Blockade, New York, May 4, 1949

The Governments of France, the Union of Soviet Socialist Republics, the United Kingdom, and the United States have reached the following agreement:

1. All the restrictions imposed since March 1, 1948 by the Government of the Union of Soviet Socialist Republics on communications, transportation, and trade between Berlin and the Western zones of Germany and between the Eastern zone and the Western zones will be removed on May 12, 1949.

2. All the restrictions imposed since March 1, 1948 by the Governments of France, the United Kingdom, and the United States, or any one of them, on communication, transportation, and trade between Berlin and the Eastern zone and between the Western and Eastern zones of Germany will also be moved on May 12, 1949.

3. Eleven days subsequent to the removal of the restrictions referred to in paragraphs one and two, namely, on May 23, 1949, a meeting of the Council of Foreign Ministers will be convened in Paris to consider questions relating to Germany and problems arising out of the situation in Berlin, including also the question of currency in Berlin.

Documents on Germany, 1944–1961, 90–91.

DOCUMENT 31

ESTABLISHMENT OF THE FEDERAL REPUBLIC OF GERMANY, SEPTEMBER 21, 1949

After the three western zones of Germany had been merged into an economic unit, the Germans worked out a basic law for the area and formed the Federal Republic of Germany (May 23, 1949). On September 21, 1949, the occupying powers recognized the regime established at Bonn and regularized their relations with it.

Effective September 21, 1949, the Allied High Commissioners in Germany have been formally advised of the formation of the Federal Republic of Germany and have proclaimed that the Occupation Statute is now in force.

Under the terms of Executive Order No. 10062, dated June 6, 1949, "The United States High Commissioner for Germany, hereinafter referred to as the High Commissioner, shall be the supreme United States authority in Germany. The High Commissioner shall have the authority, under the immediate supervision of the Secretary of State (subject, however, to consultation with and ultimate direction by the President), to exercise all of the governmental functions of the United States in Germany (other than the command of troops), including representation of the United States on the Allied High Commission for Germany and the exercise of appropriate functions of a Chief of Mission within the meaning of the Foreign Service Act of 1946."

By the same Executive Order, the United States High Commissioner for Germany was designated also as "the United States Military Governor with all the powers thereof including those vested in the United States Military Governor under all international agreements" until such time as the Military Government of the United States zone of Germany shall have been terminated. Effective September 21, 1949, the Military Government of the United States zone of Germany was terminated. Therefore, by virtue of these events, the United States High Commissioner for Germany no longer exercises the role of the United States Military Governor.

The role of the United States High Commissioner for Germany as

---

Decade, 609–610.

the ECA representative for Germany is outlined in Executive Order No. 10063, dated June 13, 1949, as follows:

"1. During his tenure of office as United States High Commissioner for Germany, Mr. John J. McCloy, under the immediate supervision of the Administrator for Economic Cooperation and the coordination of the United States Special Representative for Europe (subject, however, to consultation with and ultimate direction by the President), shall be the representative of the said Administrator and the said Special Representative in all their relations and actions with respect to Germany.

"2. Mr. McCloy, in performing the duties set forth in paragraph one hereof, shall be assisted by a Chief of Special Mission who shall be appointed by the Administrator for Economic Cooperation and who shall be acceptable to Mr. McCloy. The Chief of Special Mission shall have the rank of Minister and shall act under the immediate supervision and direction of Mr. McCloy."

The United States High Commissioner for Germany is the Honorable John J. McCloy. The British High Commissioner for Germany is General Sir Brian Robertson. The French High Commissioner for Germany is His Excellency André Francois-Poncet.

DOCUMENT 32

SOVIET TRANSFER OF POWER TO THE (EAST) GERMAN DEMOCRATIC REPUBLIC, OCTOBER 10, 1949

The Soviet Union responded to the establishment of a West German government with the creation of a Communist regime in East Germany, and all efforts to reunite the country failed because of Soviet refusal to permit free elections. The following statement by General V. I. Chuikov contains the official Soviet version of the setting up of the German Democratic Republic.

Statement by Chief of the Soviet Military Administration in Germany, Army General V. I. Chuikov, in Connection with the Decisions of the German People's Council to Put Into Operation the Constitution of the German Democratic Republic and the Forma-

Ministry of Foreign Affairs of the U.S.S.R., *The Soviet Union and the Question of the Unity of Germany and the German Peace Treaty* (Moscow, 1952), 60–63.

*tion in Berlin of the Provisional Government of the German
Democratic Republic, October 10, 1949*

The Soviet Government has instructed me to make the following
statement in connection with the decisions adopted on October 7,
1949, by the German People's Council on putting into operation the
Constitution of the German Democratic Republic and on the establishment in Berlin of a Provisional Government of the German Democratic Republic.

On October 1 the Soviet Government sent to the Governments of
the United States, Great Britain and France a Note stating the position of the Soviet Union in relation to the situation which has now
arisen in Germany in connection with the formation on September 20
of this year of a separate government in the city of Bonn (western
part of Germany). At the same time the Soviet Government declared
that the formation of the Bonn separate government is a gross violation of the Potsdam decisions, according to which the Governments
of the U.S.S.R., the United States, Great Britain and France assumed
the obligation to consider Germany as one whole and to contribute
towards its transformation into a democratic and peace-loving State,
and also the obligation to conclude a peace treaty with Germany.

In compliance with the Potsdam and other joint decisions of the
Four Powers, the Soviet Government has invariably endeavoured to
prevent the splitting of Germany, directing its efforts towards the
fulfillment of these decisions, towards the accomplishment of the
democratization and demilitarization of Germany and towards ensuring the fulfillment by Germany of the obligations placed upon her
by the Potsdam Agreement of the Four Powers.

It should be clear to all that the accomplishment of the democratization and demilitarization of Germany, based on the active participation of all democratic forces of the German people, is essential in
order to prevent the restoration of Germany as an aggressive State,
which meets the interests of all peace-loving peoples of Europe and
which corresponds to the interests of the German people itself. It is
obvious that a situation in which even a part of Germany should fall
into the hands of yesterday's inspirers of the Hitler regime is incompatible with the tasks of democratizing and demilitarizing Germany.
It is universally evident that these people make no secret of their
hostile attitude to neighbouring countries and to democratic Germany

itself, and that they are imbued with open revanchist yearnings, being today, in the western part of Germany, the direct instrument of aggressive foreign circles.

The Soviet Government is confident that the German people will find ways for the restoration of the unity of Germany, which is at present violated, and will achieve the unity of the German State on a democratic and peaceful basis. The partition of Germany cannot continue for long, inasmuch as this situation is in contradiction to the deepest aspirations of the German people.

A whole series of obstacles are placed in the way to the restoration of Germany's unity. For instance, who does not understand that the puppet "government" set up in Bonn cannot help to restore a united, democratic and peace-loving Germany? On the contrary, the formation of the Bonn government is intended only to deepen the split of Germany.

Under such conditions one cannot help but recognize as legitimate the striving of German democratic circles to take into their own hands the restoration of the unity of Germany and bring about the renascence of the country on democratic and peace-loving principles. Precisely in this respect does the Soviet Government see the essence of the decisions of the German People's Council on putting into operation the Constitution of the German Democratic Republic and on the formation, in Berlin, of a Provisional Government of the German Democratic Republic.

Moreover, the Soviet Government takes note of the fact that the Provisional Government will abide by the decisions of the Potsdam Conference and will fulfill the obligations arising out of decisions jointly adopted by the Four Powers.

In connection with the above-mentioned decisions of the German People's Council, the Soviet Government has decided to transfer to the Provisional Government of the German Democratic Republic the functions of administration which hitherto belonged to the Soviet Military Administration.

In the place of the Soviet Military Administration in Germany, a Soviet Control Commission will be established charged with exercising control over the fulfillment of the Potsdam and other joint decisions of the Four Powers in respect to Germany.

FOUR

Cold and Hot War in Asia, 1945--1953

Western successes in containing Communism in Europe were not matched in Asia. Although the Soviet Union signed a Treaty of Friendship with the Nationalist Government of China, the Chinese Communists failed to abandon their policy of open warfare against Chiang Kai-shek. The United States tried to mediate; when these efforts failed, the Nationalists were defeated on the mainland and had to seek refuge on Formosa. Some of the reasons for this debacle were set forth in a White Paper published by the State Department in 1949.

The other focal point of the East-West conflict was Korea. At the end of the war, President Truman had directed General MacArthur to accept the enemy's surrender in the Japanese home islands and in that portion of Korea lying south of the Thirty-eighth parallel; the Russians were to be responsible for the area situated to the north of that line. After a vain attempt to participate in the occupation of Hokkaido, Stalin proceeded to communize northern Korea, and although the great powers agreed on the eventual unification of the country, the Soviets refused to cooperate with a United Nations Commission set up for that purpose. This impasse resulted in the establishment of two governments, a Communist regime in the North and a non-Communist administration in the South.

But the Communists did not rest. After American troops had been withdrawn from Korea and Secretary of State Acheson had failed to include the peninsula specifically in the American defense perimeter, the North Koreans, in 1950, launched an attack upon the South. In this emergency, President Truman committed American forces to meet the threat. The United Nations authorized a police action, a measure the Soviets were unable to veto because of their boycott of the Security Council in protest against the continued presence of Nationalist China. When they abandoned their boycott, they could do little but castigate the action already taken. The United Nations, however, continued to sustain the war in Korea, and the General Assembly branded Communist China an aggressor after the Peking regime had entered the conflict. Not until 1953 was a truce worked out. The United Nations had been saved and a third world war avoided, but the policy of containment had been less than a complete success.

DOCUMENT 33

TREATY OF FRIENDSHIP BETWEEN NATIONALIST CHINA AND THE U.S.S.R. AND RELATED DOCUMENTS, AUGUST 14, 1945

On August 14, 1945, the Soviet Union signed a Treaty of Friendship and Alliance with the government of Chiang Kai-shek. As related notes made clear, in return for Chinese recognition of the independence of Outer Mongolia and her acquiescence in special Russian rights in Manchuria, the Soviets promised to give aid only to the Nationalist government. Within four years, they had violated the treaty and were preparing to sign a new one with the Chinese Communists.

Treaty of Friendship and Alliance Between the Republic of China and the U.S.S.R., August 14, 1945

The President of the National Government of the Republic of China, and the Presidium of the Supreme Soviet of the U.S.S.R.,

United States Relations with China, With Special Reference to the Period 1944–1949, Department of State Publication No. 3573 (Washington, 1949), 585–589.

Desirous of strengthening the friendly relations that have always existed between China and the U.S.S.R., through an alliance and good neighborly post-war collaboration,

Determined to assist each other in the struggle against aggression on the part of enemies of the United Nations in this world war, and to collaborate in the common war against Japan until her unconditional surrender,

Expressing their unswerving aspiration to cooperate in the cause of maintaining peace and security for the benefit of the peoples of both countries and of all the peace-loving nations,

Acting upon the principles enunciated in the joint declaration of the United Nations of January 1, 1942, in the four power Declaration signed in Moscow on October 30, 1943, and in the Charter of the International Organization of the United Nations.

Have decided to conclude the present Treaty. . . .

ARTICLE I

The High Contracting Parties undertake in association with the other United Nations to wage war against Japan until final victory is won. The High Contracting Parties undertake mutually to render to one another all necessary military and other assistance and support in this war.

ARTICLE II

The High Contracting Parties undertake not to enter into separate negotiations with Japan and not to conclude, without mutual consent, any armistice or peace treaty either with the present Japanese Government or with any other government or authority set up in Japan which do not renounce all aggressive intentions.

ARTICLE III

The High Contracting Parties undertake after the termination of the war against Japan to take jointly all measures in their power to render impossible a repetition of aggression and violation of the peace by Japan.

In the event of one of the High Contracting Parties becoming involved in hostilities with Japan in consequence of an attack by the latter against the said Contracting Party, the other High Contracting Party shall at once give to the Contracting Party so involved in hostilities all the military and other support and assistance with the means in its power.

This article shall remain in force until such time as the organization "The United Nations" may on request of the two High Contracting Parties be charged with the responsibility for preventing further aggression by Japan.

ARTICLE IV

Each High Contracting Party undertakes not to conclude any alliance and not to take any part in any coalition directed against the other High Contracting Party.

ARTICLE V

The High Contracting Parties, having regard to the interests of the security and economic development of each of them, agree to work together in close and friendly collaboration after the coming of peace and to act according to the principles of mutual respect for their sovereignty and territorial integrity and of non-interference in the internal affairs of the other contracting party.

ARTICLE VI

The High Contracting Parties agree to render each other every possible economic assistance in the post-war period with a view to facilitating and accelerating reconstruction in both countries and to contributing to the cause of world prosperity.

ARTICLE VII

Nothing in this treaty shall be so construed as may affect the rights or obligations of the High Contracting Parties as members of the organization "The United Nations."

ARTICLE VIII

. . . The Treaty comes into force immediately upon its ratification and shall remain in force for a term of thirty years. . . .

EXCHANGE OF NOTES RELATING TO THE TREATY OF FRIENDSHIP AND
ALLIANCE

*The People's Commissar for Foreign Affairs (Molotov) to the
Chinese Minister for Foreign Affairs (Wang)*

August 14, 1945

YOUR EXCELLENCY, With reference to the Treaty of Friendship
and Alliance signed today between the Republic of China and the
U.S.S.R., I have the honor to put on record the understanding between the High Contracting Parties as follows:

1. In accordance with the spirit of the aforementioned Treaty,
and in order to put into effect its aims and purposes, the Government
of the U.S.S.R. agrees to render to China moral support and aid in
military supplies and other material resources, such support and aid
to be entirely given to the National Government as the central government of China.

2. In the course of conversations regarding Dairen and Port Arthur and regarding the joint operation of the Chinese Changchun
Railway, the Government of the U.S.S.R. regarded the Three Eastern
Provinces as part of China and reaffirmed its respect for China's full
sovereignty over the Three Eastern Provinces and recognize their
territorial and administrative integrity.

3. As for the recent developments in Sinkiang the Soviet Government confirms that, as stated in Article V of the Treaty of Friendship
and Alliance, it has no intention of interfering in the internal affairs
of China.

If Your Excellency will be so good as to confirm that the understanding is correct as set forth in the preceding paragraphs, the
present note and Your Excellency's reply thereto will constitute a
part of the aforementioned Treaty of Friendship and Alliance.

I take [etc.]   V. M. MOLOTOV

*The Chinese Minister for Foreign Affairs (Wang) to the People's
Commissar for Foreign Affairs (Molotov)*

August 14, 1945

YOUR EXCELLENCY: I have the honour to acknowledge receipt of
Your Excellency's Note of today's date reading as follows:

"With reference to the Treaty of Friendship and Alliance signed today between the Republic of China and the U.S.S.R., I have the honour to put on record the understanding between the High Contracting Parties as follows:

"1. In accordance with the spirit of the aforementioned Treaty, and in order to put into effect its aims and purposes, the Government of the U.S.S.R., agrees to render to China moral support and aid in military supplies and other material resources, such support and aid to be entirely given to the National Government as the central Government of China.

"2. In the course of conversations regarding Dairen and Port Arthur and regarding the joint operation of the Chinese Changchun Railway, the Government of the U.S.S.R. regarded the Three Eastern Provinces as part of China and reaffirmed its respect for China's full sovereignty over the Three Eastern Provinces and recognize their territorial and administrative integrity.

"3. As for the recent developments in Sinkiang the Soviet Government confirms that, as stated in Article V of the Treaty of Friendship and Alliance, it has no intention of interfering in the internal affairs of China.

"If Your Excellency will be so good as to confirm that the understanding is correct as set forth in the preceding paragraphs, the present note and Your Excellency's reply thereto will constitute a part of the aforementioned Treaty of Friendship and Alliance."

I have the honour to confirm that the understanding is correct as set forth above.

I avail [etc.]   WANG SHIH-CHIEH

EXCHANGE OF NOTES ON OUTER MONGOLIA

The Chinese Minister for Foreign Affairs (Wang) to the People's Commissar for Foreign Affairs (Molotov)

August 14, 1945

YOUR EXCELLENCY: In view of the desire repeatedly expressed by the people of Outer Mongolia for their independence, the Chinese Government declares that after the defeat of Japan should a plebiscite of the Outer Mongolian people confirm this desire, the Chinese

Government will recognize the independence of Outer Mongolia with the existing boundary as its boundary.

The above declaration will become binding upon the ratification of the Treaty of Friendship and Alliance between the Republic of China and the U.S.S.R. signed on August 14, 1945.

I avail [etc.]   WANG SHIH-CHIEH

The People's Commissar for Foreign Affairs (Molotov) to the Chinese Minister for Foreign Affairs (Wang)

August 14, 1945

YOUR EXCELLENCY: I have the honour to acknowledge receipt of Your Excellency's Note reading as follows:

"In view of the desire repeatedly expressed by the people of Outer Mongolia for their independence, the Chinese Government declares that after the defeat of Japan should a plebiscite of the Outer Mongolian people confirm this desire, the Chinese Government will recognize the independence of Outer Mongolia with the existing boundary as its boundary.

"The above declaration will become binding upon the ratification of the Treaty of Friendship and Alliance between the Republic of China and the U.S.S.R. signed on August 14, 1945."

The Soviet Government has duly taken note of the above communication of the Government of the Chinese Republic and hereby expresses its satisfaction therewith, and it further states that the Soviet Government will respect the political independence and territorial integrity of the People's Republic of Mongolia (Outer Mongolia).

I avail [etc.]   V. M. MOLOTOV

Agreement Concerning Dairen

In view of a Treaty of Friendship and Alliance having been concluded between the Republic of China and the U.S.S.R. and of the pledge by the latter that it will respect Chinese sovereignty in the control of all of Manchuria as an integral part of China; and with the object of ensuring that the U.S.S.R.'s interest in Dairen as a port of entry and exit for its goods shall be safeguarded, the Republic of China agrees:

1. To declare Dairen a free port open to the commerce and shipping of all nations.

2. The Chinese Government agrees to apportion in the mentioned port for lease to U.S.S.R. wharfs and warehouses on the basis of separate agreement.

3. The Administration in Dairen shall belong to China.

The harbor-master and deputy harbor-master will be appointed by the Chinese Eastern Railway and South Manchurian Railway in agreement with the Mayor. The harbor-master shall be a Russian national, and the deputy harbor-master shall be a Chinese national.

4. In peace time Dairen is not included in the sphere of efficacy of the naval base regulations, determined by the Agreement on Port Arthur of August 14, 1945, and shall be subject to the military supervision or control established in this zone only in case of war against Japan.

5. Goods entering the free port from abroad for through transit to Soviet territory on the Chinese Eastern and South Manchurian Railways and goods coming from Soviet territory on the said railways into the free port for export shall be free from customs duties. Such goods shall be transported in sealed cars.

Goods entering China from the free port shall pay the Chinese import duties, and goods going out of other parts of China into the free port shall pay the Chinese export duties as long as they continue to be collected.

6. The term of this Agreement shall be thirty years and this Agreement shall come into force upon its ratification.

DOCUMENT 34

SECRETARY OF STATE DEAN ACHESON'S LETTER OF TRANSMITTAL OF THE WHITE PAPER ON CHINA, JULY 30, 1949

When, in 1949, the Chinese Communists overran the mainland of China, Americans were stunned. Having attempted to create a great power in China, cooperated with Chiang Kai-shek and tried to settle the Chinese

United States Relations with China, With Special Reference to the Period 1944–1949, iii–xvii.

civil war by compromise, they could not understand why their policy had miscarried. Many looked for a scapegoat and blamed the State Department, which sought to justify American policies and explain their failure in a White Paper published on August 5, 1949. The following document consists of excerpts from Secretary Acheson's letter of transmittal of the White Paper to President Truman.

DEPARTMENT OF STATE
Washington, July 30, 1949

THE PRESIDENT: In accordance with your wish, I have had compiled a record of our relations with China, special emphasis being placed on the last five years. This record is being published and will therefore be available to the Congress and to the People of the United States. . . .

The reasons for the failures of the Chinese National Government appear in some detail in the attached record. They do not stem from any inadequacy of American aid. Our military observers on the spot have reported that the Nationalist armies did not lose a single battle during the crucial year of 1948 through lack of arms or ammunition. The fact was that the decay which our observers had detected in Chungking early in the war had fatally sapped the powers of resistance of the Kuomintang. Its leaders had proved incapable of meeting the crisis confronting them, its troops had lost the will to fight, and its Government had lost popular support. The Communists, on the other hand, through a ruthless discipline and fanatical zeal, attempted to sell themselves as guardians and liberators of the people. The Nationalist armies did not have to be defeated; they disintegrated. History has proved again and again that a regime without faith in itself and an army without morale cannot survive the test of battle.

The record obviously can not set forth in equal detail the inner history and development of the Chinese Communist Party during these years. The principal reason is that, while we had regular diplomatic relations with the National Government and had the benefit of voluminous reports from our representatives in their territories, our direct contact with the Communists was limited in the main to the mediation efforts of General Hurley and General Marshall.

Fully recognizing that the heads of the Chinese Communist Party were ideologically affiliated with Moscow, our Government nevertheless took the view, in the light of the existing balance of forces in China, that peace could be established only if certain conditions were met. The Kuomintang would have to set its own house in order and both sides would have to make concessions so that the Government of China might become, in fact as well as in name, the Government of all China and so that all parties might function within the constitutional system of the Government. Both internal peace and constitutional development required that the progress should be rapid from one party government with a large opposition party in armed rebellion, to the participation of all parties, including the moderate non-communist elements, in a truly national system of government.

None of these conditions has been realized. The distrust of the leaders of both the Nationalist and Communist Parties for each other proved too deep-seated to permit final agreement, notwithstanding temporary truces and apparently promising negotiations. The Nationalists, furthermore, embarked in 1946 on an over-ambitious military campaign in the face of warnings by General Marshall that it not only would fail but would plunge China into economic chaos and eventually destroy the National Government. General Marshall pointed out that though Nationalist armies could, for a period, capture Communist-held cities, they could not destroy the Communist armies. Thus every Nationalist advance would expose their communications to attack by Communist guerrillas and compel them to retreat or to surrender their armies together with the munitions which the United States has furnished them. No estimate of a military situation has ever been more completely confirmed by the resulting facts.

The historic policy of the United States of friendship and aid toward the people of China was, however, maintained in both peace and war. Since V–J Day, the United States Government has authorized aid to Nationalist China in the form of grants and credits totaling approximately 2 billion dollars, an amount equivalent in value to more than 50 percent of the monetary expenditures of the Chinese Government and of proportionately greater magnitude in relation to the budget of that Government than the United States has provided to any nation of Western Europe since the end of the war. In addition to these grants and credits, the United States Government has sold the Chinese Government large quantities of military and civilian war surplus property with a total procurement cost of over 1 billion dollars, for which the agreed realization to the United States was 232 million dollars. A large proportion of the military supplies furnished the Chinese armies by the United States since V–J Day has, however, fallen into the hands of the Chinese Communists through the military ineptitude of the Nationalist leaders, their defections and surrenders, and the absence among their forces of the will to fight.

It has been urged that relatively small amounts of additional aid—military and economic—to the National Government would have enabled it to destroy communism in China. The most trustworthy military, economic, and political information available to our Government does not bear out this view.

A realistic appraisal of conditions in China, past and present, leads to the conclusion that the only alternative open to the United States was full-scale intervention in behalf of a Government which had lost the confidence of its own troops and its own people. Such intervention would have required the expenditure of even greater sums than have been fruitlessly spent thus far, the command of Nationalist armies by American officers, and the probable participation of American armed forces—land, sea, and air—in the resulting war. Intervention of such a scope and magnitude would have been resented by the mass of the Chinese people, would have diametrically reversed our historic policy, and would have been condemned by the American people.

It must be admitted frankly that the American policy of assisting the Chinese people in resisting domination by any foreign power or powers is now confronted with the gravest difficulties. The heart of China is in Communist hands. The Communist leaders have foresworn their Chinese heritage and have publicly announced their subservience to a foreign power, Russia, which during the last 50 years, under czars and Communists alike, has been most assiduous in its efforts to extend its control in the Far East. In the recent past, attempts at foreign domination have appeared quite clearly to the Chinese people as external aggression and as such have been bitterly and in the long run successfully resisted. Our aid and encouragement have helped them to resist. In this case, however, the foreign domination has been masked behind the façade of a vast crusading movement which apparently has seemed to many Chinese to be wholly indigenous and national. Under these circumstances, our aid has been unavailing.

The unfortunate but inescapable fact is that the ominous result of the civil war in China was beyond the control of the government of the United States. Nothing that this country did or could have done within the reasonable limits of its capabilities could have changed that result; nothing that was left undone by this country has contributed to it. It was the product of internal Chinese forces, forces which this country tried to influence but could not. A decision was arrived at within China, if only a decision by default.

And now it is abundantly clear that we must face the situation as it exists in fact. We will not help the Chinese or ourselves by basing our policy on wishful thinking. We continue to believe that, however tragic may be the immediate future of China and however ruthlessly a major portion of this great people may be exploited by a party in the interest of a foreign imperialism, ultimately the profound civilization and the democratic individualism of China will reassert themselves and she will throw off the foreign yoke. I consider that we should encourage all developments in China which now and in the future work toward this end.

In the immediate future, however, the implementation of our historic policy of friendship for China must be profoundly affected by current developments. It will necessarily be influenced by the degree to which the Chinese people come to recognize that the Communist regime serves not their interests but those of Soviet Russia and the manner in which, having become aware of the facts, they react to this foreign domination. One point, however, is clear. Should the Communist regime lend itself to the aims of Soviet Russian imperialism and attempt to engage in aggression against China's neighbors, we and the other members of the United Nations would be confronted by a situation violative of the principles of the United Nations Charter and threatening international peace and security.

Meanwhile our policy will continue to be based upon our own respect for the Charter, our friendship for China, and our traditional support for the Open Door and for China's independence and administrative and territorial integrity.

Respectfully yours,

DEAN ACHESON

DOCUMENT 35

CORRESPONDENCE BETWEEN PRESIDENT TRUMAN AND MARSHAL STALIN CONCERNING THE SURRENDER OF JAPANESE FORCES, AUGUST, 1945

When, on August 14, 1945, Japan indicated her willingness to surrender, President Truman informed Marshal Stalin of his orders to General MacArthur to accept the surrender of Japanese forces south of the thirty-eighth parallel in Korea and on the Japanese home islands. When Stalin attempted to secure northern Hokkaido as well, Truman refused, although in accordance with the Yalta agreements, he did permit the Soviets to occupy the Kurile Islands. Stalin sent a resentful reply. This correspondence, as published by the Soviets, follows.

TOP SECRET FOR GENERALISSIMO STALIN FROM PRESIDENT TRUMAN

I have approved the following general order to General of the Army MacArthur covering details of the surrender of Japanese Armed Forces:

GENERAL ORDER NUMBER 1.

1. *Military and Naval.*

I. The Imperial General Headquarters by direction of the Emperor, and pursuant to the surrender to the Supreme Commander for the Allied Powers of all Japanese Armed Forces by the Emperor, hereby orders all of its commanders in Japan and abroad to cause the Japanese Armed Forces and Japanese-controlled forces under their command to cease hostilities at once, to lay down their arms, to remain in their present locations and to surrender unconditionally to commanders acting on behalf of the United States, The Republic of China, The United Kingdom and the British Empire, and The Union of Soviet Socialist Republics, as indicated hereafter or as may be further directed by the Supreme Commander for the Allied Powers. Immediate contact will be made with the indicated commanders, or their designated representatives, subject to any changes in detail prescribed by the Supreme Commander for the Allied Powers, and their instructions will be completely and immediately carried out.

Stalin Correspondence, II, 261–268.

a. The Senior Japanese Commanders and all ground, sea, air and auxiliary forces within China (excluding Manchuria), Formosa and French Indo-China north of 16 degrees north latitude shall surrender to Generalissimo Chiang Kai-Shek.

b. The Senior Japanese Commanders and all ground, sea, air and auxiliary forces within Manchuria, Korea north of 38 degrees north latitude and Karafuto shall surrender to the Commander-in-Chief of Soviet Forces in the Far East.

c. The Senior Japanese Commanders and all ground, sea, air and auxiliary forces within the Andamans, Nicobars, Burma, Thailand, French Indo-China south of 16 degrees north latitude, Malaya, Borneo, Netherlands Indies, New Guinea, Bismarcks, and the Solomons, shall surrender (to the Supreme Allied Commander, Southeast Asia Command, or the Commanding General, Australian Forces —the exact breakdown between Mountbatten and the Australians to be arranged between them and the details of this paragraph then prepared by the Supreme Commander for the Allied Powers).

d. The Senior Japanese Commanders and all ground, sea, air and auxiliary forces in the Japanese mandated islands, Ryukyus, Bonins, and other Pacific islands shall surrender to the Commander-in-Chief, U.S. Pacific Fleet.

e. The Imperial General Headquarters, its Senior Commanders, and all ground, sea, air and auxiliary forces in the main islands of Japan, minor islands adjacent thereto, Korea south of 38 degrees north latitude, and the Philippines shall surrender to the Commander-in-Chief, U.S. Army Forces in the Pacific.

f. The above indicated commanders are the only representatives of the Allied Powers empowered to accept surrenders, and all surrenders of Japanese forces shall be made only to them or to their representatives. . . .

This order is approved by me with the understanding that it is subject to change, both by further instructions issued through the Joint Chiefs of Staff and by changes in matters of detail made by the Supreme Commander for the Allied Powers in light of the operational situation as known by him. The action on portions of the order in parentheses is a matter for the Supreme Commander for the Allied Powers.

August 15, 1945

Your message enclosing General Order Number 1 received. I have nothing against the substance of the order. It is understood that the Liaotung Peninsula is an integral part of Manchuria. However, I suggest amending General Order Number 1 as follows:

1. To include in the area to be surrendered by the Japanese armed forces to the Soviet troops all the Kurile Islands which, according to the three-Power decision taken in the Crimea, are to pass into the possession of the Soviet Union.

2. To include in the area to be surrendered by the Japanese armed forces to Soviet troops the northern half of the Island of Hokkaido adjoining in the north La Perouse Strait, which lies between Karafuto and Hokkaido. To draw the demarcation line between the northern and southern halves of Hokkaido along a line running from the town of Kushiro on the east coast of the island to the town of Rumoe on the west coast of the island, including the said towns in the northern half of the island.

This last point is of special importance to Russian public opinion. As is known, in 1919–21 the Japanese occupied the whole of the Soviet Far East. Russian public opinion would be gravely offended if the Russian troops had no occupation area in any part of the territory of Japan proper.

I am most anxious that the modest suggestions set forth above should not meet with any objections.

August 16, 1945
Received on August 18, 1945

TOP SECRET

Replying to your message of August 16, I agree to your request to modify General Order Number 1 to include all the Kurile Islands in the area to be surrendered to the Commander-in-Chief of the Soviet Forces in the Far East. However, I should like it to be understood that the United States Government desires air base rights for land and sea aircraft on some one of the Kurile Islands, preferably in the central group, for military purposes and for commercial use. I should be glad if you would advise me that you will agree to such an arrangement, the location and other details to be worked out through the appointment of special representatives of our two Governments for this purpose.

Regarding your suggestion as to the surrender of Japanese forces on the Island Hokkaido to Soviet forces, it is my intention and arrangements have been made for the surrender of Japanese forces on all the islands of Japan proper, Hokkaido, Honshu, Shikoku and Kyushu, to General MacArthur.

General MacArthur will employ Allied token forces, which, of course, includes Soviet forces, in so much of a temporary occupation of Japan proper as he considers it necessary to occupy in order to accomplish our Allied surrender terms.

PERSONAL AND SECRET FROM PREMIER J. V. STALIN TO THE PRESIDENT, MR. H. TRUMAN

Your message of August 18 to hand.

I understand your message to imply refusal to accede to the Soviet Union's request that the northern half of Hokkaido be included in the area of surrender of Japanese armed forces to Soviet troops. I must say that I and my colleagues had not anticipated that such would be your reply.

2. As regards your demand for a permanent air base on one of the Kurile Islands, which, in keeping with the three-Power decision taken in the Crimea, are to pass into the possession of the Soviet Union, I consider it my duty to say the following. First, I must point out that no such measure was envisaged by the tripartite decision either in the Crimea or at Berlin, nor does it in any way follow from the decisions adopted there. Second, demands of this kind are usually laid either before a vanquished country or before an allied country that is unable to defend a particular part of its territory and expresses, therefore, readiness to grant its ally an appropriate base. I do not think the Soviet Union can be classed in either category. Third, since your message furnishes no reasons for the demand that a permanent base be granted, I must tell you in all frankness that neither I nor my colleagues understand the circumstances in which this claim on the Soviet Union could have been conceived.

August 22, 1945

DOCUMENT 36

COMMUNIQUÉ OF THE MOSCOW CONFERENCE OF FOREIGN MINISTERS: DECLARATION CONCERNING THE RE-ESTABLISHMENT OF KOREA AS AN INDEPENDENT STATE, DECEMBER 27, 1945

When the Foreign Ministers of the United States, the Soviet Union, Great Britain and France met at Moscow in December, 1945, they included in the final communiqué issued by the conference a joint statement promising eventual unity and independence to Korea.

1. With a view to the re-establishment of Korea as an independent state, the creation of conditions for developing the country on democratic principles and the earliest possible liquidation of the disastrous results of the protracted Japanese domination in Korea, there shall be set up a provisional Korean democratic government which shall take all the necessary steps for developing the industry, transport and agriculture of Korea and the national culture of the Korean people.

2. In order to assist the formation of a provisional Korean government and with a view to the preliminary elaboration of the appropriate measures, there shall be established a Joint Commission consisting of representatives of the United States command in southern Korea and the Soviet command in northern Korea. In preparing their proposals the Commission shall consult with the Korean democratic parties and social organizations. The recommendations worked out by the Commission shall be presented for the consideration of the Governments of the Union of Soviet Socialist Republics, China, the United Kingdom and the United States prior to final decision by the two Governments represented on the Joint Commission.

3. It shall be the task of the Joint Commission, with the participation of the provisional Korean democratic government and of the Korean democratic organizations to work out measures also for helping and assisting (trusteeship) the political, economic and social progress of the Korean people, the development of democratic self-government and the establishment of the national independence of Korea.

The proposals of the Joint Commission shall be submitted, following consultation with the provisional Korean Government for the

Department of State *Bulletin*, XIII (1945), 1030.

joint consideration of the Governments of the United States, Union of Soviet Socialist Republics, United Kingdom and China for the working out of an agreement concerning a four-power trusteeship of Korea for a period of up to five years.

4. For the consideration of urgent problems affecting both southern and northern Korea and for the elaboration of measures establishing permanent coordination in administrative-economic matters between the United States command in southern Korea and the Soviet command in northern Korea, a conference of the representatives of the United States and Soviet commands in Korea shall be convened within a period of two weeks.

DOCUMENT 37

ESTABLISHMENT OF THE UNITED NATIONS TEMPORARY COMMISSION ON KOREA AND SOVIET REFUSAL TO GRANT ACCESS TO NORTH KOREA

Unable to agree with the Soviets on a plan for Korean unification, the United States brought the matter before the United Nations in 1947. On November 14, 1947, the General Assembly set up a Temporary Commission on Korea to expedite free elections throughout the country, but the Soviet Union refused to admit the Commission to its zone. On February 6, 1948, the Commission adopted a statement taking note of Soviet refusal to cooperate with it.

RESOLUTION OF THE GENERAL ASSEMBLY OF THE UNITED NATIONS
ADOPTED NOVEMBER 14, 1947

A

INASMUCH AS the Korean question which is before the General Assembly is primarily a matter for the Korean people itself and concerns its freedom and independence, and

RECOGNIZING that this question cannot be correctly and fairly resolved without the participation of representatives of the indigenous population,

The General Assembly

1. *Resolves* that elected representatives of the Korean people be invited to take part in the consideration of the question;

2. *Further resolves* that in order to facilitate and expedite such

Korea, 1945–1948, Department of State Publication No. 3305 (Washington, 1948), 66–69.

participation and to observe that the Korean representatives are in fact duly elected by the Korean people and not mere appointees by military authorities in Korea, there be forthwith established a United Nations Temporary Commission on Korea, to be present in Korea, with right to travel, observe and consult throughout Korea.

B

The General Assembly,

RECOGNIZING the urgent and rightful claims to independence of the people of Korea;

BELIEVING that the national independence of Korea should be re-established and all occupying forces then withdrawn at the earliest practicable date;

RECALLING its previous conclusion that the freedom and inde- pendence of the Korean people cannot be correctly or fairly resolved without the participation of representatives of the Korean people, and its decision to establish a United Nations Temporary Commis- sion on Korea (hereinafter called the "Commission") for the purpose of facilitating and expediting such participation by elected repre- sentatives of the Korean people,

1. *Decides* that the Commission shall consist of representatives of Australia, Canada, China, El Salvador, France, India, Philippines, Syria, Ukrainian Soviet Socialist Republic;

2. *Recommends* that the elections be held not later than 31 March 1948 on the basis of adult suffrage and by secret ballot to choose representatives with whom the Commission may consult regarding the prompt attainment of the freedom and independence of the Ko- rean people and which respresentatives, constituting a National As- sembly, may establish a National Government of Korea. The number of representatives from each voting area or zone should be propor- tionate to the population, and the elections should be under the observation of the Commission;

3. *Further recommends* that as soon as possible after the elections, the National Assembly should convene and form a National Govern- ment and notify the Commission of its formation;

4. *Further recommends* that immediately upon the establishment of a National Government, that Government should, in consultation with the Commission: (*a*) constitute its own national security forces and dissolve all military or semi-military formations not included

therein: (*b*) take over the functions of government from the military commands and civilian authorities of north and south Korea, and (*c*) arrange with the occupying Powers for the complete withdrawal from Korea of their armed forces as early as practicable and if possible within ninety days;

5. *Resolves* that the Commission shall facilitate and expedite the fulfillment of the foregoing programme for the attainment of the national independence of Korea and withdrawal of occupying forces, taking into account its observations and consultations in Korea. The Commission shall report, with its conclusions, to the General Assembly and may consult with the Interim Committee (if one be established) with respect to the application of this resolution in the light of developments;

6. *Calls upon* the Member States concerned to afford every assistance and facility to the Commission in the fulfillment of its responsibilities;

7. *Calls upon* all Members of the United Nations to refrain from interfering in the affairs of the Korean people during the interim period preparatory to the establishment of Korean independence, except in pursuance of the decisions of the General Assembly; and thereafter, to refrain completely from any and all acts derogatory to the independence and sovereignty of Korea.

ADOPTED FEBRUARY 6, 1948

The United Nations Temporary Commission on Korea has taken note of the following facts:

That the Commission was informed by the Secretary-General of the United Nations on 25 January 1948 that the attitude of the Government of the Ukrainian Soviet Socialist Republic in the matter of appointing a representative to the Temporary Commission on Korea remains the same as presented by the Ukrainian delegation at the second session of the General Assembly;

That a cable was received by the Secretariat of the Commission from the United Nations headquarters on 23 January 1948 quoting the Permanent Representative of the Union of Soviet Socialist Republics to the United Nations, Mr. Gromyko, as follows:

"In connection with your letter of 18 January 1948 transmitting the text of a letter from the Acting Chairman of the Commission on Korea, in which he expresses desire to visit the Commander of Soviet troops in Northern Korea, we find it necessary to remind you of the negative attitude taken by the Soviet Government towards the establishment of the United Nations Temporary Commission on Korea as already stated by the Soviet delegation during the second session of the General Assembly of the United Nations";

That the Commission requested the Secretary-General of the United Nations, on 16 January 1948, to remind the Government of the Soviet Union of the Secretary-General's letter of 24 November 1947 drawing attention to paragraph 6 of the substantive part of the General Assembly resolution calling on Member States concerned to afford every assistance and facility to the Commission in the fulfillment of its responsibilities, and that no reply has been received from the Soviet Government either to the letter of 24 November 1947 or to the reminder;

That, up to date, the Commission has received no reply to the letter addressed to General Korotkov expressing the desire of the Acting Chairman of the Commission to exchange the appropriate courtesies with the officers commanding the armed forces in North and South Korea, which letter was despatched to North Korea by train on 20 January 1948, while the train which left Pyongyang on 30 January 1948 did not carry any message from the Soviet authorities in North Korea;

That efforts were made to deliver other communications from the United Nations Temporary Commission on Korea to North Korea, but that the Soviet officials would neither sign for nor accept the communications transmitted by the Commission.

DOCUMENT 38

UNITED STATES RECOGNITION OF THE REPUBLIC OF KOREA, JANUARY 1, 1949

After the Soviets refused to cooperate with the United Nations Temporary Commission on Korea, elections were held in that part of the country accessible to the Commission. On August 15, 1948, a new government was inaugurated there under the Presidency of Syngman Rhee and recognized by the General Assembly of the United Nations on December 12, 1948. The United States extended full recognition to the South Korean Government on January 1, 1949.

Decade, 679.

On December 12, 1948, the United Nations General Assembly adopted a resolution approving the conclusions of the report of the United Nations Temporary Commission on Korea and declaring in part "that there has been established a lawful government (the Government of the Republic of Korea), having effective control and jurisdiction over that part of Korea where the Temporary Commission was able to observe and consult and in which the great majority of the people of all Korea reside; that this Government is based on elections which were a valid expression of the free will of the electorate of that part of Korea and which were observed by the Temporary Commission; and that this is the only such Government in Korea." The resolution of December 12 concluded with the recommendation that member states and other nations take the foregoing facts into consideration in establishing their relations with the Government of Korea.

In the light of this action by the General Assembly, and taking into account the facts set forth in the statement issued by this Government on August 12, 1948, concerning the new Korean Government, the United States Government has decided to extend full recognition to the Government of the Republic of Korea. Incidental to this step it is anticipated that, by agreement with that Government, the Mission of the United States Special Representative in Korea will in the near future be raised to Embassy rank.

In conformity with the General Assembly resolution of December 12, the United States Government will endeavor to afford every assistance and facility to the new United Nations Commission on Korea established thereunder in its efforts to help the Korean people and their lawful Government to achieve the goal of a free and united Korea.

DOCUMENT 39

SOVIET RECOGNITION OF THE KOREAN PEOPLE'S DEMOCRATIC REPUBLIC, OCTOBER 12, 1949

The Soviet reply to the establishment of a non-Communist government in South Korea was the creation of a Communist regime in the north. In a letter to Kim Il Sung, Marshal Stalin, on October 12, 1948, an-

Ministry of Foreign Affairs of the U.S.S.R., *The Soviet Union and the Korean Question, Documents* (Moscow, 1948), 84.

nounced his intention of entering into diplomatic relations with the new government.

MR. KIM IL SUNG
Chairman of the Ministerial Cabinet
of the Korean People's Democratic Republic,
Phyöngyang

I acknowledge the receipt of your letter of October 8 in which you state that the Government of the Korean People's Democratic Republic has entered on the performance of its duties, and propose the establishment of diplomatic relations with the U.S.S.R. and exchange of ambassadors, as well as the establishment of corresponding economic relations between our two States.

The Soviet Government, which unswervingly upholds the right of the Korean people to create their united independent State, welcomes the formation of the Korean Government and wishes it success in its activities in behalf of the national resurgence and democratic development of Korea. The Soviet Government expresses its readiness for the establishment of diplomatic relations between the U.S.S.R. and the Korean People's Democratic Republic and exchange of ambassadors, and parallel with this, for the establishment of corresponding economic relations.

J. STALIN,
*Chairman of the Council of Ministers
of the U.S.S.R.*

October 12, 1948

DOCUMENT 40

EXCERPTS FROM REMARKS MADE BY DEAN ACHESON AT THE NATIONAL PRESS CLUB IN WASHINGTON, JANUARY 12, 1950, ON FAR EASTERN POLICIES

In an address before the National Press Club in Washington on January 12, 1950, Secretary of State Dean Acheson spoke of an American defense perimeter running from the Ryukyus to the Philippine Islands. Critics charged afterward that his failure to include Korea specifically might have encouraged the Communists to launch their attack upon South Korea a few months later.

Department of State *Bulletin*, XXII (January 23, 1950), 115–116.

. . . What does that mean for us? It means something very, very significant. It means that nothing that we do and nothing that we say must be allowed to obscure the reality of this fact. All the efforts of propaganda will not be able to obscure it. The only thing that can obscure it is the folly of ill-conceived adventures on our part which easily could do so, and I urge all who are thinking about these foolish adventures to remember that we must not seize the unenviable position which the Russians have carved out for themselves. We must not undertake to deflect from the Russians to ourselves the righteous anger, and the wrath, and the hatred of the Chinese people which must develop. It would be folly to deflect it to ourselves. We must take the position we have always taken—that anyone who violates the integrity of China is the enemy of China and is acting contrary to our own interest. That, I suggest to you this afternoon, is the first and the greatest rule in regard to the formulation of American policy toward Asia.

I suggest that the second rule is very like the first. That is to keep our own purposes perfectly straight, perfectly pure, and perfectly aboveboard and do not get them mixed-up with legal quibbles or the attempt to do one thing and really achieve another.

The consequences of this Russian attitude and this Russian action in China are perfectly enormous. They are saddling all those in China who are proclaiming their loyalty to Moscow, and who are allowing themselves to be used as puppets of Moscow, with the most awful responsibility which they must pay for. Furthermore, these actions of the Russians are making plainer than any speech, or any utterance, or any legislation can make throughout all of Asia, what the true purposes of the Soviet Union are and what the true function of communism as an agent of Russian imperialism is. These I suggest to you are the fundamental factors, fundamental realities of attitude out of which our relations and policies must grow.

Now, let's in the light of that consider some of these policies. First of all, let's deal with the question of military security. I deal with it first because it is important and because, having stated our policy in that regard, we must clearly understand that the military menace is not the most immediate.

What is the situation in regard to the military security of the Pacific area, and what is our policy in regard to it?

In the first place, the defeat and the disarmament of Japan has placed upon the United States the necessity of assuming the military defense of Japan so long as that is required, both in the interest of our security and in the interests of the security of the entire Pacific area and, in all honor, in the interest of Japanese security. We have American—and there are Australian—troops in Japan. I am not in a position to speak for the Australians, but I can assure you that there is no intention of any sort of abandoning or weakening the defenses of Japan and that whatever arrangements are to be made either through permanent settlement or otherwise, that defense must and shall be maintained.

This defensive perimeter runs along the Aleutians to Japan and then goes to the Ryukyus. We hold important defense positions in the Ryukyu Islands, and those we will continue to hold. In the interest of the population of the Ryukyu Islands, we will at an appropriate time offer to hold these islands under trusteeship of the United Nations. But they are essential parts of the defensive perimeter of the Pacific, and they must and will be held.

The defensive perimeter runs from the Ryukyus to the Philippine Islands. Our relations, our defensive relations with the Philippines are contained in agreements between us. Those agreements are being loyally carried out and will be loyally carried out. Both peoples have learned by bitter experience the vital connections between our mutual defense requirements. We are in no doubt about that, and it is hardly necessary for me to say an attack on the Philippines could not and would not be tolerated by the United States. But I hasten to add that no one perceives the imminence of any such attack.

So far as the military security of other areas in the Pacific is concerned, it must be clear that no person can guarantee these areas against military attack. But it must also be clear that such a guarantee is hardly sensible or necessary within the realm of practical relationship.

Should such an attack occur—one hesitates to say where such an armed attack could come from—the initial reliance must be on the people attacked to resist it and then upon the commitments of the entire civilized world under the Charter of the United Nations which so far has not proved a weak reed to lean on by any people who are determined to protect their independence against outside aggression. But it is a mistake, I think, in considering Pacific and Far Eastern problems to become obsessed with military considerations. Important as they are, there are other problems that press, and these other problems are not capable of solution through military means. These other problems arise out of the susceptibility of many areas, and many countries in the Pacific area, to subversion and penetration. That cannot be stopped by military means.

The susceptibility to penetration arises because in many areas there are new governments which have little experience in governmental administration and have not become firmly established, or perhaps firmly accepted in their countries. They grow, in part, from very serious economic problems, some of them growing out directly from the last war, others growing indirectly out of the war because of the disruptions of trade with other parts of the world, with the disruption of arrangements which furnished credit and management in these areas for many years. That has resulted in dislocation of economic effort and in a good deal of suffering among the peoples concerned. In part this susceptibility to penetration comes from the great social upheaval about which I have been speaking, an upheaval which was carried on and confused a great deal by the Japanese occupation and by the propaganda which has gone on from Soviet sources since the war.

Here, then, are the problems in these other areas which require some policy on our part, and I should like to point out two facts to you and to discuss in more detail some of these areas.

The first fact is the great difference between our responsibility and our opportunities in the northern part of the Pacific area and in the southern part of the Pacific area. In the north, we have direct responsibility in Japan and we have direct opportunity to act. The same thing to a lesser degree is true in Korea. There we had direct responsibility, and there we did act, and there we have a greater opportunity to be effective than we have in the more southerly part. . . .

DOCUMENT 41

RESOLUTION OF THE UNITED NATIONS SECURITY COUNCIL CALLING FOR A NORTH KOREAN WITHDRAWAL, JUNE 25, 1950

On June 25, 1950, North Korean armed forces crossed the thirty-eighth parallel for an attack upon the Republic of Korea, from which virtually all American troops had been recalled. The Security Council thereupon called upon the North Koreans to withdraw. Because they were boycotting the Security Council in protest against the continued presence of the Nationalist Chinese, the Soviets were unable to exercise their veto.

The Security Council

Recalling the finding of the General Assembly in its resolution of 21 October 1949 that the Government of the Republic of Korea is a lawfully established government having effective control and jurisdiction over that part of Korea where the United Nations Temporary Commission on Korea was able to observe and consult and in which the great majority of the people of Korea reside; and that this Government is based on elections which were a valid expression of the free will of the electorate of that part of Korea and which were observed by the Temporary Commission; and that this is the only such government in Korea;

Mindful of the concern expressed by the General Assembly in its resolutions of 12 December 1948 and 21 October 1949 of the consequences which might follow unless Member States refrained from acts derogatory to the results sought to be achieved by the United Nations in bringing about the complete independence and unity of Korea; and the concern expressed that the situation described by the United Nations Commission on Korea in its report menaces the safety and well being of the Republic of Korea and of the people of Korea and might lead to open military conflict there;

Noting with grave concern the armed attack on the Republic of Korea by forces from North Korea,

Determines that this action constitutes a breach of the peace,

I. *Calls for* the immediate cessation of hostilities; and

Calls upon the authorities in North Korea to withdraw forthwith their armed forces to the 38th parallel;

II. *Requests* the United Nations Commission on Korea

(a) To communicate its fully considered recommendations on the situation with the least possible delay.

(b) To observe the withdrawal of North Korean forces to the 38th parallel, and

American Foreign Policy, 1950–1955, Department of State Publication No. 6446, General Foreign Policy Series 117, II, 2538–2539.

(c) To keep the Security Council informed on the execution of this resolution;

III. *Calls upon* all Members to render every assistance to the United Nations in the execution of this resolution and to refrain from giving assistance to the North Korean authorities.

DOCUMENT 42

RESOLUTION OF THE UNITED NATIONS SECURITY COUNCIL CALLING FOR UNITED NATIONS ASSISTANCE TO THE REPUBLIC OF KOREA, JUNE 27, 1950

When the Communists failed to heed the Security Council's call for a withdrawal of North Korean troops, the Security Council passed a resolution calling on members to furnish military aid to the Republic of Korea (June 27, 1950). The Soviet delegation still persisted in its boycott and was unable to veto the resolution.

The Security Council

Having determined that the armed attack upon the Republic of Korea by forces from North Korea constitutes a breach of the peace;

Having called for an immediate cessation of hostilities; and

Having called upon the authorities of North Korea to withdraw forthwith their armed forces to the 38th parallel; and

Having noted from the report of the United Nations Commission for Korea that the authorities in North Korea have neither ceased hostilities nor withdrawn their armed forces to the 38th parallel, and that urgent military measures are required to restore international peace and security; and

Having noted the appeal from the Republic of Korea to the United Nations for immediate and effective steps to secure peace and security,

Recommends that the Members of the United Nations furnish such assistance to the Republic of Korea as may be necessary to repel the armed attack and to restore international peace and security in the area.

American Foreign Policy, 1950–1955, II, 2540–2541.

DOCUMENT 43

STATEMENT BY PRESIDENT TRUMAN ORDERING U.S. FORCES INTO SUPPORTING ACTION IN KOREA, JUNE 27, 1950

In consonance with the Security Council's resolution calling on the United Nations to assist the Republic of Korea, President Truman, on June 27, 1950, issued a statement announcing that he had ordered American sea and air forces into action against the North Korean invaders. At the same time, he interposed the Seventh Fleet between the Chinese Nationalists on Formosa and the Communists on the mainland. A few days later, American ground forces were also committed in Korea, and other nations followed suit.

In Korea, the Government forces, which were armed to prevent border raids and to preserve internal security, were attacked by invading forces from North Korea. The Security Council of the United Nations called upon the invading troops to cease hostilities and to withdraw to the 38th Parallel. This they have not done but, on the contrary, have pressed the attack. The Security Council called upon all members of the United Nations to render every assistance to the United Nations in the execution of this resolution. In these circumstances, I have ordered United States air and sea forces to give the Korean Government troops cover and support.

The attack upon Korea makes it plain beyond all doubt that communism has passed beyond the use of subversion to conquer independent nations and will now use armed invasion and war. It has defied the orders of the Security Council of the United Nations issued to preserve international peace and security. In these circumstances, the occupation of Formosa by Communist forces would be a direct threat to the security of the Pacific area and to United States forces performing their lawful and necessary functions in that area.

Accordingly, I have ordered the Seventh Fleet to prevent any attack on Formosa. As a corollary of this action, I am calling upon the Chinese Government on Formosa to cease all air and sea operations against the mainland. The Seventh Fleet will see that this is done.

Department of State *Bulletin*, XXIII (July 3, 1950), 5.

The determination of the future status of Formosa must await the restoration of security in the Pacific, a peace settlement with Japan, or consideration by the United Nations.

I have also directed that United States forces in the Philippines be strengthened and that military assistance to the Philippine Government be accelerated.

I have similarly directed acceleration in the furnishing of military assistance to the forces of France and the Associated States in Indochina and the dispatch of a military mission to provide close working relations with those forces.

I know that all members of the United Nations will consider carefully the consequences of this latest aggression in Korea in defiance of the Charter of the United Nations. A return to the rule of force in international affairs would have far-reaching effects. The United States will continue to uphold the rule of law.

I have instructed Ambassador Austin, as the representative of the United States to the Security Council, to report these steps to the Council.

DOCUMENT 44

SOVIET CHARGES OF AGGRESSION IN KOREA: REMARKS BY JACOB MALIK IN THE SECURITY COUNCIL, AUGUST 1, 1950

When the Soviet Union abandoned its boycott of the Security Council, its representatives returned to castigate the United States for aggression in Korea and to link the Korean war with the question of the recognition of Communist China. The following consists of excerpts from his remarks on August 1, 1950.

MR. MALIK:

. . . The ruling circles of the United States have chosen the path of aggression against the Korean people, they have chosen to unleash war; hence they are afraid that, if the Security Council were to op-

United Nations, Security Council, *Official Records*, 5th Year, 480th Meeting, No. 22, 19–21.

erate with its full legal membership, they would not succeed in transforming it into their obedient tool of aggression against the Korean people, for cloaking new acts of aggression and unleashing war. . . .

Mr. Austin referred to the tragic fate of Korean victims of war. It is appropriate to ask the representative of the United States who is to blame for the tragic fate of many thousands of Korean mothers, children and old people, who have lost their nearest and dearest. The culprits are the ruling circles of the United States.

The whole world and the United Nations are now confronted with the fact of gross and overt aggression on the part of the United States Government against the Korean people. Having provoked, on 25 June, an armed assault by their South Korean puppets against the frontier areas of the Democratic People's Republic of Korea, the ruling circles of the United States have used this armed provocation to justify their long-planned and long-prepared armed aggression in Korea against the Korean people, and in the Far East and Asia as a whole against several other nations: against the Chinese, by the seizure and the virtual occupation of Formosa; against the Vietnamese, by sending military missions there and increasing the flow of arms; and also against the people of the Philippines.

That is why the representative of the United States in the Security Council has so stubbornly opposed the consideration of the question of the recognition of the representative of the People's Republic of China as the representative of China and the adoption of a decision on that question.

The Korean question and that of the representation of China in the United Nations are inseparably linked together. Settlement of the Korean question through the Security Council, as of any other question affecting peace, is the normal, rational and equitable course. But that requires that the Security Council should begin to function normally, with its lawful composition; and that is impossible without the participation of China and the Soviet Union in its work. The Security Council is not the Security Council when it fails to act in strict conformity with the Charter and, in particular, with Article 27 of the Charter; when it acts in the absence of two of the five permanent members of the Security Council whose participation and unanimity are an essential prerequisite for the legality of the Council's decisions.

The rejection by Washington of Mr. Nehru's appeal, and the proposal submitted today by the United States representative for the rejection of the U.S.S.R. proposal that the agenda should include both the question of the recognition of the representative of the Central People's Government of the People's Republic of China as the representative of China and the question of the peaceful settlement of the Korean question, show that the ruling circles of the United States aim at seizing Korea, and do not even want to hear of the cessation of aggression, of putting an end to armed intervention, and of the termination of hostilities. By these acts, they proclaim to the world their intention to pursue the armed struggle, to continue their intervention, to maintain their aggression against the Koreans and other Asian peoples. That is the real situation.

As to who it was that linked up the Korean and Chinese questions, it was the President of the United States who did it. In ordering his armed forces to open hostilities, to launch their aggressive operations against the people of Korea and to begin armed intervention in Korea's domestic affairs, the President of the United States also decided, in passing, to seize the Chinese island of Formosa by ordering the United States Seventh Fleet virtually to occupy that island.

What grounds, then, has the United States representative for asserting now that these are two absolutely distinct questions? There is no logic in such a statement. Mr. Austin apparently does not agree with the decision of the President of the United States.

All this leads to but one conclusion. Those who hold the interests of the world dear, those who sincerely desire a peaceful settlement of the Korean question, should not only support the U.S.S.R. delegation's proposal for a discussion in the Security Council of the two items submitted by that delegation, but should also adopt the decisions on those items necessary to restore to force the provisions of the Charter violated by the ruling circles of the United States, to restore that legality which is necessary before we can take the steps required to achieve the purposes and objectives of the United Nations —the strengthening and maintenance of peace.

Those who attempt through diversion to prevent the discussion of these questions and by a variety of manoeuvres divert the attention of the world and of the United Nations from the peaceful settlement of the Korean question reveal themselves to be enemies of the peaceful settlement of that question, and announce for all to hear their intention to continue hostilities in Korea, to intensify their aggression against the people of Korea and to extend the scope of the war they have unleashed.

Naturally the U.S.S.R. delegation vehemently objects to such diversion and manoeuvres on the part of the United States delegation, and will vote against the proposal to discuss as the first and only item of the agenda the United States draft resolution aimed at intensifying aggression.

As President of the Council I can agree to the item submitted by the United States delegation being included as item 3, to be discussed in due course.

The U.S.S.R. delegation, however, insists that the items which it has submitted on the representation of China and the peaceful settlement of the Korean question should be urgently considered by the Security Council.

It is the Security Council's duty to take immediate steps to settle the Korean question, to save the peoples of Asia from the aggression with which they are threatened by the ruling circles of the United States, which have decided on the course of aggression and armed intervention against the Korean people and are trying to intensify that aggression, that war, and to draw into it the Governments of other countries. . . .

DOCUMENT 45

RESOLUTION OF THE U.N. GENERAL ASSEMBLY NAMING THE COMMUNIST CHINESE AS AGGRESSORS IN KOREA, FEBRUARY 1, 1951

After United Nations forces had completely routed the North Koreans and were approaching the Yalu River, the Chinese Communists intervened. Thereupon, the General Assembly branded them as aggressors and called upon them to withdraw (February 1, 1951).

The Record on Korean Unification, 1943–1960, Department of State Publication No. 7084 (Washington, 1960), 123–124.

(Resolution adopted on the report of the First Committee)

The General Assembly,

Noting that the Security Council, because of lack of unanimity of the permanent members, has failed to exercise its primary responsibility for the maintenance of international peace and security in regard to Chinese Communist intervention in Korea,

Noting that the Central People's Government of the People's Republic of China has not accepted United Nations proposals to bring about a cessation of hostilities in Korea with a view to peaceful settlement, and that its armed forces continue their invasion of Korea and their large-scale attacks upon United Nations forces there,

1. *Finds* that the Central People's Government of the People's Republic of China, by giving direct aid and assistance to those who were already committing aggression in Korea and by engaging in hostilities against United Nations forces there, has itself engaged in aggression in Korea;

2. *Calls upon* the Central People's Government of the People's Republic of China to cause its forces and nationals in Korea to cease hostilities against the United Nations forces and to withdraw from Korea;

3. *Affirms* the determination of the United Nations to continue its action in Korea to meet the aggression;

4. *Calls upon* all States and authorities to continue to lend every assistance to the United Nations action in Korea;

5. *Calls upon* all States and authorities to refrain from giving any assistance to the aggressors in Korea;

6. *Requests* a Committee composed of the members of the Collective Measures Committee as a matter of urgency to consider additional measures to be employed to meet this aggression and to report thereon to the General Assembly, it being understood that the Committee is authorized to defer its report if the Good Offices Committee referred to in the following paragraph reports satisfactory progress in its efforts;

7. *Affirms* that it continues to be the policy of the United Nations to bring about a cessation of hostilities in Korea and the achievement of United Nations objectives in Korea by peaceful means, and re-

quests the President of the General Assembly to designate forthwith two persons who would meet with him at any suitable opportunity to use their good offices to this end.

DOCUMENT 46

KOREAN ARMISTICE, JULY 27, 1953

After the Chinese invaders had been pushed back beyond the thirty-eighth parallel, armistice talks were begun (July 10, 1951). It was not until two years later, after Stalin had died, that an agreement was finally concluded. In the main, the armistice of July 27, 1953, restored the status quo.

Armistice Agreement Between the United Nations Commander in Korea and the Commanders of Communist Forces in Korea, July 27, 1953

PREAMBLE

The undersigned, the Commander-in-Chief, United Nations Command, on the one hand, and the Supreme Commander of the Korean People's Army and the Commander of the Chinese People's Volunteers, on the other hand, in the interest of stopping the Korean conflict, with its great toll of suffering and bloodshed on both sides, and with the objective of establishing an armistice which will insure a complete cessation of hostilities and of all acts of armed force in Korea until a final peaceful settlement is achieved, do individually, collectively, and mutually agree to accept and to be bound and governed by the conditions and terms of armistice set forth in the following Articles and Paragraphs, which said conditions and terms are intended to be purely military in character and to pertain solely to the belligerents in Korea.

ARTICLE I

MILITARY DEMARCATION LINE AND DEMILITARIZED ZONE

1. A Military Demarcation Line shall be fixed and both sides shall withdraw two (2) kilometers from this line so as to establish a De-

militarized Zone between the opposing forces. A Demilitarized Zone shall be established as a buffer zone to prevent the occurrence of incidents which might lead to a resumption of hostilities.

2. The Military Demarcation Line is located as indicated on the attached map (Map 1).

3. The Demilitarized Zone is defined by a northern and a southern boundary as indicated on the attached map (Map 1).

4. The Military Demarcation Line shall be plainly marked as directed by the Military Armistice Commission hereinafter established. The Commanders of the opposing sides shall have suitable markers erected along the boundary between the Demilitarized Zone and their respective areas. The Military Armistice Commission shall supervise the erection of all markers placed along the Military Demarcation Line and along the boundaries of the Demilitarized Zone.

5. The waters of the Han River Estuary shall be open to civil shipping of both sides wherever one bank is controlled by one side and the other bank is controlled by the other side. The Military Armistice Commission shall prescribe rules for the shipping in that part of the Han River Estuary indicated on the attached map (Map 2). Civil shipping of each side shall have unrestricted access to the land under the military control of that side.

6. Neither side shall execute any hostile act within, from, or against the Demilitarized Zone.

7. No person, military or civilian, shall be permitted to cross the Military Demarcation Line unless specifically authorized to do so by the Military Armistice Commission.

8. No person, military or civilian, in the Demilitarized Zone shall be permitted to enter the territory under the military control of either side unless specifically authorized to do so by the Commander into whose territory entry is sought.

9. No person, military or civilian, shall be permitted to enter the Demilitarized Zone except persons concerned with the conduct of civil administration and relief and persons specifically authorized to enter by the Military Armistice Commission.

10. Civil administration and relief in that part of the Demilitarized Zone which is south of the Military Demarcation Line shall be the responsibility of the Commander-in-Chief, United Nations Command; and civil administration and relief in that part of the Demilitarized Zone which is north of the Military Demarcation Line shall

be the joint responsibility of the Supreme Commander of the Korean People's Army and the Commander of the Chinese People's Volunteers. The number of persons, military or civilian, from each side who are permitted to enter the Demilitarized Zone for the conduct of civil administration and relief shall be as determined by the respective Commanders, but in no case shall the total number authorized by either side exceed one thousand (1,000) persons at any one time. The number of civil police and the arms to be carried by them shall be as prescribed by the Military Armistice Commission. Other personnel shall not carry arms unless specifically authorized to do so by the Military Armistice Commission.

11. Nothing contained in this Article shall be construed to prevent the complete freedom of movement to, from, and within the Demilitarized Zone by the Military Armistice Commission, its assistants, its Joint Observer Teams with their assistants, the Neutral Nations Supervisory Commission hereinafter established, its assistants, its Neutral Nations Inspection Teams with their assistants, and of any other persons, materials, and equipment specifically authorized to enter the Demilitarized Zone by the Military Armistice Commission. Convenience of movement shall be permitted through the territory under the military control of either side over any route necessary to move between points within the Demilitarized Zone where such points are not connected by roads lying completely within the Demilitarized Zone. . . .

FIVE

The Cold War and the
Eisenhower Administration

The year 1953 was marked by a change in leadership in both the United States and the Soviet Union, the two main protagonists in the Cold War. General Dwight D. Eisenhower took office as President of the United States in January; Joseph Stalin died in March, and a period of uncertainty about the succession set in in Russia, with Nikita S. Khrushchev finally emerging as the leader of the Soviet state.

In spite of these developments and much talk about a new departure in the United States—Secretary of State John Foster Dulles spoke of massive retaliation—the Eisenhower administration generally continued the policy of containment. In Asia, the Geneva agreements dividing Indo-China were followed by the conclusion of a treaty setting up SEATO, and, in 1955, by an American commitment to defend Formosa; in Europe, the West Germans were admitted to membership in NATO. The Russians retaliated with a military alliance of satellites in the Warsaw Pact, but they were willing to countenance a slight reduction of tensions by agreeing to the neutralization of Austria and participating in the first summit meeting since the war. Khrushchev even accused Stalin of excesses when the new Chairman delivered a secret speech to the Twentieth Communist Party Congress. When a revolt broke out in Hungary, however, Soviet tanks crushed the revolution despite promises and a pathetic appeal by Imre Nagy to the United Nations. A General Assembly resolution condemning the intervention had no effect. At the same time, the United States joined with the Soviet Union in a resolution to end the Suez war, President Eisenhower explaining to the world why America had censured its allies.

A stalemate had again been reached. To bolster the Middle East against Communism, Congress endorsed the Eisenhower Doctrine in 1957. Khrushchev, however, chose to strike again in Europe, where, in November, 1958, he set off another Berlin crisis by demanding a settlement within six months. Although he visited President Eisenhower in the United States in 1959, the tension died down only temporarily. In 1960, the Soviets captured a U-2 pilot; the United States assumed responsibility, and Khrushchev broke up the international conference which had gathered in Paris. The emergence of new leaders in the two countries had, in the last analysis, brought little change.

DOCUMENT 47

OFFICIAL ANNOUNCEMENT OF STALIN'S DEATH, MARCH 6, 1953

On March 5, 1953, Joseph V. Stalin died. His passing inspired hope for an improvement in the relations between the Soviet Union and the West. The following consists of excerpts from the official announcement of his death.

Following is the Text of Moscow's Announcement of Premier Stalin's Death:

From the Central Committee of the Communist party of the Soviet Union, the U.S.S.R. Council of Ministers and the U.S.S.R. Presidium of the Supreme Soviet—

To all members of the party, to all workers of the Soviet Union:

Dear comrades and friends: The Central Committee of the Communist party of the Soviet Union, the U.S.S.R. Council of Ministers and the Presidium of the U.S.S.R. Supreme Soviet announce with

---

New York Times, March 6, 1953, 8.

profound sorrow to the party and all workers of the Soviet Union that on the 5th of March, at 2150 hours (9:50 P.M., Moscow time, or 1:50 P.M., Eastern Standard Time), after a grave illness, the Chairman of the U.S.S.R. Council of Ministers and the Secretary of the Central Committee of the Communist party of the Soviet Union, Joseph Vissarionovitch Stalin, died.

The heart of the comrade and inspired continuer of Lenin's will, the wise leader and teacher of the Communist Party and the Soviet people—Joseph Vissarionovitch Stalin—has stopped beating.

Stalin's name is boundlessly dear to our party, to the Soviet people, to the workers of the world.

Together with Lenin, Comrade Stalin created the mighty party of Communists, reared and forged that party.

Together with Lenin, Comrade Stalin was the inspirer and leader of the great October Socialist Revolution, founder of the world's first Socialist state.

Continuing Lenin's immortal cause, Comrade Stalin led the Soviet people to a world-historic victory of Socialism in our land.

Comrade Stalin led our country to victory over fascism in the second World War which wrought a radical change in the entire international scene.

Comrade Stalin's death—the man who devoted all his life to the unselfish service of the Communist cause—is a tremendous loss to the party, to the workers of the Soviet Union and to the whole world.

Comrade Stalin armed the party and all the people with a great and lucid program of building communism in the U.S.S.R.

The news of Comrade Stalin's death will bring profound pain to the hearts of the workers, the collective farmers, the intelligentsia, and all the workers of our Motherland, to the hearts of the warriors of our glorious Army and Navy, to the hearts of millions of workers in all countries of the world.

In these sorrowful days, all the peoples of our country are rallying even closer in a great fraternal family under the tested leadership of the Communist party, created and reared by Lenin and Stalin.

The Soviet people have boundless faith in and are permeated with deep love for their Communist party, for they know that the supreme law governing all the activity of the party is service in the interests of the people.

The workers, collective farmers, Soviet intelligentsia, and all workers of our country steadfastly pursue the policy mapped out by our party, which is in conformity with the vital interests of the workers and pursues the continued consolidation of the might of our Socialist Motherland.

The correctness of this policy of the Communist party has been proved by decades of struggle.

It has led the workers of the Soviet country to historic victories of socialism.

Inspired by this policy, the peoples of the Soviet Union under the leadership of the party advance confidently towards fresh successes of Communist construction in our land. . . .

Dear Comrades and Friends:

The great directing and guiding force of the Soviet people in the struggle for the building of Communism is to be found in our Communist party.

The steel-like unity and monolithic unity of the ranks of the party constitutes the main condition for its strength and might.

Our task is to guard like the apple of our eye the unity of the party, to educate Communists as active political fighters for the implementation of policy and decisions of the party, to strengthen even more the party's ties with all the workers, collective farmers, and intelligentsia—for in this indissoluble link with the people lies the strength and invincibility of our party.

The party regards as one its most essential tasks the education of all Communists and workers in a spirit of high political vigilance, irreconcilability and stalwartness in the struggle against internal and external foes.

The Central Committee of the Communist party of the Soviet Union, the U.S.S.R. Council of Ministers, and the Presidium of the U.S.S.R. Supreme Soviet, appealing in these sorrowful days to the party and the people, express their firm conviction that the party and all the workers of our Motherland will rally even closer around the Central Committee and the Soviet Government, will mobilize all their forces and creative energy in the great cause of building Communism in our land.

The immortal name of Stalin will live forever in the hearts of the Soviet people and all progressive mankind.

Long live the great and all-conquering teachings of Marx, Engels, Lenin and Stalin!

Long live our mighty Socialist Motherland!

Long live our heroic Soviet people!

Long live the great Communist party of Soviet Union!

THE CENTRAL COMMITTEE OF THE COMMUNIST PARTY OF THE U.S.S.R.

THE U.S.S.R. COUNCIL OF MINISTERS.

THE U.S.S.R. SUPREME SOVIET'S PRESIDIUM

DOCUMENT 48

SECRETARY OF STATE JOHN FOSTER DULLES' ADDRESS BEFORE THE COUNCIL ON FOREIGN RELATIONS, NEW YORK, JANUARY 12, 1954, CONCERNING "MASSIVE RETALIATORY POWER"

John Foster Dulles, the new Secretary of State, seemed to give American diplomacy a new look when, in an address before the Council on Foreign Relations on January 12, 1954, he spoke of the need for reliance on "massive retaliatory power." Although this policy appealed to economy-minded statesmen, in the long run it meant little.

Excerpts From Dulles' Speech

It is now nearly a year since the Eisenhower Administration took office. During that year I have often spoken of various parts of our foreign policies. Tonight I should like to present an over-all view of those policies which relate to our security.

First of all, let us recognize that many of the preceding foreign policies were good. Aid to Greece and Turkey had checked the Communist drive to the Mediterranean. The European Recovery Program had helped the peoples of Western Europe to pull out of the post-war morass. The Western powers were steadfast in Berlin and overcame the blockade with their airlift. As a loyal member of the United Nations, we had reacted with force to repel the Communist attack in Korea. When that effort exposed our military weakness, we rebuilt rapidly our military establishment. We also sought a quick buildup of armed strength in Western Europe.

These were the acts of a nation which saw the danger of Soviet Communism; which realized that its own safety was tied up with that of others; which was capable of responding boldly and promptly to emergencies. These are precious values to be acclaimed. Also, we can pay tribute to Congressional bi-partisanship which puts the nation above politics.

But we need to recall that what we did was in the main emergency action, imposed on us by our enemies.

Let me illustrate.

1. We did not send our army into Korea because we judged, in advance, that it was sound military strategy to commit our Army to fight land battles in Asia. Our decision had been to pull out of Korea. It was Soviet-inspired action that pulled us back.

2. We did not decide in advance that it was wise to grant billions annually as foreign economic aid. We adopted that policy in response to the Communist efforts to sabotage the free economies of Western Europe.

3. We did not build up our military establishment at a rate which involved huge budget deficits, a depreciating currency and a feverish economy, because this seemed, in advance, a good policy. Indeed, we decided otherwise until the Soviet military threat was clearly revealed.

We live in a world where emergencies are always possible and our survival may depend upon our capacity to meet emergencies. Let us pray that we shall always have that capacity. But, having said that, it is necessary also to say that emergency measures—however good for the emergency—do not necessarily make good permanent policies. Emergency measures are costly, they are superficial and they imply that the enemy has the initiative. They cannot be depended on to serve our long-time interests.

This "long time" factor is of critical importance. The Soviet Communists are planning for what they call "an entire historical era," and we should do the same. They seek, through many types of maneuvers, gradually to divide and weaken the free nations by overextending them in efforts which, as Lenin put it, are "beyond their strength, so that they come to practical bankruptcy." Then, said Lenin, "our victory is assured." Then, said Stalin, will be "the moment for the decisive blow."

In the face of this strategy, measures cannot be judged adequate merely because they ward off an immediate danger. It is essential to do this, but it is also essential to do so without exhausting ourselves.

When the Eisenhower Administration applied this test, we felt that some transformations were needed.

It is not sound military strategy permanently to commit U.S. land forces to Asia to a degree that leaves us no strategic reserves.

It is not sound economics, or good foreign policy, to support permanently other countries; for in the long run, that creates as much ill will as good will.

Also, it is not sound to become permanently committed to military expenditures so vast that they lead to "practical bankruptcy."

Change was imperative to assure the stamina needed for permanent security. But it was equally imperative that change should be accompanied by understanding of our true purposes. Sudden and spectacular change had to be avoided. Otherwise, there might have been a panic among our friends, and miscalculated aggression by our enemies. We can, I believe, make a good report in these respects.

We need allies and collective security. Our purpose is to make these relations more effective, less costly. This can be done by placing more reliance on deterrent power, and less dependence on local defensive power.

This is accepted practice so far as local communities are concerned. We keep locks on our doors; but we do not have an armed guard in every home. We rely principally on a community security system so well equipped to punish any who break in and steal that, in fact, would-be aggressors are generally deterred. That is the modern way of getting maximum protection at a bearable cost.

What the Eisenhower Administration seeks is a similar international security system. We want, for ourselves and the other free nations, a maximum deterrent at a bearable cost.

Local defense will always be important. But there is no local defense which alone will contain the mighty land power of the Communist world. Local defenses must be reinforced by the further deterrent of massive retaliatory power. A potential aggressor must know that he cannot always prescribe battle conditions that suit him. Otherwise, for example, a potential aggressor, who is glutted with manpower, might be tempted to attack in confidence that resistance would be confined to manpower. He might be tempted to attack in places where his superiority was decisive.

The way to deter aggression is for the free community to be willing and able to respond vigorously at places and with means of its own choosing.

So long as our basic policy concepts were unclear, our military leaders could not be selective in building our military power. If an enemy could pick his time and place and method of warfare—and if our policy was to remain the traditional one of meeting aggression by direct and local opposition—then we needed to be ready to fight in the Arctic and in the tropics; in Asia, the Near East and in Europe; by sea, by land and by air; with old weapons and with new weapons.

The total cost of our security efforts, at home and abroad, was over $50,000,000,000 per annum, and involved, for 1953, a projected budgetary deficit of $9,000,000,000; and $11,000,000,000 for 1954. This was on top of taxes comparable to war-time taxes; and the dollar was depreciating in effective value. Our allies were similarly weighed down. This could not be continued for long without grave budgetary, economic and social consequences.

But before military planning could be changed, the President and his advisers, as represented by the National Security Council, had to take some basic policy decisions. This has been done. The basic decision was to depend primarily upon a great capacity to retaliate, instantly, by means and at places of our choosing. Now the Department of Defense and the Joint Chiefs of Staff can shape our military establishment to fit what is our policy, instead of having to try to be ready to meet the enemy's many choices. That permits of a selection of military means instead of a multiplication of means. As a result, it is now possible to get, and share, more basic security at less cost.

DOCUMENT 49

FINAL DECLARATION OF THE GENEVA CONFERENCE ON THE PROBLEM OF RESTORING PEACE IN INDO-CHINA, JULY 21, 1954

When the French attempted to re-establish their colonial rule in Indo-China after the war, they were confronted with a vigorous independence movement in which the Communists played a prominent part. Afraid of the

American Foreign Policy, 1950–1955, I, 785–787.

consequences of a Communist victory in Southeast Asia, the United States contemplated intervention to save the French from defeat at Dien Bien Phu, but finally decided against such action. In April, 1954, a conference of interested powers met at Geneva to work out a settlement. The outcome was an armistice dividing Vietnam at the seventeenth parallel and agreements providing for French withdrawal from Laos and Cambodia as well. The elections in Vietnam provided for in the arrangement were never held; as in Korea, the military dividing line became a political border also. Although the United States was not a party to the armistice, it was unable to escape the consequences of the arrangement.

FINAL DECLARATION, dated the 21st July, 1954, of the Geneva Conference on the problem of restoring peace in Indo-China, in which the representatives of Cambodia, the Democratic Republic of Viet-Nam, France, Laos, the People's Republic of China, the State of Viet-Nam, the Union of Soviet Socialist Republics, the United Kingdom, and the United States of America took part.

1. The Conference takes note of the agreements ending hostilities in Cambodia, Laos and Viet-Nam and organizing international control and the supervision of the execution of the provisions of these agreements.

2. The Conference expresses satisfaction at the ending of hostilities in Cambodia, Laos and Viet-Nam; the Conference expresses its conviction that the execution of the provisions set out in the present declaration and in the agreements on the cessation of hostilities will permit Cambodia, Laos and Viet-Nam henceforth to play their part, in full independence and sovereignty, in the peaceful community of nations.

3. The Conference takes note of the declarations made by the Governments of Cambodia and of Laos of their intention to adopt measures permitting all citizens to take their place in the national community, in particular by participating in the next general elections, which, in conformity with the constitution of each of these countries, shall take place in the course of the year 1955, by secret ballot and in conditions of respect for fundamental freedoms.

4. The Conference takes note of the clauses in the agreement on the cessation of hostilities in Viet-Nam prohibiting the introduction into Viet-Nam of foreign troops and military personnel as well as of all kinds of arms and munitions. The Conference also takes note of

the declarations made by the Governments of Cambodia and Laos of their resolution not to request foreign aid, whether in war material, in personnel or in instructors except for the purpose of the effective defence of their territory and, in the case of Laos, to the extent defined by the agreements on the cessation of hostilities in Laos.

5. The Conference takes note of the clauses in the agreement on the cessation of hostilities in Viet-Nam to the effect that no military base under the control of a foreign State may be established in the regrouping zones of the two parties, the latter having the obligation to see that the zones allotted to them shall not constitute part of any military alliance and shall not be utilized for the resumption of hostilities or in the service of an aggressive policy. The Conference also takes note of the declarations of the Governments of Cambodia and Laos to the effect that they will not join in any agreement with other States if this agreement includes the obligation to participate in a military alliance not in conformity with the principles of the Charter of the United Nations or, in the case of Laos, with the principles of the agreement on the cessation of hostilities in Laos or, so long as their security is not threatened, the obligation to establish bases on Cambodian or Laotian territory for the military forces of foreign Powers.

6. The Conference recognizes that the essential purpose of the agreement relating to Viet-Nam is to settle military questions with a view to ending hostilities and that the military demarcation line is provisional and should not in any way be interpreted as constituting a political or territorial boundary. The Conference expresses its conviction that the execution of the provisions set out in the present declaration and in the agreement on the cessation of hostilities creates the necessary basis for the achievement in the near future of a political settlement in Viet-Nam.

7. The Conference declares that, so far as Viet-Nam is concerned, the settlement of political problems, effected on the basis of respect for the principles of independence, unity and territorial integrity, shall permit the Viet-Namese people to enjoy the fundamental freedoms, guaranteed by democratic institutions established as a result of free general elections by secret ballot. In order to ensure that sufficient progress in the restoration of peace has been made, and that all the necessary conditions obtain for free expression of the national will,

general elections shall be held in July 1956, under the supervision of an international commission composed of representatives of the Member States of the International Supervisory Commission, referred to in the agreement on the cessation of hostilities. Consultations will be held on this subject between the competent representative authorities of the two zones from 20 July 1955 onwards.

8. The provisions of the agreements on the cessation of hostilities intended to ensure the protection of individuals and of property must be most strictly applied and must, in particular, allow everyone in Viet-Nam to decide freely in which zone he wishes to live.

9. The competent representative authorities of the Northern and Southern zones of Viet-Nam, as well as the authorities of Laos and Cambodia, must not permit any individual or collective reprisals against persons who have collaborated in any way with one of the parties during the war, or against members of such persons' families.

10. The Conference takes note of the declaration of the Government of the French Republic to the effect that it is ready to withdraw its troops from the territory of Cambodia, Laos and Viet-Nam, at the request of the governments concerned and within periods which shall be fixed by agreement between the parties except in the cases where, by agreement between the two parties, a certain number of French troops shall remain at specified points and for a specified time.

11. The Conference takes note of the declaration of the French Government to the effect that for the settlement of all the problems connected with the re-establishment and consolidation of peace in Cambodia, Laos and Viet-Nam, the French Government will proceed from the principle of respect for the independence and sovereignty, unity and territorial integrity of Cambodia, Laos and Viet-Nam.

12. In their relations with Cambodia, Laos and Viet-Nam, each member of the Geneva Conference undertakes to respect the sovereignty, the independence, the unity and the territorial integrity of the abovementioned states, and to refrain from any interference in their internal affairs.

13. The members of the Conference agree to consult one another on any question which may be referred to them by the International Supervisory Commission, in order to study such measures as may prove necessary to ensure that the agreements on the cessation of hostilities in Cambodia, Laos and Viet-Nam are respected.

DOCUMENT 50

THE SOUTHEAST ASIA COLLECTIVE DEFENSE TREATY, SEPTEMBER 8, 1954

In order to build a wall against Communist expansion in Southeast Asia, Secretary Dulles sought to unite as many countries as possible in military alliances. The Southeast Asia Collective Defense Treaty setting up SEATO, signed at Manila on September 8, 1954, was an example of this policy. The signatories were the United States, Australia, France, New Zealand, Pakistan, the Philippines, Thailand, and the United Kingdom.

The Parties to this Treaty,

Recognizing the sovereign equality of all the Parties,

Reiterating their faith in the purposes and principles set forth in the Charter of the United Nations and their desire to live in peace with all peoples and all governments,

Reaffirming that, in accordance with the Charter of the United Nations, they uphold the principle of equal rights and self-determination of peoples, and declaring that they will earnestly strive by every peaceful means to promote self-government and to secure the independence of all countries whose peoples desire it and are able to undertake its responsibilities,

Desiring to strengthen the fabric of peace and freedom and to uphold the principles of democracy, individual liberty and the rule of law, and to promote the economic well-being and development of all peoples in the treaty area,

Intending to declare publicly and formally their sense of unity, so that any potential aggressor will appreciate that the Parties stand together in the area, and

Desiring further to coordinate their efforts for collective defense for the preservation of peace and security,

Therefore agree as follows:

ARTICLE I

The Parties undertake, as set forth in the Charter of the United Nations, to settle any international disputes in which they may be involved by peaceful means in such a manner that international peace and security and justice are not endangered, and to refrain in their international relations from the threat or use of force in any manner inconsistent with the purposes of the United Nations.

ARTICLE II

In order more effectively to achieve the objectives of this Treaty, the Parties, separately and jointly, by means of continuous and effective self-help and mutual aid will maintain and develop their individual and collective capacity to resist armed attack and to prevent and counter subversive activities directed from without against their territorial integrity and political stability.

ARTICLE III

The Parties undertake to strengthen their free institutions and to cooperate with one another in the further development of economic measures, including technical assistance, designed both to promote economic progress and social well-being and to further the individual and collective efforts of governments toward these ends.

ARTICLE IV

1. Each Party recognizes that aggression by means of armed attack in the treaty area against any of the Parties or against any State or territory which the Parties by unanimous agreement may hereafter designate, would endanger its own peace and safety, and agrees that it will in that event act to meet the common danger in accordance with its constitutional processes. Measures taken under this paragraph shall be immediately reported to the Security Council of the United Nations.

2. If, in the opinion of any of the Parties, the inviolability or the integrity of the territory or the sovereignty or political independence of any Party in the treaty area or of any other State or territory to which the provisions of paragraph 1 of this Article from time to time apply is threatened in any way other than by armed attack or is affected or threatened by any fact or situation which might endanger the peace of the area, the Parties shall consult immediately in order to agree on the measures which should be taken for the common defense.

3. It is understood that no action on the territory of any State designated by unanimous agreement under paragraph 1 of this Article

or on any territory so designated shall be taken except at the invitation or with the consent of the government concerned.

ARTICLE V

The Parties hereby establish a Council, on which each of them shall be represented, to consider matters concerning the implementation of this Treaty. The Council shall provide for consultation with regard to military and any other planning as the situation obtaining in the treaty area may from time to time require. The Council shall be so organized as to be able to meet at any time. . . .

UNDERSTANDING OF THE UNITED STATES OF AMERICA

The United States of America in executing the present Treaty does so with the understanding that its recognition of the effect of aggression and armed attack and its agreement with reference thereto in Article IV, paragraph 1, apply only to communist aggression but affirms that in the event of other aggression or armed attack it will consult under the provisions of Article IV, paragraph 2.

In witness whereof, the undersigned Plenipotentiaries have signed this Treaty.

Done at Manila, this eighth day of September, 1954.

DOCUMENT 51

PROTOCOL TO THE NORTH ATLANTIC TREATY ON THE ACCESSION OF THE FEDERAL REPUBLIC OF GERMANY, OCTOBER 23, 1954

The problem of Germany was as baffling in the fifties as it had been in the forties. Unwilling to abide by the results of a free election throughout the country, the Soviets refused to agree to German unification except on their own terms. The Western powers thereupon sought to integrate West Germany more closely with western Europe, first by her inclusion in a European Defense Community which failed to materialize, and then in NATO. The following protocol became effective on May 5, 1955.

The Parties to the North Atlantic Treaty signed at Washington on 4th April, 1949,

---

Documents on Germany, 1944–1961, 173–174.

Being satisfied that the security of the North Atlantic area will be enhanced by the accession of the Federal Republic of Germany to that Treaty, and

Having noted that the Federal Republic of Germany has by a declaration dated 3rd October, 1954, accepted the obligations set forth in Article 2 of the Charter of the United Nations and has undertaken upon its accession to the North Atlantic Treaty to refrain from any action inconsistent with the strictly defensive character of that Treaty, and

Having further noted that all member governments have associated themselves with the declaration also made on 3rd October, 1954, by the Governments of the United States of America, the United Kingdom of Great Britain and Northern Ireland and the French Republic in connection with the aforesaid declaration of the Federal Republic of Germany,

Agree as follows:

ARTICLE I

Upon the entry into force of the present Protocol, the Government of the United States of America shall on behalf of all the Parties communicate to the Government of the Federal Republic of Germany an invitation to accede to the North Atlantic Treaty. Thereafter the Federal Republic of Germany shall become a Party to that Treaty on the date when it desposits its instruments of accession with the Government of the United States of America in accordance with Article 10 of that Treaty. . . .

Signed at Paris the twenty-third day of October nineteen hundred and fifty-four.

For Belgium:
    P. H. SPAAK
For Canada:
    L. B. PEARSON
For Denmark:
    H. C. HANSEN
For France:
    P. MENDÈS-FRANCE
For Greece:
    S. STEPHANOPOULOS

For Iceland:
  KRISTINN GUDMUNDSON
For Italy:
  G. MARTINO
For the Grand-Duchy of Luxemburg:
  JOS BECH
For Netherlands:
  J. W. BEYEN
For Norway:
  HALVARD LANGE
For Portugal:
  PAULO CUNHA

DOCUMENT 52

JOINT RESOLUTION ON DEFENSE OF FORMOSA, JANUARY 29, 1955

Determined not to allow the Chinese Communists to dislodge their adversaries on Formosa, the United States reacted vigorously to attacks upon offshore islands still in Nationalist hands. Upon the request of President Eisenhower, Congress passed a Joint Resolution giving the President power to defend Formosa, the Pescadores, and such related positions as he might judge to be necessary. A formal Treaty of Alliance had already been signed with Chiang Kai-shek on December 2, 1954.

Text of Joint Resolution on Defense of Formosa

Whereas the primary purpose of the United States, in its relations with all other nations, is to develop and sustain a just and enduring peace for all; and

Whereas certain territories in the West Pacific under the jurisdiction of the Republic of China are now under armed attack, and threats and declarations have been and are being made by the Chinese Communists that such armed attack is in aid of and in preparation for armed attack on Formosa and the Pescadores,

Whereas such armed attack if continued would gravely endanger the peace and security of the West Pacific Area and particularly of Formosa and the Pescadores; and

Department of State, *Bulletin*, XXXII (February 7, 1955), 213.

Whereas the secure possession by friendly governments of the Western Pacific Island chain, of which Formosa is a part, is essential to the vital interests of the United States and all friendly nations in or bordering upon the Pacific Ocean; and

Whereas the President of the United States on January 6, 1955, submitted to the Senate for its advice and consent to ratification a Mutual Defense Treaty between the United States of America and the Republic of China, which recognizes that an armed attack in the West Pacific area directed against territories, therein described, in the region of Formosa and the Pescadores, would be dangerous to the peace and safety of the parties to the treaty: Therefore be it

Resolved by the Senate and House of Representatives of the United States of America in Congress assembled, That the President of the United States be and he hereby is authorized to employ the Armed Forces of the United States as he deems necessary for the specific purpose of securing and protecting Formosa and the Pescadores against armed attack, this authority to include the securing and protection of such related positions and territories of that area now in friendly hands and the taking of such other measures as he judges to be required or appropriate in assuring the defense of Formosa and the Pescadores.

This resolution shall expire when the President shall determine that the peace and security of the area is reasonably assured by international conditions created by action of the United Nations or otherwise, and shall so report to the Congress.

DOCUMENT 53

THE WARSAW SECURITY PACT, MAY 14, 1955

The Soviet Union countered West Germany's admission into NATO by concluding a security pact with her satellites (May 14, 1955).

Treaty of Friendship, Cooperation and Mutual Assistance Between the People's Republic of Albania, the People's Republic of Bulgaria, the Hungarian People's Republic, the German Democratic Republic, the Polish People's Republic, the Rumanian

American Foreign Policy, 1950–1955, I, 1239–1242.

*People's Republic, the Union of Soviet Socialist Republics and
the Czechoslovak Republic, May 14, 1955*

The Contracting Parties,

reaffirming their desire for the establishment of a system of European collective security based on the participation of all European states irrespective of their social and political systems, which would make it possible to unite their efforts in safeguarding the peace of Europe;

mindful, at the same time, of the situation created in Europe by the ratification of the Paris agreements, which envisage the formation of a new military alignment in the shape of "Western European Union," with the participation of a remilitarized Western Germany and the integration of the latter in the North-Atlantic bloc, which increased the danger of another war and constitutes a threat to the national security of the peaceable states;

being persuaded that in these circumstances the peaceable European states must take the necessary measures to safeguard their security and in the interests of preserving peace in Europe;

guided by the objects and principles of the Charter of the United Nations Organization;

being desirous of further promoting and developing friendship, cooperation and mutual assistance in accordance with the principles of respect for the independence and sovereignty of states and of non-interference in their internal affairs,

have decided to conclude the present Treaty of Friendship, Cooperation and Mutual Assistance and have for that purpose appointed as their plenipotentiaries:

. . . who, having presented their full powers, found in good and due form, have agreed as follows:

Article 1

The Contracting Parties undertake, in accordance with the Charter of the United Nations Organization, to refrain in their international relations from the threat or use of force, and to settle their international disputes peacefully and in such manner as will not jeopardize international peace and security.

Article 2

The Contracting Parties declare their readiness to participate in a spirit of sincere cooperation in all international actions designed to safeguard international peace and security, and will fully devote their energies to the attainment of this end.

The Contracting Parties will furthermore strive for the adoption, in agreement with other states which may desire to cooperate in this, of effective measures for universal reduction of armaments and prohibition of atomic, hydrogen and other weapons of mass destruction.

Article 3

The Contracting Parties shall consult with one another on all important international issues affecting their common interests, guided by the desire to strengthen international peace and security.

They shall immediately consult with one another whenever, in the opinion of any one of them, a threat of armed attack on one or more of the Parties to the Treaty has arisen, in order to ensure joint defense and the maintenance of peace and security.

Article 4

In the event of armed attack in Europe on one or more of the Parties to the Treaty by any state or group of states, each of the Parties to the Treaty, in the exercise of its right to individual or collective self-defence in accordance with Article 51 of the Charter of the United Nations Organization, shall immediately, either individually or in agreement with other Parties to the Treaty, come to the assistance of the state or states attacked with all such means as it deems necessary, including armed force. The parties to the Treaty shall immediately consult concerning the necessary measures to be taken by them jointly in order to restore and maintain international peace and security.

Measures taken on the basis of this Article shall be reported to the Security Council in conformity with the provisions of the Charter of the United Nations Organization. These measures shall be discontinued immediately the Security Council adopts the necessary measures to restore and maintain international peace and security.

Article 5

The Contracting Parties have agreed to establish a Joint Command of the armed forces that by agreement among the Parties shall be assigned to the Command, which shall function on the basis of jointly established principles. They shall likewise adopt other agreed measures necessary to strengthen their defensive power, in order to protect the peaceful labours of their peoples, guarantee the inviolability of their frontiers and territories, and provide defence against possible aggression.

Article 6

For the purpose of the consultations among the Parties envisaged in the present Treaty, and also for the purpose of examining questions which may arise in the operation of the Treaty, a Political Consultative Committee shall be set up, in which each of the Parties to the Treaty shall be represented by a member of its Government or by another specifically appointed representative.

The Committee may set up such auxiliary bodies as may prove necessary.

Article 7

The Contracting Parties undertake not to participate in any coalitions or alliances and not to conclude any agreements whose objects conflict with the objects of the present Treaty.

The Contracting Parties declare that their commitments under existing international treaties do not conflict with the provisions of the present Treaty.

Article 8

The Contracting Parties declare that they will act in a spirit of friendship and cooperation with a view to further developing and fostering economic and cultural intercourse with one another, each adhering to the principle of respect for the independence and sovereignty of the others and non-interference in their internal affairs.

Article 9

The present Treaty is open to the accession of other states, irrespective of their social and political systems, which express their readiness by participation in the present Treaty to assist in uniting the efforts of the peaceable states in safeguarding the peace and security of the peoples. Such accession shall enter into force with the agreement of the Parties to the Treaty after the declaration of accession has been deposited with the Government of the Polish People's Republic. . . .

Article 11

The present Treaty shall remain in force for twenty years. For such Contracting Parties as do not at least one year before the expiration of this period present to the Government of the Polish People's Republic a statement of denunciation of the Treaty, it shall remain in force for the next ten years.

Should a system of collective security be established in Europe, and a General European Treaty of Collective Security concluded for this purpose, for which the Contracting Parties will unswervingly strive, the present Treaty shall cease to be operative from the day the General European Treaty enters into force.

Done in Warsaw on May 14, 1955, in one copy each in the Russian, Polish, Czech and German languages, all texts being equally authentic. . . .

DOCUMENT 54

AUSTRIAN STATE TREATY, MAY 15, 1955, AND AUSTRIAN NEUTRALITY RESOLUTION

In spite of trouble in Asia and Europe, the death of Stalin did bring about a slight relaxation of tensions. The main beneficiary of this development was Austria, which regained its independence as a result of the Austrian State Treaty of May 15, 1955. Occupation forces were withdrawn, and the Austrian Parliament subsequently adopted a resolution of perpetual neutrality.

AUSTRIAN STATE TREATY, MAY 15, 1955

PREAMBLE

The Union of Soviet Socialist Republics, the United Kingdom of Great Britain and Northern Ireland, the United States of America, and France, hereinafter referred to as "the Allied and Associated Powers," of the one part and Austria, of the other part;

Whereas on 13th March, 1938, Hitlerite Germany annexed Austria by force and incorporated its territory in the German Reich;

American Foreign Policy, 1950–1955, I, 643–652, 688.

Whereas in the Moscow Declaration published on 1st November, 1943, the Governments of the Union of Soviet Socialist Republics, the United Kingdom and the United States of America declared that they regarded the annexation of Austria by Germany on 13th March, 1938, as null and void and affirmed their wish to see Austria re-established as a free and independent State, and the French Committee of National Liberation made a similar declaration on 16th November, 1943;

Whereas as a result of the Allied victory Austria was liberated from the domination of Hitlerite Germany;

Whereas the Allied and Associated Powers, and Austria, taking into account the importance of the efforts which the Austrian people themselves have made and will have to continue to make for the restoration and democratic reconstruction of their country, desire to conclude a treaty re-establishing Austria as a free, independent and democratic State, thus contributing to the restoration of peace in Europe;

Whereas the Allied and Associated Powers desire by means of the present Treaty to settle in accordance with the principles of justice all questions which are still outstanding in connection with the events referred to above, including the annexation of Austria by Hitlerite Germany and participation of Austria in the war as an integral part of Germany; and

Whereas the Allied and Associated Powers and Austria are desirous for these purposes of concluding the present Treaty to serve as the basis of friendly relations between them, thereby enabling the Allied and Associated Powers to support Austria's application for admission to the United Nations Organization,

Have therefore appointed the undersigned Plenipotentiaries who, after presentation of their full powers, found in good and due form, have agreed on the following provisions:

PART I

POLITICAL AND TERRITORIAL CLAUSES

ARTICLE 1

Re-Establishment of Austria as a Free and Independent State

The Allied and Associated Powers recognize that Austria is re-established as a sovereign, independent and democratic State.

ARTICLE 2

Maintenance of Austria's Independence

The Allied and Associated Powers declare that they will respect the independence and territorial integrity of Austria as established under the present Treaty.

ARTICLE 3

Recognition by Germany of Austrian Independence

The Allied and Associated Powers will incorporate in the German Peace Treaty provisions for securing from Germany the recognition of Austria's sovereignty and independence and the renunciation by Germany of all territorial and political claims in respect of Austria and Austrian territory.

ARTICLE 4

Prohibition of Anschluss

1. The Allied and Associated Powers declare that political or economic union between Austria and Germany is prohibited. Austria fully recognizes its responsibilities in this matter and shall not enter into political or economic union with Germany in any form whatsoever.

2. In order to prevent such union Austria shall not conclude any agreement with Germany, nor do any act, nor take any measures likely, directly or indirectly, to promote political or economic union with Germany, or to impair its territorial integrity or political or economic independence. Austria further undertakes to prevent within its territory any act likely, directly or indirectly, to promote such union and shall prevent the existence, resurgence and activities of any organizations having as their aim political or economic union with Germany, and pan-German propaganda in favor of union with Germany.

ARTICLE 5

Frontiers of Austria

The frontiers of Austria shall be those existing on 1st January, 1938. . . .

ARTICLE 8

Democratic Institutions

Austria shall have a democratic government based on elections by secret ballot and shall guarantee to all citizens free, equal and universal suffrage as well as the right to be elected to public office without discrimination as to race, sex, language, religion or political opinion. . . .

PART III

ARTICLE 20

Withdrawal of Allied Forces

1. The Agreement on the Machinery of Control in Austria of 28th June, 1946 shall terminate on the coming into force of the present Treaty.

2. On the coming into force of the present Treaty, the Inter-Allied Command established under paragraph 4 of the Agreement on Zones of Occupation in Austria and the Administration of the City of Vienna of 9th July, 1945, shall cease to exercise any functions with respect to the administration of the City of Vienna. The Agreement on Zones of Occupation of Austria shall terminate upon completion of the withdrawal from Austria of the forces of the Allied and Associated Powers in accordance with paragraph 3 of the present Article.

3. The forces of the Allied and Associated Powers and members of the Allied Commission for Austria shall be withdrawn from Austria within ninety days from the coming into force of the present Treaty, and in so far as possible not later than 31st December, 1955.

4. The Government of Austria shall accord to the forces of the Allied and Associated Powers and the members of the Allied Commission for Austria pending their withdrawal from Austria the same rights, immunities and facilities as they enjoyed immediately before the coming into force of the present Treaty. . . .

AUSTRIAN NEUTRALITY RESOLUTION

Austria declares, with the object of the lasting and perpetual maintenance of her independence from without and the inviolability of her territory, as well as in the interest of maintenance of internal law and order, of her own free will her perpetual neutrality, and is resolved to maintain and defend it with all means at her disposal.

Austria, in order to secure these, will in the future, join no military alliances and will not permit the establishment of military bases of foreign states on her territory.

Austria, in this connection, declares her desire to observe at all times in her relations with other states the principles laid down in the United Nations Charter, and once again voices her willingness and ability to accede to and observe the obligations contained in the charter.

In addition, the Federal Government is requested—

To submit to the Nationalrat (Parliament) the draft of a federal constitutional law regulating the neutrality;

To take all steps in order to achieve the final admission to the organization of the United Nations, for which Austria has already applied;

To inform all states of this law with the request for recognition of Austria's neutrality as soon as the Austrian State Treaty has entered into effect and Austria has been evacuated of the occupation forces.

DOCUMENT 55

THE GENEVA CONFERENCE, JULY 1955: DIRECTIVE OF THE HEADS OF GOVERNMENT OF THE FOUR POWERS TO THE FOREIGN MINISTERS, JULY 23, 1955

The relaxation of tensions following the death of Stalin was highlighted by a "summit" conference at Geneva in July, 1955. President Eisenhower, Premier Bulganin, Prime Minister Eden and Premier Faure met for several days to discuss the world's problems (July 18–23, 1955). Nikita Khrushchev was also present. While no positive steps were taken by the conferees, the final directive to their foreign ministers indicated a renewed willingness to negotiate.

The Geneva Conference of Heads of Government, July 18–23, 1955, Department of State Publication No. 6046 (Washington, 1955), 67–68.

[At this meeting the Heads of Government agreed on the definitive phraseology of the final directive to the Foreign Ministers. The directive was formally adopted at the Eighth Plenary Meeting.]

Directive of the Heads of Government of the Four Powers to the Foreign Ministers

The Heads of Government of France, the United Kingdom, the U.S.S.R. and the U.S.A., guided by the desire to contribute to the relaxation of international tension and to the consolidation of confidence between states, instruct their Foreign Ministers to continue the consideration of the following questions with regard to which an exchange of views has taken place at the Geneva Conference; and to propose effective means for their solution, taking account of the close link between the reunification of Germany and the problems of European security, and the fact that the successful settlement of each of these problems would serve the interests of consolidating peace.

1. *European Security and Germany.* For the purpose of establishing European security with due regard to the legitimate interests of all nations and their inherent right to individual and collective self-defense, the Ministers are instructed to consider various proposals to this end, including the following: A security pact for Europe or for a part of Europe, including provisions for the assumption by member nations of an obligation not to resort to force and to deny assistance to an aggressor; limitation, control, and inspection in regard to armed forces and armaments; establishment between East and West of a zone in which the disposition of armed forces will be subject to mutual agreement; and also to consider other possible proposals pertaining to the solution of this problem.

The Heads of Government, recognizing their common responsibility for the settlement of the German question and the re-unification of Germany, have agreed that the settlement of the German question and the re-unification of Germany by means of free elections shall be carried out in conformity with the national interests of the German people and the interests of European security. The Foreign Ministers will make whatever arrangements they may consider desirable for the participation of, or for consultation with, other interested parties.

2. *Disarmament*

The Four Heads of Government,

Desirous of removing the threat of war and lessening the burden of armaments,

Convinced of the necessity, for secure peace and for the welfare of mankind, of achieving a system for the control and reduction of all armaments and armed forces under effective safeguards,

Recognizing that achievements in this field would release vast material resources to be devoted to the peaceful economic development of nations, for raising their well-being, as well as for assistance to underdeveloped countries,

Agree:

(1) for these purposes to work together to develop an acceptable system for disarmament through the Sub–Committee of the United Nations Disarmament Commission;

(2) to instruct their representatives in the Sub–Committee in the discharge of their mandate from the United Nations to take account in their work of the views and proposals advanced by the Heads of Government at this Conference;

(3) to propose that the next meeting of the Sub–Committee be held on August 29, 1955, at New York;

(4) to instruct the Foreign Ministers to take note of the proceedings in the Disarmament Commission, to take account of the views and proposals advanced by the Heads of Government at this Conference and to consider whether the four Governments can take any further useful initiative in the field of disarmament.

3. *Development of Contacts between East and West*

The Foreign Ministers should by means of experts study measures, including those possible in organs and agencies of the United Nations, which could (a) bring about a progressive elimination of barriers which interfere with free communications and peaceful trade between people and (b) bring about such freer contacts and exchanges as are to the mutual advantage of the countries and peoples concerned.

4. The Foreign Ministers of the Four Powers will meet at Geneva during October to initiate their consideration of these questions and to determine the organisation of their work.

DOCUMENT 56

SPEECH OF NIKITA KHRUSHCHEV BEFORE A CLOSED SESSION OF THE XXTH CONGRESS OF THE COMMUNIST PARTY OF THE SOVIET UNION ON FEBRUARY 25, 1956

That Stalin's death might have some beneficial results for the world became clear with Nikita Khrushchev's secret speech to the Twentieth Party Congress of the Soviet Union on February 25, 1956. Castigating the former Soviet leader for sundry crimes, his successor seemed to confirm many of the non-Communist explanations for the West's difficulty with Stalin, at least by indirection.

EXCERPTS FROM KHRUSHCHEV'S SPEECH

. . . The negative characteristics of Stalin, which, in Lenin's time, were only incipient, transformed themselves during the last years into a grave abuse of power by Stalin, which caused untold harm to our Party.

We have to consider seriously and analyze correctly this matter in order that we may preclude any possibility of a repetition in any form whatever of what took place during the life of Stalin, who absolutely did not tolerate colleagiality in leadership and in work, and who practiced brutal violence, not only toward everything which opposed him, but also toward that which seemed to his capricious and despotic character, contrary to his concepts.

Stalin acted not through persuasion, explanation, and patient co-operation with people, but by imposing his concepts and demanding absolute submission to his opinion. Whoever opposed this concept or tried to prove his viewpoint, and the correctness of his position—was doomed to removal from the leading collective and to subsequent

---

Speech of Nikita Khrushchev Before a Closed Session of the XXth Congress of the Communist Party of the Soviet Union on February 25, 1956, 85th Cong., 1st Sess., Subcommittee to Investigate the Administration of the Internal Security Act and Other Internal Security Laws of the Committee on the Judiciary, United States Senate (Washington, 1957), 27–33, 37, 42.

moral and physical annihilation. This was especially true during the period following the XVIIth Party Congress, when many prominent Party leaders and rank-and-file Party workers, honest and dedicated to the cause of Communism, fell victim to Stalin's despotism.

We must affirm that the Party had fought a serious fight against the Trotskyites, rightists and bourgeois nationalists, and that it disarmed ideologically all the enemies of Leninism. This ideological fight was carried on successfully as a result of which the Party became strengthened and tempered. Here Stalin played a positive role.

The Party led a great political ideological struggle against those in its own ranks who proposed anti-Leninist theses, who represented a political line hostile to the Party and to the cause of Socialism. This was a stubborn and a difficult fight but a necessary one, because the political line of both the Trotskyite-Zinovievite bloc and of the Bukharinites led actually toward the restoration of capitalism and capitulation to the world bourgeoisie. Let us consider for a moment what would have happened if in 1928–1929 the political line of right deviation had prevailed among us, or orientation toward "cotton-dress industrialization," or toward the kulak, etc. We would not now have a powerful heavy industry, we would not have the Kolkhozes, we would find ourselves disarmed and weak in a capitalist encirclement. . . .

Worth noting is the fact that even during the progress of the furious ideological fight against the Trotskyites, the Zinovievites, the Bukharinites and others—extreme repressive measures were not used against them. The fight was on ideological grounds. But some years later when Socialism in our country was fundamentally constructed, when the exploiting classes were generally liquidated, when the Soviet social structure had radically changed, when the social basis for political movements and groups hostile to the Party had violently contracted, when the ideological opponents of the Party were long since defeated politically—then the repression directed against them began.

It was precisely during this period (1935–1937–1938) that the practice of mass repression through the government apparatus was born, first against the enemies of Leninism—Trotskyites, Zinovievites, Bukharinites, long since politically defeated by the Party, and subsequently also against many honest Communists, against those Party cadres who had borne the heavy load of the Civil War and the first and most difficult years of industrialization and collectivization, who actively fought against the Trotskyites and the rightists for the Leninist Party line.

Stalin originated the concept "enemy of the people." This term automatically rendered it unnecessary that the ideological errors of a man or men engaged in a controversy be proven; this term made possible the usage of the most cruel repression, violating all norms of revolutionary legality, against anyone who in any way disagreed with Stalin, against those who were only suspected of hostile intent, against those who had bad reputations. This concept, "enemy of the people," actually eliminated the possibility of any kind of ideological fight or the making of one's views known on this or that issue, even those of a practical character. In the main, and in actuality, the only proof of guilt used, against all norms of current legal science, was the "confession" of the accused himself; and, as subsequent probing proved, "confessions" were acquired through physical pressures against the accused.

This led to glaring violations of revolutionary legality, and to the fact that many entirely innocent persons, who in the past had defended the Party line, became victims.

We must assert that, in regard to those persons who in their time had opposed the Party line, there were often no sufficiently serious reasons for their physical annihilation. The formula, "enemy of the people" was specifically introduced for the purpose of physically annihilating such individuals.

It is a fact that many persons, who were later annihilated as enemies of the Party [were] people who had worked with Lenin during his life. Some of these persons had made errors during Lenin's life, but, despite this, Lenin benefited by their work, he corrected them and he did everything possible to retain them in the ranks of the Party; he induced them to follow him. . . .

Lenin's wisdom in dealing with people was evident in his work with cadres.

An entirely different relationship with people characterized Stalin. Lenin's traits—patient work with people; stubborn and painstaking education of them; the ability to induce people to follow him without using compulsion, but rather through the ideological influence on them of the whole collective—were entirely foreign to Stalin. He (Stalin) discarded the Leninist method of convincing and educating; he abandoned the method of ideological struggle for that of administrative violence, mass repressions, and terror. He acted on an increasingly larger scale and more stubbornly through punitive organs, at the same time often violating all existing norms of morality and of Soviet laws.

Arbitrary behavior by one person encouraged and permitted arbitrariness in others. Mass arrests and deportations of many thousands of people, execution without trial and without normal investigation created conditions of insecurity, fear, and even desperation.

This, of course, did not contribute toward unity of the Party ranks and of all strata of working people, but on the contrary brought about annihilation and the expulsion from the Party of workers who were loyal but inconvenient to Stalin. . . .

In practice Stalin ignored the norms of Party life and trampled on the Leninist principle of collective Party leadership.

Stalin's wilfulness vis-a-vis the Party and its Central Committee became fully evident after the XVIIth Party Congress which took place in 1934.

Having at its disposal numerous data showing brutal willfulness toward Party cadres, the Central Committee had created a Party Commission under the control of the Central Committee Presidium; it was charged with investigating what made possible the mass repressions against the majority of the Central Committee members and candidates elected at the XVIIth Congress of the All-Union Communist Party (Bolsheviks).

The Commission has become acquainted with a large quantity of materials in the NKVD archives and with other documents and has established many facts pertaining to the fabrication of cases against Communists, to false accusations, to glaring abuses of Socialist legality—which resulted in the death of innocent people. It became apparent that many Party, Soviet and economic activists, who were branded in 1937–1938 as "enemies," were actually never enemies, spies, wreckers, etc., but were always honest Communists; they were only so stigmatized and often, no longer able to bear barbaric tortures, they charged themselves (at the order of the investigative judges—falsifiers) with all kinds of grave and unlikely crimes. The Commission has presented to the Central Committee Presidium lengthy and documented materials pertaining to mass repressions against the delegates to the XVIIth Party Congress and against members of the Central Committee elected at that Congress. These materials have been studied by the Presidium of the Central Committee.

It was determined that of the 139 members and candidates of the Party's Central Committee who were elected at the XVIIth Congress, 98 persons, i.e., 70 percent, were arrested and shot (mostly in 1937–1938). [Indignation in the hall.]

What was the composition of the delegates to the XVIIth Congress? It is known that eighty percent of the voting participants of the XVIIth Congress joined the Party during the years of conspiracy before the Revolution and during the Civil War; this means before 1921. By social origin the basic mass of the delegates to the Congress were workers (60 percent of the voting members).

For this reason, it was inconceivable that a Congress so composed would have elected a Central Committee, a majority of whom would prove to be enemies of the Party. The only reason why 70 percent of Central Committee members and candidates elected at the XVIIth Congress were branded as enemies of the Party and of the people was because honest Communists were slandered, accusations against them were fabricated, and revolutionary legality was gravely undermined. . . .

The majority of the Central Committee members and candidates elected at the XVIIth Congress and arrested in 1937–1938 were expelled from the Party illegally through the brutal abuse of the Party Statute, because the question of their expulsion was never studied at the Central Committee Plenum.

Now when the cases of some of these so-called "spies" and "saboteurs" were examined it was found that all their cases were fabricated. Confessions of guilt of many arrested and charged with enemy activity were gained with the help of cruel and inhuman tortures.

At the same time Stalin, as we have been informed by members of the Political Bureau of that time, did not show them the statements of many accused political activists when they retracted their confessions before the military tribunal and asked for an objective examination of their cases. There were many such declarations, and Stalin doubtlessly knew of them.

The Central Committee considers it absolutely necessary to inform the Congress of many such fabricated "cases" against the members of the Party's Central Committee elected at the XVIIth Party Congress. . . .

Facts prove that many abuses were made on Stalin's orders without reckoning with any norms of Party and Soviet legality. Stalin was a very distrustful man, sickly suspicious; we knew this from our work with him. He could look at a man and say: "Why are your eyes so shifty today," or "Why are you turning so much today and avoiding to look me directly in the eyes?" The sickly suspicion created in him a general distrust even toward eminent Party workers whom he had known for years. Everywhere and in everything he saw "enemies," "two-facers" and "spies."

Possessing unlimited power he indulged in great willfulness and choked a person morally and physically. A situation was created when one could not express one's own will.

When Stalin said that one or another should be arrested, it was necessary to accept on faith that he was an "enemy of the people." Meanwhile, Beria's gang, which ran the organs of state security, outdid itself in proving the guilt of the arrested and the truth of materials which it falsified. And what proofs were offered? The confessions of the arrested, and the investigative judges accepted these "confessions." And how is it possible that a person confesses to crimes which he has not committed? Only in one way—because of application of physical methods of pressuring him, tortures, bringing him to a state of unconsciousness, deprivation of his judgment, taking away of his human dignity. In this manner were "confessions" acquired.

When the wave of mass arrests began to recede in 1939, and the leaders of territorial Party organizations began to accuse the NKVD workers of using methods of physical pressure on the arrested, Stalin dispatched a coded telegram on 20 January 1939, to the committee secretaries of oblasts and krais, to the Central Committees of republic Communist Parties, to the People's Commissars of Internal Affairs and to the heads of NKVD organizations. This telegram stated:

"The Central Committee of the All-Union Communist Party (Bolsheviks) explains that the application of methods of physical pressure in NKVD practice is permissible from 1937 on in accordance with permission of the Central Committee of the All-Union Communist Party (Bolsheviks). . . . It is known that all bourgeois intelligence services use methods of physical influence against the representatives of the Socialist proletariat and that they use them in their most scandalous forms. The question arises as to why the Socialist intelligence service should be more humanitarian against the mad agents of the bourgeoisie, against the deadly enemies of the working class and of the Kolkhoz workers. The Central Committee of the All-Union Communist Party (Bolsheviks) considers that physical pressure should still be used obligatorily, as an exception applicable to known and obstinate enemies of the people, as a method both justifiable and appropriate."

Thus, Stalin had sanctioned in the name of the Central Committee of the All-Union Communist Party (Bolsheviks) the most brutal violation of Socialist legality, torture and oppression, which led as we have seen to the slandering and self-accusation of innocent people. . . .

DOCUMENT 57

THE HUNGARIAN REVOLUTION: DECLARATION OF THE U.S.S.R. GOVERNMENT ON THE BASIS OF THE DEVELOPMENT AND FURTHER STRENGTHENING OF FRIENDSHIP AND COOPERATION BETWEEN THE SOVIET UNION AND OTHER SOCIALIST STATES, OCTOBER 30, 1956

Khrushchev's loosening of the Communist system brought about unrest in the Eastern European Soviet satellites. Dissatisfaction in Poland was brought under control before it turned into open revolution; in Hungary, however, an armed revolt broke out. On October 28, 1956, Imre Nagy, the new President of the Council of Ministers of Hungary, announced that the Soviets had consented to withdraw their troops, and on October 30, Moscow radio broadcast a statement setting forth its willingness to negotiate.

The principles of peaceful coexistence, friendship, and cooperation among all states have always been and still form the unshakable foundation of the foreign relations of the U.S.S.R. This policy finds its most profound and consistent expression in the relationship with socialist countries. United by the common ideal of building a socialist society and the principles of proletarian internationalism, the countries of the great commonwealth of socialist nations can build

Department of State *Bulletin*, XXXV (November 12, 1956), 745–746.

their relations only on the principle of full equality, respect of territorial integrity, state independence and sovereignty, and noninterference in one another's domestic affairs.

This does not exclude, but on the contrary presupposes, close fraternal cooperation and mutual aid between the countries of the socialist commonwealth in the economic, political, and cultural spheres. It is on this basis that after World War II and after the rout of fascism the regimes of the people's democracies came into being in a number of countries of Europe and Asia, which were strengthened and display great vitality.

In the process of the establishment of the new regime and the deep revolutionary transformation in social relations there were not a few difficulties, unsolved problems, and out-and-out mistakes, including some in the relations between the socialist states—violations and mistakes which infringed the principles of equality in relations between socialist states. . . .

It is known that, in accordance with the Warsaw Treaty and with government agreements, Soviet units are stationed in the Hungarian and the Rumanian Republics. In the Polish Republic, Soviet military units are stationed on the basis of the Potsdam Four-Power Agreement and the Warsaw Treaty. In other people's democratic countries there are no Soviet military units.

With a view to insuring the mutual security of the socialist countries, the Soviet Government is ready to examine with other socialist countries that are parties to the Warsaw Treaty the question of Soviet troops stationed on the territory of these countries. In this the Soviet Government proceeds from the general principle that the stationing of troops of one state that is a party to the Warsaw Treaty on the territory of another state that is a party to the Warsaw Treaty should take place on the basis of an agreement among all its participants and not only with the agreement of the state on whose territory these troops are stationed or are planned to be stationed at its request.

The Soviet Government regards it as indispensable to make a statement in connection with the events in Hungary.

The course of the events has shown that the working people of Hungary, who have achieved great progress on the basis of their people's democratic order, correctly raise the question of the necessity of eliminating serious shortcomings in the field of economic building, the further raising of the material well-being of the population, and the struggle against bureaucratic excesses in the state apparatus.

However, this just and progressive movement of the working people was soon joined by forces of black reaction and counterrevolution, which are trying to take advantage of the discontent of part of the working people to undermine the foundations of the people's democratic order in Hungary and to restore the old landlord and capitalist order.

The Soviet Government and all the Soviet people deeply regret that the development of events in Hungary has led to bloodshed. On the request of the Hungarian People's Government the Soviet Government consented to the entry into Budapest of the Soviet Army units to assist the Hungarian People's Army and the Hungarian authorities to establish order in the town. Believing that the further presence of Soviet Army units in Hungary can serve as a cause for even greater deterioration of the situation, the Soviet Government has given instructions to its military command to withdraw the Soviet Army units from Budapest as soon as this is recognized as necessary by the Hungarian Government.

At the same time, the Soviet Government is ready to enter into relevant negotiations with the Government of the Hungarian People's Republic and other participants of the Warsaw Treaty on the question of the presence of Soviet troops on the territory of Hungary.

The defense of socialist achievements by the people's democracy of Hungary is at the present moment the chief and sacred duty of workers, peasants, and intelligentsia, and of all the Hungarian working people.

The Soviet Government expresses confidence that the peoples of the socialist countries will not permit foreign and internal reactionary forces to undermine the basis of the people's democratic regimes, won and consolidated by the heroic struggle and toil of the workers, peasants, and intelligentsia of each country.

They will make all efforts to remove all obstacles that lie in the path of further strengthening the democratic basis of the independence and sovereignty of their countries, to develop further the socialist basis of each country, its economy and culture, for the sake of the constant growth of the material welfare and the cultural level of all the workers. They will consolidate the fraternal unity and mutual assistance of the socialist countries for the strengthening of the great cause of peace and socialism.

DOCUMENT 58

THE HUNGARIAN REVOLUTION: HUNGARY'S APPEAL TO THE UNITED NATIONS, NOVEMBER 2, 1956

In spite of Russian promises, Soviet forces not only failed to leave Hungary but were reinforced to squelch the revolution. In desperation, Imre Nagy addressed the United Nations in a plea for assistance.

Letter Dated 2 November 1956, to the Secretary-General from the President of the Council of Ministers and Acting Foreign Minister of the Hungarian People's Republic

Budapest, 2 November 1956

As the President of the Council of Ministers and designated Foreign Minister of the Hungarian People's Republic I have the honour to bring to the attention of Your Excellency the following additional information:

I have already mentioned in my letter of 1 November 1956 that new Soviet military units entered Hungary and that the Hungarian Government informed the Soviet Ambassador in Budapest of this fact, at the same time terminated the Treaty of Warsaw, declared the neutrality of Hungary and requested the United Nations to guarantee the neutrality of the country.

On 2 November 1956 further an exact information, mainly military reports, reached the Government of the Hungarian People's Republic, according to which large Soviet military units crossed the border of the country, marching towards Budapest. They occupy railway lines, railway stations and railway safety equipment. Reports also have come about that Soviet military movements of east-west direction are being observed on the territory of Western Hungary.

On the basis of the above-mentioned facts the Hungarian Government deemed it necessary to inform the Embassy of the U.S.S.R. and

United Nations, Security Council, *Official Records*, 11th Year, Supplement for October, November, and December 1956, U. N. Document S/3726.

all the other diplomatic missions in Budapest about these steps directed against our People's Republic.

At the same time, the Government of the Hungarian People's Republic forwarded concrete proposals on the withdrawal of Soviet troops stationed in Hungary as well as the place of negotiations concerning the execution of the termination of the Treaty of Warsaw and presented a list containing the names of the members of the Government's delegation. Furthermore, the Hungarian Government made a proposal to the Soviet Embassy in Budapest to form a mixed committee to prepare the withdrawal of the Soviet troops.

I request Your Excellency to call upon the great powers to recognize the neutrality of Hungary and ask the Security Council to instruct the Soviet and Hungarian Governments to start the negotiations immediately.

I also request Your Excellency to make known the above to the members of the Security Council.

(*Signed*) IMRE NAGY
President of the Council of Ministers
Acting Minister for Foreign Affairs

DOCUMENT 59

THE HUNGARIAN REVOLUTION: RESOLUTION ADOPTED BY THE GENERAL ASSEMBLY ON NOVEMBER 4, 1956

Soviet repression of the Hungarian revolution by armed force led the General Assembly of the United Nations to pass a resolution calling upon the Soviet Union to withdraw from Hungary. The resolution was submitted by the United States and adopted, on November 4, 1956, by a vote of 50 to 8, with 15 abstentions. The Soviet Union defied it.

The General Assembly,

Considering that the United Nations is based on the principle of the sovereign equality of all its Members,

Recalling that the enjoyment of human rights and of fundamental freedom in Hungary was specifically guaranteed by the Peace Treaty between Hungary and the Allied and Associated Powers signed at Paris on 10 February 1947 and that the general principle of these

Department of State *Bulletin*, XXXV (November 19, 1956), 803–804.

rights and this freedom is affirmed for all peoples in the Charter of the United Nations,

Convinced that recent events in Hungary manifest clearly the desire of the Hungarian people to exercise and to enjoy fully their fundamental rights, freedom and independence,

Condemning the use of Soviet military forces to suppress the efforts of the Hungarian people to reassert their rights,

Noting moreover the declaration by the Government of the Union of Soviet Socialist Republics of 30 October 1956, of its avowed policy of non-intervention in the internal affairs of other States,

Noting the communication of 1 November 1956 of the Government of Hungary to the Secretary-General regarding demands made by that Government to the Government of the Union of Soviet Socialist Republics for the instant and immediate withdrawal of Soviet forces,

Noting further the communication of 2 November 1956 from the Government of Hungary to the Secretary-General asking the Security Council to instruct the Government of the Union of Soviet Socialist Republics and the Government of Hungary to start the negotiations immediately on withdrawal of Soviet forces,

Noting that the intervention of Soviet military forces in Hungary has resulted in grave loss of life and widespread bloodshed among the Hungarian people,

Taking note of the radio appeal of Prime Minister Imre Nagy of 4 November 1956,

1. *Calls upon* the Government of the Union of Soviet Socialist Republics to desist forthwith from all armed attack on the peoples of Hungary and from any form of intervention, in particular armed intervention, in the internal affairs of Hungary;

2. *Calls upon* the Union of Soviet Socialist Republics to cease the introduction of additional armed forces into Hungary and to withdraw all of its forces without delay from Hungarian territory;

3. *Affirms* the right of the Hungarian people to a government responsive to its national aspirations and dedicated to its independence and well-being;

4. *Requests* the Secretary-General to investigate the situation caused by foreign intervention in Hungary, to observe the situation directly through representatives named by him, and to report thereon to the General Assembly at the earliest moment, and as soon as pos-

sible suggest methods to bring an end to the foreign intervention in Hungary in accordance with the principles of the Charter of the United Nations;

5. *Calls upon* the Government of Hungary and the Government of the Union of Soviet Socialist Republics to permit observers designated by the Secretary-General to enter the territory of Hungary, to travel freely therein, and to report their findings to the Secretary-General;

6. *Calls upon* all Members of the United Nations to cooperate with the Secretary-General and his representatives in the execution of his functions;

7. *Requests* the Secretary-General in consultation with the heads of appropriate specialized agencies to inquire, on an urgent basis, into the needs of the Hungarian people for food, medicine and other similar supplies, and to report to the General Assembly as soon as possible;

8. *Requests* all Members of the United Nations, and invites national and international humanitarian organizations to co-operate in making available such supplies as may be required by the Hungarian people.

DOCUMENT 60

THE SUEZ CRISIS: EXCERPTS FROM PRESIDENT EISENHOWER'S ADDRESS OF OCTOBER 31, 1956

In October, 1956, the crisis in the Middle East also reached a boiling point. After seizing the Suez Canal in July, 1956, President Nasser of Egypt had found himself involved in severe altercations with Great Britain and France. As the Soviets were preoccupied with the Hungarian revolution, Israel, a country he had long vowed to destroy, seized the opportunity to launch an attack upon Egypt in order to end incursions into her territory and to open the Gulf of Aqaba and the canal. Great Britain and France then intervened also. President Eisenhower, unwilling to risk or condone war, promptly condemned this action and explained his course in a radio and television address on October 31, 1956.

. . . I now turn to that other part of the world where, at this moment, the situation is somber. It is not a situation that calls for extravagant fear or hysteria. It invites our most serious concern.

Department of State *Bulletin*, XXXV (November 19, 1956), 744–745.

I speak, of course, of the Middle East. This ancient crossroads of the world was, as we all know, an area long subject to colonial rule. This rule ended after World War II, when all countries there won full independence. Out of the Palestinian mandated territory was born the new State of Israel.

These historic changes could not, however, instantly banish animosities born of the ages. Israel and her Arab neighbors soon found themselves at war with one another. And the Arab nations showed continuing anger toward their former colonial rulers, notably Great Britain and France.

The United States through all the years since the close of World War II has labored tirelessly to bring peace and stability to this area.

We have considered it a basic matter of United States policy to support the new State of Israel and at the same time to strengthen our bonds both with Israel and with the Arab countries. But unfortunately, through all these years, passion in the area threatened to prevail over peaceful purpose and, in one form or another, there has been almost continuous fighting.

This situation recently was aggravated needlessly by an Egyptian policy including rearmament with Communist weapons. We, for our part, felt this to be a misguided policy on the part of the Government of Egypt. The State of Israel, for its part, felt increasing anxiety for its safety. And Great Britain and France feared more and more that Egyptian policies threatened what they regard as their "lifeline" of the Suez Canal.

These matters came to a crisis on July 26th of this year, when the Egyptian Government seized the Universal Suez Canal Company. For 90 years, ever since the inauguration of the canal, that company had operated the canal, largely under British and French technical supervision.

There were some among our allies who urged an immediate reaction to this event by use of force. We insistently urged otherwise, and our wish prevailed—through a long succession of conferences and negotiations for weeks and months, with participation by the United Nations. And there, only a short while ago, on the basis of agreed principles, it seemed that an acceptable accord was within our reach. But the direct relations of Egypt with both Israel and France kept worsening to a point at which first Israel, then France and

Great Britain also, determined that, in their judgment, there could be no protection of their vital interests without resort to force.

Upon this decision, events followed swiftly. On Sunday [October 28] the Israeli Government ordered total mobilization. On Monday, their armed forces penetrated deeply into Egypt and to the vicinity of the Suez Canal, nearly 100 miles away. And on Tuesday, the British and French Governments delivered a 12-hour ultimatum to Israel and Egypt—now followed up by armed attack against Egypt.

The United States was not consulted in any way about any phase of these actions. Nor were we informed of them in advance.

As it is the manifest right of any of these nations to take such decisions and actions, it is likewise our right—if our judgment so dictates—to dissent. We believe these actions to have been taken in error. For we do not accept the use of force as a wise or proper instrument for the settlement of international disputes.

To say this in this particular instance is in no way to minimize our friendship with these nations nor our determination to retain and to strengthen the bonds among us. And we are fully aware of the grave anxieties of Israel, of Britain, and of France. We know that they have been subjected to grave and repeated provocations.

The present fact, nonetheless, seems clear: The actions taken can scarcely be reconciled with the principles and purposes of the United Nations to which we have all subscribed. And, beyond this, we are forced to doubt even if resort to war will for long serve the permanent interests of the attacking nations.

Now we must look to the future.

In the circumstances I have described, there will be no United States involvement in these present hostilities. I therefore have no plan to call the Congress in special session. Of course, we shall continue to keep in contact with congressional leaders of both parties. At the same time it is—and it will remain—the dedicated purpose of your Government to do all in its power to localize the fighting and to end the conflict.

We took our first measure in this action yesterday. We went to the United Nations Security Council with a request that the forces of Israel return to their own land and that hostilities in the area be brought to a close. This proposal was not adopted, because it was vetoed by Great Britain and France.

The processes of the United Nations, however, are not exhausted.

It is our hope and intent that this matter will be brought before the United Nations General Assembly. There, with no veto operating, the opinion of the world can be brought to bear in our quest for a just end to this tormenting problem. In the past the United Nations has proved able to find a way to end bloodshed. We believe it can and will do so again.

My fellow citizens, as I review the march of world events in recent years, I am ever more deeply convinced that the processes of the United Nations need further to be developed and strengthened. I speak particularly of increasing its ability to secure justice under international law.

In all the recent troubles in the Middle East, there have indeed been injustices suffered by all nations involved. But I do not believe that another instrument of injustice—war—is the remedy for these wrongs.

There can be no peace without law. And there can be no law if we were to invoke one code of international conduct for those who oppose us and another for our friends.

The society of nations has been slow in developing means to apply this truth. But the passionate longing for peace on the part of all peoples of the earth compels us to speed our search for new and more effective instruments of justice. The peace we seek and need means much more than mere absence of war. It means the acceptance of law, and the fostering of justice, in all the world. To our principles guiding us in this quest we must stand fast. In so doing we can honor the hopes of all men for a world in which peace will truly and justly reign.

DOCUMENT 61

THE SUEZ CRISIS: GENERAL ASSEMBLY RESOLUTION ON MIDDLE EAST, NOVEMBER 2, 1956

In spite of Israel's great military success and the Soviet Union's preoccupation in Hungary, the United States, on November 2, 1956, joined with its Cold War antagonist in urging an immediate cease-fire and withdrawal in the Middle East. President Nasser was thus saved from disaster and Western influence in the region suffered a severe blow.

Department of State *Bulletin*, XXXV (November 12, 1956), 754.

The General Assembly,

Noting the disregard on many occasions by parties to the Israel-Arab Armistice Agreements of 1948 of the terms of such agreements, and that the armed forces of Israel have penetrated deeply into Egyptian territory in violation of the General Armistice Agreement between Egypt and Israel,

Noting that armed forces of France and the United Kingdom are conducting military operations against Egyptian territory,

Noting that traffic through the Suez Canal is now interrupted to the serious prejudice of many nations,

Expressing its grave concern over these developments,

1. *Urges* as a matter of priority that all parties now involved in hostilities in the area agree to an immediate cease-fire and as part thereof halt the movement of military forces and arms into the area;

2. *Urges* the parties to the Armistice Agreements promptly to withdraw all forces behind the Armistice lines, to desist from raids across the Armistice lines into neighbouring territory, and to observe scrupulously the provisions of the Armistice Agreements;

3. *Recommends* that all Members refrain from introducing military goods in the area of hostilities and in general refrain from any acts which would delay or prevent the implementation of this resolution;

4. *Urges* that upon the cease-fire being effective steps be taken to reopen the Suez Canal and restore secure freedom of navigation;

5. *Requests* the Secretary-General to observe and promptly report on the compliance with this resolution, to the Security Council and to the General Assembly, for such further action as they may deem appropriate in accordance with the Charter;

6. *Decides* to remain in emergency session pending compliance with this resolution.

DOCUMENT 62

THE EISENHOWER DOCTRINE: JOINT RESOLUTION TO PROMOTE PEACE AND STABILITY IN THE MIDDLE EAST, MARCH 9, 1957

The Suez debacle resulted in renewed anti-Western threats in the Middle East. In order to meet the danger, President Eisenhower, on January 5,

1957, asked Congress for authority to assist Middle Eastern nations in their fight against Communism. A Joint Resolution embodying this policy was signed by the President on March 9, 1957.

Resolved by the Senate and House of Representatives of the United States of America in Congress assembled,

That the President be and hereby is authorized to cooperate with and assist any nation or group of nations in the general area of the Middle East desiring such assistance in the development of economic strength dedicated to the maintenance of national independence.

SEC. 2. The President is authorized to undertake, in the general area of the Middle East, military assistance programs with any nation or group of nations of that area desiring such assistance. Furthermore, the United States regards as vital to the national interest and world peace the preservation of the independence and integrity of the nations of the Middle East. To this end, if the President determines the necessity thereof, the United States is prepared to use armed forces to assist any such nation or group of such nations requesting assistance against armed aggression from any country controlled by international communism: *Provided,* That such employment shall be consonant with the treaty obligations of the United States and with the Constitution of the United States.

SEC. 3. The President is hereby authorized to use during the balance of fiscal year 1957 for economic and military assistance under this joint resolution not to exceed $200,000,000 from any appropriation now available for carrying out the provisions of the Mutual Security Act of 1954, as amended, in accord with the provisions of such Act: *Provided,* That, whenever the President determines it to be important to the security of the United States, such use may be under the authority of section 401 (a) of the Mutual Security Act of 1954, as amended (except that the provisions of section 105 (a) thereof shall not be waived), and without regard to the provisions of section 105 of the Mutual Security Appropriation Act, 1957: *Provided further,* That obligations incurred in carrying out the purposes of the first sentence of section 2 of this joint resolution shall be paid only

Department of State *Bulletin,* XXXVI (March 25, 1957), 481.

out of appropriations for military assistance, and obligations incurred in carrying out the purposes of the first section of this joint resolution shall be paid only of appropriations other than those for military assistance. This authorization is in addition to other existing authorizations with respect to the use of such appropriations. None of the additional authorization contained in this section shall be used until fifteen days after the Committee on Foreign Relations of the Senate, the Committee on Foreign Affairs of the House of Representatives, the Committees on Appropriations of the Senate and the House of Representatives and, when military assistance is involved, the Committees on Armed Services of the Senate and the House of Representatives have been furnished a report showing the object of the proposed use, the country for the benefit of which such use is intended, and the particular appropriation or appropriations for carrying out the provisions of the Mutual Security Act of 1954, as amended, from which the funds are proposed to be derived: *Provided,* That funds available under this section during the balance of fiscal year 1957 shall, in the case of any such report submitted during the last fifteen days of the fiscal year, remain available for use under this section for the purposes stated in such report for a period of twenty days following the date of submission of such report. Nothing contained in this joint resolution shall be construed as itself authorizing the appropriation of additional funds for the purpose of carrying out the provisions of the first section or of the first sentence of section 2 of this joint resolution.

SEC. 4. The President should continue to furnish facilities and military assistance, within the provisions of applicable law and established policies, to the United Nations Emergency Force in the Middle East, with a view to maintaining the truce in that region.

SEC. 5. The President shall within the months of January and July of each year report to the Congress his action hereunder.

SEC. 6. This joint resolution shall expire when the President shall determine that the peace and security of the nations in the general area of the Middle East are reasonably assured by international conditions created by action of the United Nations or otherwise except that it may be terminated earlier by a concurrent resolution of the two Houses of Congress.

DOCUMENT 63

NOTE FROM THE SOVIET FOREIGN MINISTRY TO THE AMERICAN AMBASSADOR AT MOSCOW (THOMPSON), REGARDING BERLIN, NOVEMBER 27, 1958

In Europe, Germany remained the most serious obstacle to an improvement of international relations. A new Berlin crisis was precipitated by Premier Khrushchev when, in an address at a Moscow Soviet-Polish meeting, he announced his intention of ending the occupation regime in the former German capital (November 10, 1958). Three weeks later, on November 27, 1958, in a note to the American ambassador at Moscow, the Soviets clarified these proposals and made them more ominous by the addition of a six-month time limit.

[Department of State translation]

The Government of the Union of Soviet Socialist Republics addresses the Government of the United States of America as one of the signatory powers of the Potsdam Agreement on the urgent question of the status of Berlin.

The problem of Berlin, which is situated in the center of the German Democratic Republic but the western part of which is cut off from the GDR as a result of foreign occupation, deeply affects not only the national interests of the German people but also the interests of all nations desirous of establishing lasting peace in Europe. Here in the historic capital of Germany two worlds are in direct contact and at every turn there tower the barricades of the "cold war." A situation of constant friction and tension has prevailed for many years in this city, which is divided into two parts. Berlin, which witnessed the greatest triumph of the joint struggle of our countries against Fascist aggression, has now become a dangerous center of contradiction between the Great Powers, allies in the last war. Its role in the relations between the Powers may be compared to a smoldering fuse that has been connected to a powder keg. Incidents arising here, even if they seem to be of local significance, may, in an atmosphere of heated passions, suspicion, and mutual apprehensions, cause a conflagration which will be difficult to extinguish. This is the sad pass to which has come, after the 13 postwar years, the once joint and concerted policy of the Four Powers—the U.S.S.R., the U.S.A., Great Britain and France—with regard to Germany. . . .

When the peoples were celebrating victory over Hitlerite Germany a conference of the heads of government of the Soviet Union, the U.S.A. and Great Britain was held in Potsdam in order to work out a joint policy with respect to post-war Germany. The Potsdam Agreement, to which France acceded soon after it was signed, generalized the historical experience of the struggle waged by the peoples to prevent aggression by German militarism. The entire content of this agreement was directed toward creating conditions precluding the possibility of yet another attack by Germany against peace-loving states, toward preventing German militarists from unleashing another world war so that Germany, having abandoned forever the mirage of a policy of conquest, might make a firm start on the road to peaceful development. . . .

The Potsdam Agreement contained important provisions whereby Germany was to be regarded as a single economic entity, even during the occupation period. The agreement also provided for the creation of central German administrative departments. The Council for Foreign Ministers, established by a decision of the Potsdam Conference, was instructed to prepare a peace settlement for Germany.

The implementation of all these measures should have enabled the German people to effect a fundamental reconstruction of their life and to ensure the creation of a united, peace-loving, democratic German state. . . .

Actually, of all the Allied agreements on Germany, only one is being carried out today. It is the agreement on the so-called quadripartite status of Berlin. On the basis of that status, the Three Western Powers are ruling the roost in West Berlin, turning it into a kind of state within a state and using it as a center from which to pursue subversive activity against the GDR, the Soviet Union, and the other parties of the Warsaw Treaty. The United States, Great Britain, and France are freely communicating with West Berlin through lines of communication passing through the territory and the airspace of the German Democratic Republic, which they do not even want to recognize. . . .

At present, the U.S.A., Great Britain, and France are opposed, as follows from their notes of September 30 of this year, to the latest proposals for a peaceful settlement with Germany put forward by the Soviet Union and the GDR, while making no proposals of their own on this question, just as they have made none throughout the postwar period. As a matter of fact, the last note of the U.S. Government is a restatement of the position that proved to be utterly unrealistic, whereby Germany's national unity is to be re-established by the U.S.S.R, the U.S.A., Great Britain, and France rather than by the German states that are to unite. It also follows from the U.S. Government's note that it is once again avoiding negotiations with the Soviet Union and the other interested states for the purpose of preparing a peace treaty with Germany. The result is a veritable vicious circle: The U.S. Government is objecting to the drafting of a German peace treaty by referring to the absence of a united German state while at the same time hampering the reunification of Germany by rejecting the only real possibility of solving this problem through agreement between the two German states.

Is it not because the Western Powers would like to prolong indefinitely their privileges in West Germany and the occupation regime in West Berlin that they take this position on the question of drafting a peace treaty? It is becoming increasingly clear that such is the actual state of affairs.

The Soviet Government reaffirms its readiness to participate at any time in negotiations to draft a peace treaty with Germany. However, the absence of a peace treaty can by no means be an excuse now for attempting to maintain the occupation regime anywhere in Germany. . . .

In this connection, the Government of the U.S.S.R. hereby notifies the United States Government that the Soviet Union regards as null and void, the "Protocol of the Agreement between the Governments of the Union of Soviet Socialist Republics, the United States of America, and the United Kingdom on the zones of operation in Germany and on the administration of Greater Berlin," of September 12, 1944, and the related supplementary agreements, including the agreement on the control machinery in Germany, concluded between the governments of the U.S.S.R., the U.S.A., Great Britain, and France on May 1, 1945, i.e., the agreements that were intended to be in effect during the first years after the capitulation of Germany.

It is easy to see that all the Soviet Government is doing by making this statement is to recognize the actual state of affairs, which consists in the fact that the U.S.A., Great Britain, and France have long since rejected the essentials of the treaties and agreements concluded during the war against Hitler Germany and after its defeat. The Soviet Government is doing no more than drawing conclusions that inevitably ensue for the Soviet Union from this actual state of affairs.

Pursuant to the foregoing and proceeding from the principle of respect for the sovereignty of the German Democratic Republic, the Soviet Government will enter into negotiations with the Government of the GDR at an appropriate time with a view to transferring to the German Democratic Republic the functions temporarily performed by the Soviet authorities by virtue of the above-mentioned Allied agreements and under the agreement between the U.S.S.R. and the GDR of September 20, 1955. The best way to solve the Berlin problem would undoubtedly be to adopt a decision based on the enforcement of the Potsdam Agreement on Germany. But this is possible only in the event that the three Western Powers return to a policy in German affairs that would be pursued jointly with the U.S.S.R. and in conformity with the spirit and principles of the Potsdam Agreement. In the present circumstances this would mean the withdrawal of the Federal Republic of Germany from NATO with the simultaneous withdrawal of the German Democratic Republic from the Warsaw Treaty [organization], and an agreement whereby, in accordance with the principles of the Potsdam Agreement, neither of the two German states would have any armed forces except those needed to maintain law and order at home and guard the frontiers.

Should the Government of the United States be unwilling to contribute in such a way to the implementation of the political principles of the Allied agreements on Germany, it will have no reason, either legal or moral, for insisting on the preservation of the Four-Power status of Berlin. Some ill-wishers of the Soviet Union may of course try to interpret the position of the Soviet Government in the question of the occupation regime in Berlin as the striving for some sort of annexation. It goes without saying that such an interpretation has nothing in common with reality. The Soviet Union, just as the other Socialist states, has no territorial claims. In its policy, it is firmly guided by the principle of condemning annexation, i.e., the seizure of foreign territories and forced annexation of foreign peoples. This principle was proclaimed by Lenin, the founder of the Soviet state, as far back as the first days of Soviet power in Russia.

The U.S.S.R. does not seek any conquests. All it wants is to put an end to the abnormal and dangerous situation that has developed in Berlin because of the continued occupation of its western sectors by the U.S.A., Great Britain, and France.

An independent solution to the Berlin problem must be found in the very near future since the Western Powers refuse to take part in the preparation of a peace treaty with Germany and the Government of the FRG, supported by the same powers, is pursuing a policy hampering the unification of Germany. It is necessary to prevent West Berlin from being used any longer as a springboard for intensive espionage, sabotage, and other subversive activities against Socialist countries, the GDR, and the U.S.S.R. or, to quote the leaders of the United States Government, to prevent its being used for "indirect aggression" against the countries of the Socialist camp. . . .

One cannot of course fail to take into account the fact that the political and economic development of West Berlin during the period of its occupation by the three Western powers has progressed in a different direction from the development of East Berlin and the GDR, as a result of which the way of life in the two parts of Berlin are at the present time entirely different. The Soviet Government considers that when the foreign occupation is ended the population of West Berlin must be granted the right to have whatever way of life it wishes for itself. If the inhabitants of West Berlin desire to preserve the present way of life, based on private capitalistic ownership, that is up to them. The U.S.S.R, for its part, would respect any choice of the West Berliners in this matter.

In view of all these considerations, the Soviet Government on its part would consider it possible to solve the West Berlin question at the present time by the conversion of West Berlin into an independent political unit—a free city, without any state, including both existing German states, interfering in its life. Specifically, it might be possible to agree that the territory of the free city be demilitarized and that no armed forces be contained therein. The free city, West Berlin, could have its own government and run its own economic, administrative, and other affairs.

The Four Powers which shared in the administration of Berlin after the war could, as well as both of the German states, undertake to respect the status of West Berlin as a free city, just as was done, for instance, by the Four Powers with respect to the neutral status which was adopted by the Austrian Republic.

For its part, the Soviet Government would have no objection to the United Nations also sharing, in one way or other, in observing the free-city status of West Berlin.

It is obvious that, considering the specific position of West Berlin, which lies within the territory of the GDR and is cut off from the outside world, the question would arise of some kind of arrangement with the German Democratic Republic concerning guarantees of un-hindered communications between the free city and the outside world —both to the East and to the West—with the object of free move-ment of passenger and freight traffic. In its turn West Berlin would undertake not to permit on its territory any hostile subversive ac-tivity directed against the GDR or any other state.

The above-mentioned solution of the problem of West Berlin's status would be an important step toward normalizing the situation in Berlin, which, instead of being a hotbed of unrest and tension, could become a center for contacts and cooperation between both parts of Germany in the interest of her peaceful future and the unity of the German nation. . . .

In case the Government of the U.S.A. and the governments of Great Britain and France express their agreement to consider the question of liquidating the present occupation regime in West Berlin by setting up a free city within its territory, the Soviet government would be willing on behalf of the Four Powers to enter into official contact on this matter with the government of the German Demo-cratic Republic, with which it has already had preliminary consulta-tions prior to the sending of the present note. . . .

It should also be taken into consideration that the necessity may arise for talks between the municipal authorities of both parts of Berlin and also between the GDR and the FRG to settle any ques-tions that may arise. In view of this, the Soviet Government proposes to make no changes in the present procedure for military traffic of the U.S.A., Great Britain, and France from West Berlin to the FRG for half a year. It regards such a period as fully sufficient to provide a sound basis for the solution of the questions connected with the change in Berlin's situation and to prevent a possibility of any com-plications, provided, naturally, that the governments of the Western powers do not deliberately seek such complications. During the above-mentioned period the parties will have an opportunity to prove in practice their desire to ease international tension by settling the Berlin question.

If the above-mentioned period is not utilized to reach an adequate agreement, the Soviet Union will then carry out the planned measures through an agreement with the GDR. It is envisaged that the German Democratic Republic, like any other independent state, must fully deal with questions concerning its space, i.e., exercise its sovereignty on land, on water, and in the air. At the same time, there will terminate all contacts still maintained between representatives of the armed forces and other officials of the Soviet Union in Germany and corresponding representatives of the armed forces and other officials of the U.S.A., Great Britain, and France on questions pertaining to Berlin. . . .

DOCUMENT 64
JOINT COMMUNIQUÉ BY THE UNITED STATES AND THE SOVIET UNION, REGARDING CAMP DAVID CONVERSATIONS OF PRESIDENT EISENHOWER AND PREMIER KHRUSHCHEV, SEPTEMBER 27, 1959

When the Western powers refused to accede to Khrushchev's terms for a German settlement, he permitted his time limit to lapse, and the Berlin crisis eased. Relaxation of tensions reached a high point when the Soviet leader visited the United States in 1959. A Joint Communiqué concerning his conversations with President Eisenhower at Camp David, Maryland, was issued on September 27, 1959.

The Chairman of the Council of Ministers of the U.S.S.R., N. S. Khrushchev, and President Eisenhower have had a frank exchange of opinions at Camp David. In some of these conversations United States Secretary of State Herter and Soviet Foreign Minister Gromyko, as well as other officials from both countries, participated.

Chairman Khrushchev and the President have agreed that these discussions have been useful in clarifying each other's position on a number of subjects. The talks were not undertaken to negotiate issues. It is hoped, however, that their exchanges of views will contribute to a better understanding of the motives and positions of each and thus to the achievement of a just and lasting peace.

The Chairman of the Council of Ministers of the U.S.S.R. and the President of the United States agreed that the question of general disarmament is the most important one facing the world today. Both governments will make every effort to achieve a constructive solution of this problem.

In the course of the conversations an exchange of views took place on the question of Germany including the question of a peace treaty with Germany, in which the positions of both sides were expounded.

With respect to the specific Berlin question, an understanding was reached, subject to the approval of the other parties directly concerned, that negotiations would be reopened with a view to achieving a solution which would be in accordance with the interests of all concerned and in the interest of the maintenance of peace.

In addition to these matters useful conversations were held on a number of questions affecting the relations between the Union of Soviet Socialist Republics and the United States. These subjects included the question of trade between the two countries. With respect to an increase in exchanges of persons and ideas, substantial progress was made in discussions between officials and it is expected that certain agreements will be reached in the near future.

The Chairman of the Council of Ministers of the U.S.S.R. and the President of the United States agreed that all outstanding international questions should be settled not by the application of force but by peaceful means through negotiation.

Finally it was agreed that an exact date for the return visit of the President to the Soviet Union next spring would be arranged through diplomatic channels.

DOCUMENT 65

THE U–2 INCIDENT: EXCERPTS FROM PREMIER KHRUSH-CHEV'S REMARKS ON U.S. PLANE INCIDENT, MAY 7, 1960

Just as an improvement in relations between East and West seemed possible at a new summit meeting in Paris, the Soviet Union, in May 1960,

Background Documents on Events Incident to the Summit Conference, Senate Committee on Foreign Relations, 86th Cong., 2d Ses. (Washington, 1960), 6–11.

announced that it had captured an American pilot within its borders. Admitting that a plane was missing, the United States insisted that it was a weather craft which had gone astray near the Turkish border. On May 7, 1960, Premier Khrushchev refuted this version by his announcement that the pilot was still alive.

[From *The New York Times,* May 8, 1960]

Following are excerpts from the concluding speech to the meeting of the Supreme Soviet in Moscow yesterday by Premier Khrushchev, as provided in English in New York by Tass, the official Soviet press agency:

The aggressive act committed by the American Air Force against the Soviet Union has justifiably incensed the Deputies and all the Soviet people. Numerous inquiries and appeals are being received by the session and the Soviet Government. In view of this permit me to dwell on this question once again and to furnish certain new data.

After my report to the Supreme Soviet, in which I dwelt on this fact, the United States Department of State claimed in an official press statement that the point in question was a violation of the Soviet State Frontier by an American aircraft of the "Lockheed U–2" type, which allegedly was studying weather conditions in the upper layers of the atmosphere in the area of the Turkish-Soviet frontier.

This plane had allegedly strayed off its course because the pilot had oxygen trouble. The State Department asserts that the pilot lost consciousness and, steered by its automatic pilot, the plane flew into Soviet territory. According to the Department of State, the pilot only had time to report back about the failure of his oxygen equipment to the Turkish airdrome in Adana, whence it flew, an airdrome which allegedly does not belong to the military but to the National Aeronautics and Space Research Administration.

Soon after that, the National Aeronautics and Space Research Administration issued a statement with a view to confirming the State Department's version.

Comrades, I must tell you a secret. When I was making my report I deliberately did not say that the pilot was alive and in good health and that we have got parts of the plane. We did so deliberately because had we told everything at once, the Americans would have invented another version.

And now, just look how many silly things they have said—Van Lake, scientific research and so on and so forth. Now that they know that the pilot is alive they will have to invent something else and they will do it.

[Mr. Khrushchev read from the United States statement issued after his first announcement; it was printed in the New York Times last Friday.]

These are the official versions put into circulation by American officials to mislead the public opinion of their country and the world.

I must declare, comrade Deputies, that these versions are completely untrue and calculated for gullible people.

The authors of these versions supposed that if the plane was shot down, the pilot most probably perished too. So there will be nobody to ask how everything actually happened, there will be no way to check what sort of plane it was and what instruments it carried.

First of all, I wish to announce that the pilot of the shot-down American plane is alive and in good health. He is now in Moscow. Brought here also are the remains of this plane and its special instrumentation, discovered during the investigation.

The name of this pilot is Francis Gary Powers. He is 30 years old. He says he is a first lieutenant of the United States Air Force, where he served till 1956, that is, to the day when he went over to the Central Intelligence Agency.

Francis Powers reported, incidentally, that while serving with the American Air Force he used to get $700 a month, but when he went over to the intelligence service and started carrying out spying assignments to glean secret information, he began getting $2,500 a month. That is how capital buys lives, buys people. The flier testified that he had no dizziness, nor had his oxygen apparatus failed. He was flying along the assigned course, accurately executing his chief's orders, switching on and off the equipment over the preselected targets for gleaning intelligence on the Soviet Union's military and industrial establishments, and flew on until the very moment his piratical flight into this country's interior was cut short.

I want to tell something about the results of the examination of the plane that has been shot down and its equipment, as well as of the questioning of the pilot. The inquiry still continues, but the picture is fairly clear already.

To start with, this was, indeed, a high-altitude, low-speed "Lockheed U–2." They banked on its high altitude and believed that this plane cannot be brought down by any fighter or antiaircraft artillery. That is why they thought it could fly over Soviet territory with immunity. In fact, the plane flew at a great altitude and it was hit by the rocket at an altitude of 20,000 meters [65,000 feet]. And if they fly higher, we will also hit them! The plane was in no way equipped for "upper atmosphere research" or for taking "air samples," as official American spokesmen assert.

Not at all. This was a real military reconnaissance aircraft fitted with various instruments for collecting intelligence and, among other things, for aerial photography. . . .

But the installation of the infernal machine was not the only precaution taken. To cover up the tracks of the crime the pilot was told that he must not fall alive in the hands of the Soviet authorities. For this reason he was supplied with a special pin. He was to have pricked himself with this poisoned pin, resulting in instantaneous death.

What a barbarism! Here is this instrument—the latest achievement of American technology for the killing of their own people (a photograph is produced).

But everything alive wants to live and when the plane was brought down the pilot bailed out by parachute. And when he landed he did not follow the advice of those who sent him on his anti-Soviet predatory assignment but remained alive.

It is alleged that the flight was made for scientific purposes to investigate the upper layers of the atmosphere. The question arises why the pilot then had to be armed with a noiseless pistol. He was given it for some emergency, not to take air samples but to blow people's brains out. All this we shall present to the public as material evidence. This is what, so to say, such Christians are like.

He was given this pistol after making low bows as they do in churches. And yet they call us godless atheists. Yet we have never committed such crimes against humanity and never will. If the pilot was given a pistol to defend himself against wild beasts in case of a forced landing, the question arises, why a pistol with a silencer? This also shows what so-called scientific purposes were pursued by the plane.

The pilot who was supposed to explore the atmosphere was given

7,500 rubles in Soviet currency. The question arises, when and where was he to have spent them and for what purposes, for he did not fly to exchange old rubles for new?

The pilot was also given French gold francs. I have seen these gold francs with my own eyes. And you can see them here in the photograph. They are covered with cellophane on both sides of the coins. Done in a cultured, American way. But what did the pilot need these francs for? He also had West German, Italian, and other currency. Besides his own watch he was also given for his trip another two gold watches and seven gold rings for ladies. Why was all this necessary in the upper layers of the atmosphere? Or, maybe, the pilot was to have flown still higher to Mars and was going to lead astray Martian ladies?

You see how thoroughly American pilots are equipped before setting off on a flight to take samples of air in the upper layers of the atmosphere. Thus, no concocted version can save the reputation of those who bear the responsibility for this perfidious act.

Thus, no concocted version can save the reputation of those who bear the responsibility for this perfidious action. They were caught red-handed as organizers of the incursion in the airspace of the Soviet Union not long before the meeting of the heads of government in Paris, not long before the visit to the Soviet Union of the President of the United States. I believe that this is a bad preparation for serious talks on easing international tension.

I am now reading in the Western press comments on these events and there are some people who accuse us, Khrushchev, of wanting to undermine the summit meeting because otherwise he would not have presented this fact at the session of the Supreme Soviet but raised it through some other channels but what did you expect, gentlemen? You are accustomed to make mischief and some people regard this as all but a good thing and keep silent. No, we are not such kind of people: if you made mischief bear the responsibility for this openly.

They live according to the law; if one is rich, one will not be imprisoned. This is true for the capitalist because he always can buy himself off. But there is another country, the country of socialism, where law protects the state, protects society, protects everyone living in this state.

What could be the reason for such a reckless step? This was evidently done because someone in the United States was obsessed by the idea of intelligence. The United States proposal on the "open sky" is well known. We rejected this proposal and the American military then decided to "open" the Soviet sky by themselves.

But there are rules of international laws, there are national frontiers and no one has the right to disregard these laws and to cross the frontiers of other countries.

From the lofty rostrum of the Supreme Soviet we warn once again those countries that make their territory available for the take-off of planes with anti-Soviet intentions—do not play with fire, gentlemen!

The governments of the three countries—Turkey, Pakistan and Norway—must be clearly aware that they were accomplices of this flight because they permitted the use of their airfields against the Soviet Union.

DOCUMENT 66

THE U–2 INCIDENT: TEXT OF THE STATEMENT BY PRESIDENT EISENHOWER, FOLLOWING THE MAY 16, 1960, MEETING OF THE FOUR HEADS OF GOVERNMENT

When the United States admitted responsibility for the U–2 flight over Russia, Premier Khrushchev torpedoed the summit conference at Paris by demanding an apology and punishment for the perpetrators of the flights. He also withdrew his invitation to President Eisenhower for a return visit to Russia. The President thereupon issued a statement explaining his position and deploring the breakdown of the conference.

[Department of State press release No. 271, May 17, 1960]

Having been informed yesterday by General de Gaulle and Prime Minister Macmillan of the position which Mr. Khrushchev has taken in regard to this Conference during his calls yesterday morning on them, I gave most careful thought as to how this matter should best be handled. Having in mind the great importance of this Conference and the hopes that the peoples of all the world have reposed in this meeting, I concluded that in the circumstances it was best to see if at today's private meeting any possibility existed through the exercise of reason and restraint to dispose of this matter of the overflights, which would have permitted the Conference to go forward.

Background Documents on Events Incident to the Summit Conference, 45–47.

I was under no illusion as to the probability of success of any such approach but I felt that in view of the great responsibility resting on me as President of the United States, this effort should be made.

In this I received the strongest support of my colleagues, President de Gaulle and Prime Minister Macmillan. Accordingly, at this morning's private session, despite the violence and inaccuracy of Mr. Khrushchev's statements, I replied to him on the following terms:

I had previously been informed of the sense of the statement just read by Premier Khrushchev.

In my statement of May 11 and in the statement of Secretary Herter of May 9 the position of the United States was made clear with respect to the distasteful necessity of espionage activities in a world where nations distrust each other's intentions. We pointed out that these activities had no aggressive intent but rather were to assure the safety of the United States and the free world against surprise attack by a power which boasts of its ability to devastate the United States and other countries by missiles armed with atomic warheads. As is well known, not only the United States but most other countries are constantly the targets of elaborate and persistent espionage of the Soviet Union.

There is in the Soviet statement an evident misapprehension on one key point. It alleges that the United States has, through official statements, threatened continued overflights. The importance of this alleged threat was emphasized and repeated by Mr. Khrushchev. The United States has made no such threat. Neither I nor my Government has intended any. The actual statements go no further than to say that the United States will not shirk its responsibility to safeguard against surprise attack.

In point of fact, these flights were suspended after the recent incident and are not to be resumed. Accordingly, this cannot be the issue.

I have come to Paris to seek agreements with the Soviet Union which would eliminate the necessity for all forms of espionage, including overflights. I see no reason to use this incident to disrupt the conference.

Should it prove impossible, because of the Soviet attitude, to come to grips here in Paris with this problem and the other vital issues threatening world peace, I am planning in the near future to submit to the United Nations a proposal for the creation of a United Nations aerial surveillance to detect preparations for attack. This plan I had intended to place before this conference. This surveillance system would operate in the territories of all nations prepared to accept such inspection. For its part, the United States is prepared not only to accept United Nations aerial surveillance, but to do everything in its power to contribute to the rapid organization and successful operation of such international surveillance.

We of the United States are here to consider in good faith the important problems before this Conference. We are prepared either to carry this point no further, or to undertake bilateral conversations between the United States and the U.S.S.R. while the main Conference proceeds.

My words were seconded and supported by my Western colleagues, who also urged Mr. Khrushchev to pursue the path of reason and commonsense, and to forget propaganda. Such an attitude would have permitted the Conference to proceed. Mr. Khrushchev was left in no doubt by me that his ultimatum would never be acceptable to the United States.

Mr. Khrushchev brushed aside all arguments of reason, and not only insisted upon this ultimatum, but also insisted that he was going to publish his statement in full at the time of his own choosing. It was thus made apparent that he was determined to wreck the Paris Conference.

In fact, the only conclusion that can be drawn from his behavior this morning was that he came all the way from Moscow to Paris with the sole intention of sabotaging this meeting on which so much of the hopes of the world have rested.

In spite of this serious and adverse development, I have no intention whatsoever to diminish my continuing efforts to promote progress toward a peace with justice. This applies to the remainder of my stay in Paris as well as thereafter.

SIX

The Cold War and Latin America

Even though Latin America did not seem to be immediately involved in the Cold War in the 1940's, the United States took pains to safeguard its southern flank by entering into regional understandings and military alliances with its hemispheric neighbors. The Act of Chapultepec, the Rio Treaty of Mutual Assistance, and the Organization of American States were all symptomatic of this policy.

During the 1950's, however, Communism made serious inroads upon Latin America. Poor, exploited, and ultranationalistic, the masses of the continent became an obvious target for Soviet propaganda, and in May, 1954, Communist influences were clearly felt in Guatemala when a shipment of arms arrived from eastern Europe. The leftist government of the Central American republic was overthrown by a revolution, but Latin America remained as susceptible to Communist propaganda as before. Soviet influence spread, and when, in 1959, Fidel Castro overthrew the corrupt Batista government in Cuba, he received open support from the Soviet Union. After signing a favorable trade agreement with the U.S.S.R., the Cuban government became increasingly anti-American, until the United States, in retaliation, was finally compelled to cut Cuba's sugar quota. Then Chairman Khrushchev denounced the Monroe Doctrine, and although the American states, at San José, passed a mild declaration condemning Soviet interference, the United States would have to make a major effort to prevent further Communist penetration of the Western hemisphere.

DOCUMENT 67

THE ACT OF CHAPULTEPEC, MARCH 6, 1945

The United States had sought to strengthen its ties with the Latin-American countries throughout World War II, and, by the beginning of 1945, all but Argentina had broken with the Axis. Cooperation between the American states was to be strengthened by the adoption of the Act of Chapultepec by the Inter-American Conference on Problems of Peace and War which met in Mexico City from February 21 to March 8, 1945. In effect, it internationalized the Monroe Doctrine, and even Argentina eventually adhered to it.

Act of Chapultepec

Whereas:

The peoples of the Americas, animated by a profound love of justice, remain sincerely devoted to the principles of international law;

It is their desire that such principles, notwithstanding the present difficult circumstances, prevail with even greater force in future international relations;

The inter-American conferences have repeatedly proclaimed certain fundamental principles, but these must be reaffirmed at a time when the juridical bases of the community of nations are being re-established;

The new situation in the world makes more imperative than ever the union and solidarity of the American peoples, for the defense of their rights and the maintenance of international peace; . . .

The security and solidarity of the Continent are affected to the same extent by an act of aggression against any of the American States by a non-American State, as by an act of aggression of an American State against one or more American States;

Decade, 414–417.

The Governments Represented at the Inter-American Conference on Problems of War and Peace

Declare:

1. That all sovereign States are juridically equal among themselves.

2. That every State has the right to the respect of its individuality and independence, on the part of the other members of the international community.

3. That every attack of a State against the integrity or the inviolability of the territory, or against the sovereignty or political independence of an American State, shall, comformably to Part III hereof, be considered as an act of aggression against the other States which sign this Act. In any case invasion by armed forces of one State into the territory of another trespassing boundaries established by treaty and demarcated in accordance therewith shall constitute an act of aggression.

4. That in case acts of aggression occur or there are reasons to believe that an aggression is being prepared by any other State against the integrity or inviolability of the territory, or against the sovereignty or political independence of an American State, the States signatory to this Act will consult among themselves in order to agree upon the measures it may be advisable to take.

5. That during the war, and until the treaty recommended in Part II hereof is concluded, the signatories of this Act recognize that such threats and acts of aggression, as indicated in paragraphs 3 and 4 above, constitute an interference with the war effort of the United Nations, calling for such procedures, within the scope of their constitutional powers of a general nature and for war, as may be found necessary, including: recall of chiefs of diplomatic missions; breaking of diplomatic relations; breaking of consular relations; breaking of postal, telegraphic, telephonic, radio-telephonic relations; interruption of economic, commercial and financial relations; use of armed force to prevent or repel aggression.

6. That the principles and procedure contained in this Declaration shall become effective immediately, inasmuch as any act of aggression or threat of aggression during the present state of war interferes with the war effort of the United Nations to obtain victory. Henceforth,

and to the end that the principles and procedures herein stipulated shall conform with the constitutional processes of each Republic, the respective Governments shall take the necessary steps to perfect this instrument in order that it shall be in force at all times.

PART II

The Inter-American Conference on Problems of War and Peace
Recommends:

That for the purpose of meeting threats or acts of aggression against any American Republic following the establishment of peace, the Governments of the American Republics consider the conclusion, in accordance with their constitutional processes, of a treaty establishing procedures whereby such threats or acts may be met by the use, by all or some of the signatories of said treaty, of any one or more of the following measures: recall of chiefs of diplomatic missions; breaking of diplomatic relations; breaking of consular relations; breaking of postal, telegraphic, telephonic, radio-telephonic relations; interruption of economic, commercial and financial relations; use of armed force to prevent or repel aggression.

PART III

The above Declaration and Recommendation constitute a regional arrangement for dealing with such matters relating to the maintenance of international peace and security as are appropriate for regional action in this Hemisphere. The said arrangement, and the pertinent activities and procedures, shall be consistent with the purposes and principles of the general international organization, when established.

This agreement shall be known as the "ACT OF CHAPULTEPEC."

DOCUMENT 68

INTER-AMERICAN TREATY OF RECIPROCAL ASSISTANCE (RIO PACT), SEPTEMBER 2, 1947

In spite of friction between the United States and the authoritarian government of Argentina, inter-American amity had progressed far enough by 1947 to enable the American states to sign and eventually ratify the

Decade, 421–425.

Inter-American Treaty of Reciprocal Assistance. Negotiated at the Rio de Janeiro Conference for the Maintenance of Continental Peace and Security, the Rio Pact of September 2, 1947, formally incorporated the underlying principles of the Act of Chapultepec in a regional alliance. The Americas consequently seemed to constitute a common front against aggression from within and without.

In the name of their Peoples, the Governments represented at the Inter-American conference for the Maintenance of Continental Peace and Security, desirous of consolidating and strengthening their relations of friendship and good neighborliness, and

Considering:

That Resolution VIII of the Inter-American Conference on Problems of War and Peace, which met in Mexico City, recommended the conclusion of a treaty to prevent and repeal threats and acts of aggression against any of the countries of America;

That the High Contracting Parties reiterate their will to remain united in an inter-American system consistent with the purposes and principles of the United Nations, and reaffirm the existence of the agreement which they have concluded concerning those matters relating to the maintenance of international peace and security which are appropriate for regional action;

That the High Contracting Parties reaffirm their adherence to the principles of inter-American solidarity and cooperation, and especially to those set forth in the preamble and declarations of the Act of Chapultepec, all of which should be understood to be accepted as standards of their mutual relations and as the juridical basis of the Inter-American System;

That the American States propose, in order to improve the procedures for the pacific settlement of their controversies, to conclude the treaty concerning the "Inter-American Peace System" envisaged in Resolutions IX and XXXIX of the Inter-American Conference on Problems of War and Peace,

That the obligation of mutual assistance and common defense of the American Republics is essentially related to their democratic ideals and to their will to cooperate permanently in the fulfillment of the principles and purposes of a policy of peace;

That the American regional community affirms as a manifest truth that juridical organization is a necessary prerequisite of security and peace, and that peace is founded on justice and moral order and, consequently, on the international recognition and protection of human rights and freedoms, on the indispensable well-being of the people, and on the effectiveness of democracy for the international realization of justice and security,

Have resolved, in conformity with the objectives stated above, to conclude the following Treaty, in order to assure peace, through adequate means, to provide for effective reciprocal assistance to meet armed attacks against any American State, and in order to deal with threats of aggression against any of them:

Article 1. The High Contracting Parties formally condemn war and undertake in their international relations not to resort to the threat or the use of force in any manner inconsistent with the provisions of the Charter of the United Nations or of this Treaty.

Article 2. As a consequence of the principle set forth in the preceding Article, the High Contracting Parties undertake to submit every controversy which may arise between them to methods of peaceful settlement and to endeavor to settle any such controversy among themselves by means of the procedures in force in the Inter-American System before referring it to the General Assembly or the Security Council of the United Nations.

Article 3.

1. The High Contracting Parties agree that an armed attack by any State against an American State shall be considered as an attack against all the American States and, consequently, each one of the said Contracting Parties undertakes to assist in meeting the attack in the exercise of the inherent right of individual or collective self-defense recognized by Article 51 of the Charter of the United Nations.

2. On the request of the State or States directly attacked and until the decision of the Organ of Consultation of the Inter-American System, each one of the Contracting Parties may determine the immediate measures which it may individually take in fulfillment of the obligation contained in the preceding paragraph and in accordance with the principle of continental solidarity. The Organ of Consultation shall meet without delay for the purpose of examining those measures and agreeing upon the measures of a collective character that should be taken. . . .

Article 6. If the inviolability or the integrity of the territory or the sovereignty or political independence of any American State should be affected by an aggression which is not an armed attack or by an extra-continental or intra-continental conflict, or by any other fact or situation that might endanger the peace of America, the Organ of Consultation shall meet immediately in order to agree on the measures which must be taken in case of aggression to assist the victim of the aggression or, in any case, the measures which should be taken for the common defense and for the maintenance of the peace and security of the Continent.

Article 7. In the case of a conflict between two or more American States, without prejudice to the right of self-defense in conformity with Article 51 of the Charter of the United Nations, the High Contracting Parties, meeting in consultation shall call upon the contending States to suspend hostilities and restore matters to the *status quo ante bellum,* and shall take in addition all other necessary measures to reestablish or maintain inter-American peace and security and for the solution of the conflict by peaceful means. The rejection of the pacifying action will be considered in the determination of the aggressor and in the application of the measures which the consultative meeting may agree upon.

Article 8. For the purposes of this Treaty, the measures on which the Organ of Consultation may agree will comprise one or more of the following: recall of chiefs of diplomatic missions; breaking of diplomatic relations; breaking of consular relations; partial or complete interruption of economic relations or of rail, sea, air, postal, telegraphic, telephonic, and radiotelephonic or radiotelegraphic communications; and use of armed force.

Article 9. In addition to other acts which the Organ of Consultation may characterize as aggression, the following shall be considered as such:

a. Unprovoked armed attack by a State against the territory, the people, or the land, sea or air forces of another State;

b. Invasion, by the armed forces of a State, of the territory of an American State, through the trespassing of boundaries demarcated in accordance with a treaty, judicial decision, or arbitral award, or, in the absence of frontiers thus demarcated, invasion affecting a region which is under the effective jurisdiction of another State. . . .

DOCUMENT 69

CHARTER OF THE ORGANIZATION OF AMERICAN STATES, APRIL 30, 1948

The work of unifying the continent begun at Chapultepec and carried further at Rio was brought to a climax at Bogotá. On April 30, 1948, the Ninth International Conference of American States, meeting at the Colombian capital, adopted the Charter of the Organization of American States, which created a useful organ for continental cooperation. Fear of Communist aggression and subversion had been the moving force in its establishment.

In the name of their peoples, the States represented at the Ninth International Conference of American States,

Convinced that the historic mission of America is to offer to man a land of liberty, and a favorable environment for the development of his personality and the realization of his just aspirations;

Conscious that that mission has already inspired numerous agreements, whose essential value lies in the desire of the American peoples to live together in peace, and, through their mutual understanding and respect for the sovereignty of each one, to provide for the betterment of all, in independence, in equality and under law;

Confident that the true significance of American solidarity and good neighborliness can only mean the consolidation on this continent, within the framework of democratic institutions, of a system of individual liberty and social justice based on respect for the essential rights of man;

Persuaded that their welfare and their contribution to the progress and the civilization of the world will increasingly require intensive continental cooperation;

Resolved to persevere in the noble undertaking that humanity has conferred upon the United Nations, whose principles and purposes they solemnly reaffirm;

Convinced that juridical organization is a necessary condition for security and peace founded on moral order and on justice; and

Decade, 427–435.

In accordance with Resolution IX of the Inter-American Conference on Problems of War and Peace, held at Mexico City, Have agreed upon the following

CHAPTER 1: NATURE AND PURPOSES

Part One

ARTICLE 1

The American States establish by this Charter the international organization that they have developed to achieve an order of peace and justice, to promote their solidarity, to strengthen their collaboration, and to defend their sovereignty, their territorial integrity and their independence. Within the United Nations, the Organization of American States is a regional agency.

ARTICLE 2

All American States that ratify the present Charter are Members of the Organization.

ARTICLE 3

Any new political entity that arises from the union of several Member States and that, as such, ratifies the present Charter, shall become a Member of the Organization. The entry of the new political entity into the Organization shall result in the loss of membership of each one of the States which constitute it.

ARTICLE 4

The Organization of American States, in order to put into practice the principles on which it is founded and to fulfill its regional obligations under the Charter of the United Nations, proclaims the following essential purposes:

a) To strengthen the peace and security of the continent;

b) To prevent possible causes of difficulties and to ensure the pacific settlement of disputes that may arise among the Member States;

c) To provide for common action on the part of those States in the event of aggression;

d) To seek the solution of political, juridical and economic problems that may arise among them; and

e) To promote, by cooperative action, their economic, social and cultural development.

CHAPTER II: PRINCIPLES

ARTICLE 5

The American States reaffirm the following principles:

a) International law is the standard of conduct of States in their reciprocal relations;

b) International order consists essentially of respect for the personality, sovereignty and independence of States, and the faithful fulfillment of obligations derived from treaties and other sources of international law;

c) Good faith shall govern the relations between States;

d) The solidarity of the American States and the high aims which are sought through it require the political organization of those States on the basis of the effective exercise of representative democracy;

e) The American States condemn war of aggression: victory does not give rights;

f) An act of aggression against one American State is an act of aggression against all the other American States;

g) Controversies of an international character arising between two or more American States shall be settled by peaceful procedures;

h) Social justice and social security are bases of lasting peace;

i) Economic cooperation is essential to the common welfare and prosperity of the peoples of the continent;

j) The American States proclaim the fundamental rights of the individual without distinction as to race, nationality, creed or sex;

k) The spiritual unity of the continent is based on respect for the cultural values of the American countries and requires their close cooperation for the high purposes of civilization;

1) The education of peoples should be directed toward justice, freedom and peace.

CHAPTER III: FUNDAMENTAL RIGHTS AND DUTIES OF STATES

ARTICLE 6

States are juridically equal, enjoy equal rights and equal capacity to exercise these rights, and have equal duties. The rights of each State depend not upon its power to ensure the exercise thereof, but upon the mere fact of its existence as a person under international law. . . .

CHAPTER V: COLLECTIVE SECURITY

ARTICLE 24

Every act of aggression by a State against the territorial integrity or the inviolability of the territory or against the sovereignty or political independence of an American State shall be considered an act of aggression against the other American States.

ARTICLE 25

If the inviolability or the integrity of the territory or the sovereignty or political independence of any American State should be affected by an armed attack or by an act of aggression that is not an armed attack, or by an extra-continental conflict, or by a conflict between two or more American States, or by any other fact or situation that might endanger the peace of America, the American States, in furtherance of the principles of continental solidarity or collective self-defense, shall apply the measures and procedures established in the special treaties on the subject. . . .

Part Two

CHAPTER IX: THE ORGANS

ARTICLE 32

The Organization of American States accomplishes its purposes by means of:
    a) The Inter-American Conference;

    b) The Meeting of Consultation of Ministers of Foreign Affairs;
    c) The Council;
    d) The Pan American Union;
    e) The Specialized Conferences; and
    f) The Specialized Organizations.

CHAPTER X: THE INTER-AMERICAN CONFERENCE

ARTICLE 33

The Inter-American Conference is the supreme organ of the Organization of American States. It decides the general action and policy of the Organization and determines the structure and functions of its Organs, and has the authority to consider any matter relating to friendly relations among the American States. These functions shall be carried out in accordance with the provisions of this Charter and of other inter-American treaties.

ARTICLE 34

All Member States have the right to be represented at the Inter-American Conference. Each State has the right to one vote. . . .

CHAPTER XI: THE MEETING OF CONSULTATION OF MINISTERS OF FOREIGN AFFAIRS

ARTICLE 39

The Meeting of Consultation of Ministers of Foreign Affairs shall be held in order to consider problems of an urgent nature and of common interest to the American States, and to serve as the Organ of Consultation.

ARTICLE 40

Any Member State may request that a Meeting of Consultation be called. The request shall be addressed to the Council of the Organization, which shall decide by an absolute majority whether a meeting should be held.

ARTICLE 41

The program and regulations of the Meeting of Consultation shall be prepared by the Council of the Organization and submitted to the Member States for consideration.

ARTICLE 42

If, for exceptional reasons, a Minister of Foreign Affairs is unable to attend the meeting, he shall be represented by a special delegate.

ARTICLE 43

In case of an armed attack within the territory of an American State or within the region of security delimited by treaties in force, a Meeting of Consultation shall be held without delay. Such Meeting shall be called immediately by the Chairman of the Council of the Organization, who shall at the same time call a meeting of the Council itself.

ARTICLE 44

An Advisory Defense Committee shall be established to advise the Organ of Consultation on problems of military cooperation that may arise in connection with the application of existing special treaties on collective security.

ARTICLE 45

The Advisory Defense Committee shall be composed of the highest military authorities of the American States participating in the Meeting of Consultation. Under exceptional circumstances the Governments may appoint substitutes. Each State shall be entitled to one vote.

ARTICLE 46

The Advisory Defense Committee shall be convoked under the same conditions as the Organ of Consultation, when the latter deals with matters relating to defense against aggression.

ARTICLE 47

The Committee shall also meet when the Conference or the Meeting of Consultation or the Governments, by a two-thirds majority of the Member States, assign to it technical studies or reports on specific subjects.

CHAPTER XII: THE COUNCIL

ARTICLE 48

The Council of the Organization of American States is composed of one Representative of each Member State of the Organization, especially appointed by the respective Government, with the rank of Ambassador. The appointment may be given to the diplomatic representative accredited to the Government of the country in which the Council has its seat. During the absence of the titular Representative, the Government may appoint an interim Representative.

ARTICLE 49

The Council shall elect a Chairman and a Vice Chairman, who shall serve for one year and shall not be eligible for election to either of those positions for the term immediately following. . . .

DOCUMENT 70

COMMUNIST SHIPMENT OF ARMS TO GUATEMALA: STATEMENT TO THE PRESS BY THE DEPARTMENT OF STATE, MAY 17, 1954

In spite of the efforts of the United States to present a united all-American front against Communism, Soviet ideology seemed to gain a foothold in Guatemala after Jacobo Arbenz Guzmán had become President in 1951. The Arbenz government expropriated American-owned property and took a leftist approach to many problems long before the State Department announced the arrival of Communist arms in the Central American republic on May 17, 1954. By June 18, a revolution had broken out against President Arbenz, whose government was then overthrown by Colonel Carlos Castillo Armas. The United States promptly recognized the new regime.

The Department of State is in receipt of reliable information to the effect that an important shipment of arms has been effected from Soviet-controlled territory to Guatemala.

American Foreign Policy, 1950–1955, I, 1307–1308.

On May 15, the ship *Alfhelm,* believed to be under charter, arrived at Puerto Barrios, Guatemala, carrying a large shipment of armament consigned to the Guatemalan Government. This armament is now being unloaded at Puerto Barrios. We are advised that the armament was shipped from the Communist-administered port of Stettin.

Because of the origin of these arms, the point of their embarkation, their destination, and the quantity of arms involved, the Department of State considers that this is a development of gravity.

DOCUMENT 71

AGREEMENT ON TRADE AND PAYMENTS BETWEEN THE UNION OF SOVIET SOCIALIST REPUBLICS AND THE REPUBLIC OF CUBA, FEBRUARY 13, 1960

On January 1, 1959, Fidel Castro, the Cuban insurgent leader, overthrew the government of President Fulgencio Batista. After an initial period of friendliness toward Castro, the United States became increasingly irritated by his highhanded treatment of his enemies and his nationalization of American owned properties. The Cuban leader threw down the gauntlet to his neighbor during a visit of Anastas Mikoyan to Havana. On February 13, 1960, the Castro government received a $100,000,000 credit from the Soviet Union at low interest and signed a trade pact with her. Cuba was drifting into the Soviet orbit.

The Government of the Union of Soviet Socialist Republics and the Government of the Republic of Cuba, desiring to develop trade between the two countries on the basis of equality and mutual benefit, have agreed as follows:

Article 1

The Union of Soviet Socialist Republics undertakes to purchase 425,000 tons of sugar in the Republic of Cuba in 1960, in addition to the 575,000 tons already purchased for delivery during the year. Over the succeeding four years the Union of Soviet Socialist Republics will purchase one million tons of sugar each year in the Republic of Cuba.

United Nations *Treaty Series,* 369 (New York, 1960), 26–32.

The sugar purchased by the Union of Soviet Socialist Republics in the Republic of Cuba is intended for domestic consumption, and during the period of validity of this Agreement the Union of Soviet Socialist Republics shall not export sugar to countries which are traditional importers of Cuban sugar.

The sugar purchased by the Union of Soviet Socialist Republics in the Republic of Cuba between 1961 and 1964 shall be paid for as follows: 20 per cent of the total annual quantity purchased shall be paid for in currency freely convertible into U.S. dollars, and the remainder in deliveries of goods. The 425,000 tons of sugar purchased and shipped in 1960 shall be paid for entirely in goods.

The goods to be exported from the Republic of Cuba to the Union of Soviet Socialist Republics in 1960 are listed in schedule A. Schedules of goods for export during the succeeding years shall be drawn up each year by agreement between the Parties.

Article 2

The Republic of Cuba shall purchase in the Union of Soviet Socialist Republics equipment, machinery and mechanical tools, petroleum and petroleum products, wheat, paper, non-ferrous metals, chemical products, fertilizers and other goods.

The goods to be exported from the Union of Soviet Socialist Republics to the Republic of Cuba in 1960 are listed in schedule B. Schedules of goods for export during the succeeding years shall be drawn up each year by agreement between the Parties. . . .

Article 5

The two Governments agree to grant each other unconditional most-favoured-nation treatment in all matters relating to custom duties and tariffs, consular fees and any other charges and duties which are or may become applicable in respect of the import or export of goods, as also in regard to the method of imposition of such taxes and to all customs regulations and formalities.

Article 6

The provisions of article 5 of this Agreement shall not extend to:

(*a*) Any special privileges which the Government of the Union of Soviet Socialist Republics has granted or may grant to countries adjacent to it;

(*b*) Any special privileges which the Government of the Republic of Cuba has granted or may grant to the United States of America.

Article 7

The merchant vessels of both countries shall on entering or leaving Soviet or Cuban ports and during their stay in such ports, enjoy the most favourable conditions granted under the relevant legislation to ships flying the flags of third parties in regard to harbour regulations and port operations.

Article 8

Payments in respect of the goods referred to in this Agreement, with the exceptions set forth in article 1, which are payable in currencies freely convertible into U.S. dollars, and the payment of the costs connected with the trade exchanges in question, shall be made in the Union of Soviet Socialist Republics through the State Bank and in the Republic of Cuba through the National Bank of Cuba. . . .

If the balance of the accounts opened in accordance with this article exceeds $U.S.10 million, representatives of the two Governments shall consider ways and means of liquidating the balance in excess. Interest at the rate of 2.5 per cent per annum shall be charged on any part of the balance in excess of $U.S.10 million.

The State Bank of the Union of Soviet Socialist Republics and the National Bank of Cuba shall agree upon technical procedures for accounting operations between them under this Agreement.

Article 9

On the expiry of this Agreement, any outstanding balance in the accounts referred to in article 8 shall be liquidated by the debtor Party within a period of six months by deliveries of goods agreed upon by the Parties.

If, in the course of the six months period the balance has not been liquidated by deliveries of goods, representatives of the Parties shall agree upon procedures for the liquidation of the balance remaining.

Article 10

A joint commission consisting of representatives of the two Parties shall be set up to study the question of developing trade between the two countries and to prepare appropriate recommendations for sub-mission to the respective Governments. The commission shall be convened at the request of either Party.

Article 11

Three months before the expiry of this Agreement, negotiations shall be initiated between the two countries with a view to regulating the further exchange of goods between the two countries on a mu-tually satisfactory basis.

Article 12

This Agreement shall be concluded for a period of five years. It shall be ratified by both Parties at the earliest possible date and shall enter into force on the date of exchange of the instruments of ratifi-cation.

Notwithstanding the foregoing, the Agreement shall be provision-ally effective as of the day of its signature. . . .

DOCUMENT 72

REDUCTION OF CUBAN SUGAR QUOTA: STATEMENT BY PRESIDENT EISENHOWER, JULY 6, 1960

Relations between the United States and Cuba deteriorated rapidly after the conclusion of the Cuban-Soviet trade agreement. Amid charges and countercharges, it became clear that Cuba was developing into an outpost of the Soviet bloc in the Western Hemisphere. Accordingly, on July 6, 1960, the United States reduced its Cuban sugar quota, which had been highly favorable to the island republic, from 3,119,655 to 700,000 short tons. President Eisenhower's statement explained this action.

I have today [July 6] approved legislation enacted by the Con-gress which authorizes the President to determine Cuba's sugar quota for the balance of calendar year 1960 and for the 3-month period ending March 31, 1961. In conformity with this legislation I have signed a proclamation which, in the national interest, establishes the

Department of State *Bulletin*, XLIII (July 25, 1960), 140.

Cuban sugar quota for the balance of 1960 at 39,752, short tons, plus the sugar certified for entry prior to July 3, 1960. This represents a reduction of 700,000 short tons from the original 1960 Cuban quota of 3,119,655 short tons.

The deficit will be filled by purchases from other free-world suppliers.

The importance of the United States Government's action relating to sugar quota legislation makes it desirable, I believe, to set forth the reasons which led the Congress to authorize and the Executive to take this action in the national interest.

Normally about one-third of our total sugar supply comes from Cuba. Despite every effort on our part to maintain traditionally friendly relations, the Government of Cuba is now following a course which raises serious question as to whether the United States can, in the long run, continue to rely upon that country for such large quantities of sugar. I believe that we would fail in our obligation to our people if we did not take steps to reduce our reliance for a major food product upon a nation which has embarked upon a deliberate policy of hostility toward the United States.

The Government of Cuba has committed itself to purchase substantial quantities of goods from the Soviet Union under barter arrangements. It has chosen to undertake to pay for these goods with sugar—traded at prices well below those which it has obtained in the United States. The inescapable conclusion is that Cuba has embarked on a course of action to commit steadily increasing amounts of its sugar crop to trade with the Communist bloc, thus making its future ability to fill the sugar needs of the United States ever more uncertain.

It has been with the most genuine regret that this Government has been compelled to alter the heretofore mutually beneficial sugar trade between the United States and Cuba. Under the system which has existed up to this time, the people of Cuba, particularly those who labor in the cane fields and in the mills, have benefited from the maintenance of an assured market in the United States, where Cuban sugar commands a price well above that which could be obtained in the world market. These benefits also reached many others whose livelihood was related to the sugar industry on the island.

The American people will always maintain their friendly feelings for the people of Cuba. We look forward to the day when the Cuban Government will once again allow this friendship to be fully expressed in the relations between our two countries.

DOCUMENT 73

KHRUSHCHEV'S DENUNCIATION OF THE MONROE DOCTRINE: NEWS CONFERENCE IN THE KREMLIN, JULY 12, 1960

Soviet support for Cuba became stronger and stronger as Castro veered closer to Communism. On July 12, 1960, in a press conference held at the Kremlin, Premier Khrushchev announced that he considered the Monroe Doctrine to have outlived its time. The United States issued a vigorous denial.

MR. KHRUSHCHEV—Our historians paid tribute once to the positive role of the United States foreign policy principles enunciated by President Monroe 137 years ago which came to be known as the Monroe Doctrine. This was directed against the designs of European colonialists on the countries of Latin America, and at the same time proclaimed the principle of noninterference by the United States of America in the internal affairs of the European countries. The United States of America was then still acting as a democratic nation which had the sympathies of many.

But then everything changed abruptly. Now the United States is using the Monroe Doctrine to substantiate a right to rule all the Latin-American countries, meddle in their domestic affairs, keep them under its tutelage and, of course, exploit them.

The Latin-American countries have very rich natural resources. Yet, most of the population of those countries is living under gruelling conditions. What is that due to? It cannot be explained by saying that the peoples of Latin America are averse to hard work. Not at all. They are very hard-working people and they show concern for their countries. The reason is quite different. It is that the ones who rule the roost there are the imperialists of the United States of America, the colonialists, who, like vultures, snatch the last crumb out of the mouths of the dying children and old folk just to wax fat and rich. And it is through the Monroe Doctrine that they want to assure themselves the right to go on with this robbery forever.

But the Monroe Doctrine is known to date far back to a remote past. The human race lives under different conditions today. It is Marxism-Leninism, the most progressive teaching, that is flourishing more and more in our time. It triumphs not only in the domain of theory but also in that of practice.

And the peoples see that a country's independence is the road to its liberation. The people are increasingly realizing that to enjoy the fruits of their labor and the natural resources of their land they must have independence above all else.

It goes without saying that, as a Communist, I believe that the Communist way is the best way society can develop. But this is every people's own affair and we do not impose our ideas and our form of government upon anyone.

Life moves forward, it sweeps away everything that does not correspond to the spirit of the time; it asserts the new, the progressive. We consider that the Monroe Doctrine has outlived its time, has outlived itself, has died, so to say, a natural death. Now the remains of this doctrine should best be buried as every dead body is, so that it should not poison the air by its decay. That would be the correct thing to do and this is what will happen apparently.

DOCUMENT 74

THE DECLARATION OF SAN JOSÉ, AUGUST 28, 1960

The American states reacted to the Soviet threat in Cuba by passing the Declaration of San José. Adopted during the Seventh Meeting of Consultation of the Ministers of Foreign Affairs by a vote of 19–0 (Cuba and Santo Domingo did not participate), the Declaration of August 28, 1960, reaffirmed traditional policies of rejection of extra-American interference in continental affairs. Cuba, however, was not mentioned by name.

The Seventh Meeting of Consultation of Ministers of Foreign Affairs

Department of State *Bulletin*, XLIII (September 12, 1960), 407.

1. Condemns emphatically the intervention or the threat of intervention, even when conditional, by an extracontinental power in the affairs of the American republics and declares that the acceptance of a threat of extracontinental intervention by any American state jeopardizes American solidarity and security, wherefor the Organization of American States is under obligation to disapprove it and reject it with equal vigor;

2. Rejects, also, the attempt of the Sino-Soviet powers to make use of the political, economic, or social situation of any American state, inasmuch as that attempt is capable of destroying hemispheric unity and jeopardizing the peace and the security of the hemisphere;

3. Reaffirms the principle of nonintervention by any American state in the internal or external affairs of the other American states, and reiterates that each state has the right to develop its cultural, political, and economic life freely and naturally, respecting the rights of the individual and the principles of universal morality, and as a consequence, no American state may intervene for the purpose of imposing upon another American state its ideologies or political, economic, or social principles;

4. Reaffirms that the inter-American system is incompatible with any form of totalitarianism and that democracy will achieve the full scope of its objectives in the hemisphere only when all the American republics conduct themselves in accordance with the principles stated in the Declaration of Santiago, Chile, which was approved at the Fifth Meeting of Consultation of Ministers of Foreign Affairs, the observance of which it recommends as soon as possible;

5. Proclaims that all member states of the regional organization are under obligation to submit to the discipline of the inter-American system, voluntarily and freely agreed upon, and that the soundest guarantee of their sovereignty and their political independence stems from compliance with the provisions of the Charter of the Organization of American States;

6. Declares that all controversies between member states should be resolved by the measures for peaceful solution that are contemplated in the inter-American system;

7. Reaffirms its faith in the regional system and its confidence in the Organization of American States, created to achieve an order of peace and justice that excludes any possible aggression, to promote

solidarity among its members, to strengthen their collaboration, and to defend their sovereignty, their territorial integrity, and their political independence, since it is in this Organization that the members find the best guarantee for their evolution and development;

8. Resolves that this declaration shall be known as "The Declaration of San José, Costa Rica."

SEVEN

The New Frontier and the Cold War

The return of the Democrats in the United States in 1961 brought to power a young President who held out great hopes to the world. His first major venture in foreign affairs, however, was disastrous. When Cuban exiles, encouraged by the United States, launched an invasion of their homeland, Khrushchev threatened nuclear war; the President refused to support the landing, and Fidel Castro was able to announce a great victory. To prove to the Soviet leader that the United States could not be intimidated any further, President Kennedy met his adversary in Vienna, but Khrushchev turned out to be obstinate. Launching a new campaign for the elimination of Western positions in Berlin, he caused the President to announce a partial mobilization of the reserves. Finally, to prevent the escape of East Germans to the West, the Communists, despite Western protests, erected a wall physically dividing the city.

In Latin America, the Kennedy administration now attempted to seize the initiative. Pledging American aid for an Alliance for Progress, the United States sought to attack Latin America's chief reason for discontent—its abject poverty. And when it became evident that Russian missiles were being installed in Cuba, the President quarantined the island. Khrushchev consented to a withdrawal of his weapons and the immediate crisis passed; the problem of Communisn in Cuba, however, had not been solved.

In Asia, the Cold War had given rise to intermittent guerrilla campaigns. Laos was neutralized at Geneva in 1962, but the agreement broke down, and endemic civil war continued. A Communist rebellion in South Vietnam was kept alive by North Vietnamese aid in spite of large-scale American military and economic assistance to the government at Saigon. Finally, the North Vietnamese attacked units of the United States navy in the Gulf of Tonkin; Lyndon B. Johnson, who had succeeded John F. Kennedy after the President's assassination, ordered a retaliatory air strike upon North Vietnamese bases, and Congress endorsed his action.

The situation in the Far East was complicated by the increased intransigence of Communist China, which seemed determined to prevent any sort of détente with the West. Eventually Mao Tse-tung went so far as to bring about a break with the Soviet Union. This development made possible the conclusion of a nuclear test ban on the one hand, but on the other, it aggravated the threat of war as shown by the Peking government's denunciation of the treaty. Whether the Soviets, who dismissed Khrushchev late in 1964, would be able to cope with this problem remained to be seen.

DOCUMENT 75

EXCHANGE OF MESSAGES BETWEEN PREMIER KHRUSHCHEV AND PRESIDENT KENNEDY CONCERNING THE INVASION AT THE BAY OF PIGS, APRIL 18, 1961

On April 17, 1961, a band of Cuban exiles, apparently expecting full American support, landed on the Bay of Pigs. Unwilling to risk the international complications threatened by the Soviets, President Kennedy refused to extend aid to the rebels, and the invasion failed. The notes exchanged between him and Premier Khrushchev on April 18, 1961, follow.

MR. KHRUSHCHEV TO PRESIDENT KENNEDY
[Unofficial translation]

April 18, 1961

MR. PRESIDENT: I address this message to you at an alarming hour which is fraught with danger against universal peace. An armed aggression has been started against Cuba. It is an open secret that the armed bands which have invaded that country have been prepared,

Department of State *Bulletin*, XLIV (May 8, 1961), 661–662.

equipped, and armed in the United States. The planes which bomb Cuban towns belong to the United States of America, the bombs which they drop have been put at their disposal by the American Government.

All this arouses in the Soviet Union, the Soviet Government, and the Soviet people an understandable feeling of indignation. Only recently, exchanging views through our representatives, we talked with you about the mutual wish of the parties to exert joint efforts directed toward the improvement of relations between our countries and the prevention of a danger of war. Your statement a few days ago to the effect that the United States of America would not participate in military actions against Cuba created an impression that the leading authorities of the United States are aware of the consequences which aggression against Cuba could have for the whole world and the United States of America itself.

How are we to understand what is really being done by the United States now that the attack on Cuba has become a fact?

It is yet not too late to prevent the irreparable. The Government of the U.S. can still prevent the flames of war kindled by the interventionists on Cuba from spreading into a conflagration which it will be impossible to cope with. I earnestly appeal to you, Mr. President, to call a halt to the aggression against the Republic of Cuba. The military techniques and the world political situation now are such that any so-called "small war" can produce a chain reaction in all parts of the world.

As for the U.S.S.R., there must be no mistake about our position. We will extend to the Cuban people and its Government all the necessary aid for the repulse of the armed attack on Cuba. We are sincerely interested in the relaxation of international tension, but if others go in for its aggravation, then we will answer them in full measure. In general it is impossible to carry on affairs in such a way that in one area the situation is settled and the fire is put out, and in another area a new fire is lit.

I hope that the U.S. Government will take into consideration these reasons, dictated only by concern that steps should not be permitted which might lead the world to a catastrophe of war.

KHRUSHCHEV
Chairman of the U.S.S.R. Council of Ministers

PRESIDENT KENNEDY TO MR. KHRUSHCHEV
[White House press release dated April 18]

APRIL 18, 1961

MR. CHAIRMAN: You are under a serious misapprehension in regard to events in Cuba. For months there has been evident and growing resistance to the Castro dictatorship. More than 100,000 refugees have recently fled from Cuba into neighboring countries. Their urgent hope is naturally to assist their fellow Cubans in their struggle for freedom. Many of these refugees fought alongside Dr. Castro against the Batista dictatorship; among them are prominent leaders of his own original movement and government.

These are unmistakable signs that Cubans find intolerable the denial of democratic liberties and the subversion of the 26th of July Movement by an alien-dominated regime. It cannot be surprising that, as resistance within Cuba grows, refugees have been using whatever means are available to return and support their countrymen in the continuing struggle for freedom. Where people are denied the right of choice, recourse to such struggle is the only means of achieving their liberties.

I have previously stated, and I repeat now, that the United States intends no military intervention in Cuba. In the event of any military intervention by outside force we will immediately honor our obligations under the inter-American system to protect this hemisphere against external aggression. While refraining from military intervention in Cuba, the people of the United States do not conceal their admiration for Cuban patriots who wish to see a democratic system in an independent Cuba. The United States government can take no action to stifle the spirit of liberty.

I have taken careful note of your statement that the events in Cuba might affect peace in all parts of the world. I trust that this does not mean that the Soviet government, using the situation in Cuba as a pretext, is planning to inflame other areas of the world. I would like to think that your government has too great a sense of responsibility to embark upon any enterprise so dangerous to general peace.

I agree with you as to the desirability of steps to improve the international atmosphere. I continue to hope that you will cooperate in opportunities now available to this end. A prompt cease-fire and peaceful settlement of the dangerous situation in Laos, cooperation with the United Nations in the Congo and a speedy conclusion of an acceptable treaty for the banning of nuclear tests would be constructive steps in this direction. The regime in Cuba could make a similar contribution by permitting the Cuban people freely to determine their own future by democratic processes and freely to cooperate with their Latin American neighbors.

I believe, Mr. Chairman, that you should recognize that free peoples in all parts of the world do not accept the claim of historical inevitability for Communist revolution. What your government believes is its own business; what it does in the world is the world's business. The great revolution in the history of man, past, present and future, is the revolution of those determined to be free.

JOHN F. KENNEDY

DOCUMENT 76

REPORT BROADCAST BY CUBAN NATIONAL RADIO, APRIL 20, 1961, SUMMARIZING COMMUNIQUÉ ISSUED BY PREMIER FIDEL CASTRO

The failure of the Bay of Pigs invasion led Premier Castro to issue an exultant communiqué glorifying his victory. The following summary of the communiqué was broadcast by the Cuban radio on April 20, 1961.

The militias of the revolutionary forces took by assault the last points held by the foreign mercenary invasion forces that had occupied the national territory. The communiqué adds that Playa Giron, which was the last mercenary stronghold, fell at 5:30 (Wednesday) afternoon.

It says that the revolution has emerged victorious although it had to pay a high price in precious lives of revolutionary fighters, who faced the invaders and attacked them incessantly without a single pause.

Further along, the communiqué says that in this fashion the army which was organized in the space of many months by the imperialist Government of the United States, was destroyed in less than seventy-

New York Times, April 21, 1961, 3.

two hours. The communiqué adds that the enemy has suffered a crushing defeat.

Part of the mercenaries tried to escape from the country in several ships, which were sunk by the revolutionary air force. The rest of the mercenary forces, after suffering many casualties—dead and injured —scattered in a swampy area from which there was no possible escape route.

A large quantity of arms, manufactured in the United States, were captured, including several Sherman heavy tanks. No complete count has yet been made of the captured weapons.

In the next few hours the revolutionary Government will give to the people a complete account of all the events.

DOCUMENT 77

EXCERPTS FROM AN ADDRESS BY PREMIER KHRUSH-CHEV AT MOSCOW, CONCERNING HIS MEETING AT VIENNA WITH PRESIDENT KENNEDY, JUNE 15, 1961

On June 3 and 4, 1961, President Kennedy met Premier Khrushchev at Vienna. The meeting failed to dispel the differences between them, and Khrushchev precipitated a renewed crisis when he demanded that a German peace treaty be concluded before the end of the year. Excerpts from his speech on June 15, 1961, follow.

Permit me now to turn to the German question, which occupied an important place in our talks with President Kennedy.

The Soviet Government has repeatedly stated its position on this question. And the Western powers cannot complain that they do not know our proposals sufficiently well. We have done and are doing everything to convince the Government of Britain, the United States, France and other nations which took part together with us in the war against Hitler Germany that the absence of a peace treaty with Germany has created a deeply abnormal and dangerous situation in Europe.

The question seems to be clear. A peace treaty with Germany is indispensable. Moreover, of course, there can be no question of any new changes of borders. We proceed from the premise that the peace

---

Documents on Germany, 1944–1961, 660–663.

treaty with Germany will put a seal on what has already been established by the Potsdam agreement.

The government of the German Democratic Republic has repeatedly stated that it recognizes as final the eastern border of Germany along the Oder-Neisse line, established by this agreement.

Indeed, the Governments of the Western powers obviously understand, too, how senseless it would be to raise now the question of revising Germany's boundaries. Their representatives have often told us about this during our conversations.

A simple operation, it seems—to put a seal on what actually already exists and what is long demanded by the peoples. What is it, then, that keeps the Western Governments from this step?

The reason, obviously, lies in the fact that certain people do lip service to peace while actually wishing to keep alive the smoldering coals of World War II, so as to choose a suitable moment and fan up the conflagration of a new war. . . .

West Berlin, which is situated on the territory of the German Democratic Republic, will after the signing of the peace treaty be free of all the result of the capitulation of Hitler's Germany and the introduction of the occupation regime there.

It should be said that when the question of a peace treaty with Germany, and consequently of the normalization of the situation in West Berlin, arises, the representatives of the Western powers in many cases depart from legal grounds and start appealing to questions of prestige. But these attempts are beneath criticism. . . .

And this peaceful step is called a threat or even an act of aggression! Such talk can come only from those who seek to slander or distort our intentions, to poison the minds of the peoples with lies.

We ask everyone to understand us correctly: The conclusion of a peace treaty with Germany cannot be postponed any longer. A peaceful settlement in Europe must be attained this year.

During the meetings in Vienna there was also an exchange of views on the situation in Laos and on a peaceful settlement of the Laotian question. . . .

It emerged from our talks with President Kennedy that we understand the peaceful coexistence of states differently. The President's idea is to build up something like a dam against the people's movement to establish in their countries social systems which the ruling circles of the Western powers deem unsuitable.

I must point out that on the whole I am pleased with these talks. If you were to ask me was it worthwhile negotiating this meeting, was it worth holding, I would reply without hesitation: This meeting was worthwhile; moreover, it was necessary.

DOCUMENT 78

REPORT TO THE NATION ON THE BERLIN CRISIS BY PRESIDENT KENNEDY, JULY 25, 1961

Premier Khrushchev's threats to solve the German question on his own terms within the year failed to move the United States. On July 25, 1961, President Kennedy replied by reiterating the Western position, asking for increased defense appropriations, and requesting authorization to call up certain reservists. Congress promptly responded.

Seven weeks ago tonight I returned from Europe to report on my meeting with Premier Khrushchev and the others. His grim warnings about the future of the world, his aide memoire on Berlin, his subsequent speeches and threats which he and his agents have launched, and the increase in the Soviet military budget that he has announced have all prompted a series of decisions by the administration and a series of consultations with the members of the NATO organization. In Berlin, as you recall, he intends to bring to an end, through a stroke of the pen, first, our legal rights to be in West Berlin and, secondly, our ability to make good on our commitment to the 2 million free people of that city. That we cannot permit.

We are clear about what must be done—and we intend to do it. I want to talk frankly with you tonight about the first steps that we shall take. These actions will require sacrifice on the part of many of our citizens. More will be required in the future. They will require, from all of us, courage and perseverance in the years to come. But if we and our allies act out of strength and unity of purpose—with calm determination and steady nerves, using restraint in our words as well as our weapons—I am hopeful that both peace and freedom will be sustained.

The immediate threat to free men is in West Berlin. But that iso-

lated outpost is not an isolated problem. The threat is worldwide.
Our effort must be equally wide and strong and not be obsessed by
any single manufactured crisis. We face a challenge in Berlin, but
there is also a challenge in southeast Asia, where the borders are
less guarded, the enemy harder to find, and the danger of communism
less apparent to those who have so little. We face a challenge in our
own hemisphere and indeed wherever else the freedom of human
beings is at stake. . . .

We are there as a result of our victory over Nazi Germany, and our
basic rights to be there deriving from that victory include both our
presence in West Berlin and the enjoyment of access across East Germany. These rights have been repeatedly confirmed and recognized in
special agreements with the Soviet Union. Berlin is not a part of East
Germany, but a separate territory under the control of the allied
powers. Thus our rights there are clear and deep-rooted. But in addition to those rights is our commitment to sustain—and defend, if
need be—the opportunity for more than 2 million people to determine their own future and choose their own way of life.

Thus our presence in West Berlin, and our access thereto, cannot
be ended by any act of the Soviet Government. The NATO shield
was long ago extended to cover West Berlin, and we have given our
word that an attack in that city will be regarded as an attack upon
us all.

For West Berlin, lying exposed 110 miles inside East Germany,
surrounded by Soviet troops and close to Soviet supply lines, has
many roles. It is more than a showcase of liberty, a symbol, an island
of freedom in a Communist sea. It is even more than a link with
the free world, beacon of hope behind the Iron Curtain, an escape
hatch for refugees.

West Berlin is all of that. But above all it has now become, as
never before, the great testing place of Western courage and will, a
focal point where our solemn commitments, stretching back over the
years since 1945, and Soviet ambitions now meet in basic confronta-
tion.

It would be a mistake for others to look upon Berlin, because of its
location, as a tempting target. The United States is there, the United
Kingdom and France are there, the pledge of NATO is there, and the
people of Berlin are there. It is as secure, in that sense, as the rest
of us, for we cannot separate its safety from our own.

I hear it said that West Berlin is militarily untenable. And so was Bastogne. And so, in fact, was Stalingrad. Any dangerous spot is tenable if men—brave men—will make it so.

We do not want to fight, but we have fought before. And others in earlier times have made the same dangerous mistake of assuming that the West was too selfish and too soft and too divided to resist invasions of freedom in other lands. Those who threaten to unleash the forces of war on a dispute over West Berlin should recall the words of the ancient philosopher: "A man who causes fear cannot be free from fear."

We cannot and will not permit the Communists to drive us out of Berlin, either gradually or by force. For the fulfillment of our pledge to that city is essential to the morale and security of Western Germany, to the unity of Western Europe, and to the faith of the entire free world. Soviet strategy has long been aimed not merely at Berlin but at dividing and neutralizing all of Europe, forcing us back to our own shores. We must meet our oft-stated pledge to the free peoples of West Berlin—and maintain our rights and their safety, even in the face of force—in order to maintain the confidence of other free peoples in our word and our resolve. The strength of the alliance on which our security depends is dependent in turn on our willingness to meet our commitments to them.

So long as the Communists insist that they are preparing to end by themselves unilaterally our rights in West Berlin and our commitments to its people, we must be prepared to defend those rights and those commitments. We will at all times be ready to talk, if talk will help. But we must also be ready to resist with force, if force is used upon us. Either alone would fail. Together, they can serve the cause of freedom and peace.

The new preparations that we shall make to defend the peace are part of the long-term buildup in our strength which has been under way since January. They are based on our needs to meet a worldwide threat, on a basis which stretches far beyond the present Berlin crisis. Our primary purpose is neither propaganda nor provocation—but preparation. . . .

But even more importantly, we need the capability of placing in any critical area at the appropriate time a force which, combined with those of our allies, is large enough to make clear our determination and our ability to defend our rights at all costs and to meet all levels of aggressor pressure with whatever levels of force are required. We intend to have a wider choice than humiliation or all-out nuclear action.

While it is unwise at this time either to call up or send abroad excessive numbers of these troops before they are needed, let me make it clear that I intend to take, as time goes on, whatever steps are necessary to make certain that such forces can be deployed at the appropriate time without lessening our ability to meet our commitments elsewhere.

Thus, in the days and months ahead, I shall not hesitate to ask the Congress for additional measures or exercise any of the Executive powers that I possess to meet this threat to peace. Everything essential to the security of freedom must be done; and if that should require more men, or more taxes, or more controls, or other new powers, I shall not hesitate to ask them. The measures proposed today will be constantly studied, and altered as necessary. But while we will not let panic shape our policy, neither will we permit timidity to direct our program.

Accordingly I am now taking the following steps:

(1) I am tomorrow requesting of the Congress for the current fiscal year an additional $3,247,000,000 of appropriations for the Armed Forces.

(2) To fill out our present Army divisions and to make more men available for prompt deployment, I am requesting an increase in the Army's total authorized strength from 875,000 to approximately 1 million men.

(3) I am requesting an increase of 29,000 and 63,000 men, respectively, in the active-duty strength of the Navy and the Air Force.

(4) To fulfill these manpower needs, I am ordering that our draft calls be doubled and tripled in the coming months; I am asking the Congress for authority to order to active duty certain ready reserve units and individual reservists and to extend tours of duty; and, under that authority, I am planning to order to active duty a number of air transport squadrons and Air National Guard tactical air squadrons to give us the airlift capacity and protection that we need. Other reserve forces will be called up when needed.

(5) Many ships and planes once headed for retirement are to be retained or reactivated, increasing our airpower tactically and our sealift, airlift, and antisubmarine warfare capability. In addition, our

strategic air power will be increased by delaying the deactivation of B–47 bombers.

(6) Finally, some $1.8 billion—about half of the total sum—is needed for the procurement of nonnuclear weapons, ammunition, and equipment.

The details on all these requests will be presented to the Congress tomorrow. Subsequent steps will be taken to suit subsequent needs. Comparable efforts for the common defense are being discussed with our NATO allies. For their commitment and interest are as precise as our own.

And let me add that I am well aware of the fact that many American families will bear the burden of these requests. Studies or careers will be interrupted; husbands and sons will be called away; incomes in some cases will be reduced. But these are burdens which must be borne if freedom is to be defended. Americans have willingly borne them before, and they will not flinch from the task now. . . .

For it is not the freedom of West Berlin which is "abnormal" in Germany today but the situation in that entire divided country. If anyone doubts the legality of our rights in Berlin, we are ready to have it submitted to international adjudication. If anyone doubts the extent to which our presence is desired by the people of West Berlin, compared to East German feelings about their regime, we are ready to have that question submitted to a free vote in Berlin and, if possible, among all the German people. And let us hear at that time from the 2½ million refugees who have fled the Communist regime in East Germany—voting for Western-type freedom with their feet.

The world is not deceived by the Communist attempt to label Berlin as a hotbed of war. There is peace in Berlin today. The source of world trouble and tension is Moscow, not Berlin. And if war begins, it will have begun in Moscow and not Berlin.

For the choice of peace or war is largely theirs, not ours. It is the Soviets who have stirred up this crisis. It is they who are trying to force a change. It is they who have opposed free elections. It is they who have rejected an all-German peace treaty and the rulings of international law. And as Americans know from our history on our own old frontier, gun battles are caused by outlaws and not by officers of the peace.

In short, while we are ready to defend our interests, we shall also be ready to search for peace—in quiet exploratory talks, in formal or informal meetings. We do not want military considerations to dominate the thinking of either East or West. And Mr. Khrushchev may find that his invitation to other nations to join in a meaningless treaty may lead to *their* inviting *him* to join in the community of peaceful men, in abandoning the use of force, and in respecting the sanctity of agreements. . . .

The solemn vow each of us gave to West Berlin in time of peace will not be broken in time of danger. If we do not meet our commitments to Berlin, where will we later stand? If we are not true to our word there, all that we have achieved in collective security, which relies on these words, will mean nothing. And if there is one path above all others to war, it is the path of weakness and disunity.

Today the endangered frontier of freedom runs through divided Berlin. We want it to remain a frontier of peace. This is the hope of every citizen of the Atlantic Community, every citizen of Eastern Europe, and, I am confident, every citizen of the Soviet Union. For I cannot believe that the Russian people, who bravely suffered enormous losses in the Second World War, would now wish to see the peace upset once more in Germany. The Soviet Government alone can convert Berlin's frontier of peace into a pretext for war.

DOCUMENT 79

EXCHANGE OF NOTES BETWEEN THE WESTERN AND SO-VIET COMMANDANTS AT BERLIN CONCERNING THE PHYSICAL DIVISION OF THE CITY, AUGUST 15 AND 18, 1961

When, during the night of August 12–13, 1961, the East German authorities began to erect physical barriers between East and West Berlin, the Western commandants protested. Their note was answered by their Soviet counterpart on August 18, but the physical barrier remained.

Note From the American, British, and French Commandants at Berlin to the Soviet Commandant, August 15, 1961

During the night of August 12–13 the East German authorities put into effect illegal measures designed to turn the boundaries between

Documents on Germany, 1944–1961, 726, 728–729.

the West sectors of Berlin and the Soviet sector into an arbitrary barrier to movement of German citizens resident in East Berlin and East Germany.

Not since the imposition of the Berlin blockade has there been such a flagrant violation of the four-power agreements concerning Berlin. The agreement of June 20, 1949, in which the U.S.S.R. pledged itself to facilitate freedom of movement within Berlin and between Berlin and the rest of Germany, has also been violated.

In disregard of these arrangements and of the wishes of the population of this city, for the welfare of which the four powers are jointly responsible, freedom of circulation throughout Berlin has been severely curtailed. Traffic between the east sector and the western sectors of Berlin has been disrupted by the cutting of S-Bahn and U-bahn service, the tearing up of streets, the erection of road blocks, and the stringing of barbed wire. In carrying out these illegal actions, military and paramilitary units, which were formed in violation of four-power agreements and whose very presence in East Berlin is illegal, turned the Soviet sector of Berlin into an armed camp.

Moreover, the East German authorities have now prohibited the many inhabitants of East Berlin and East Germany who were employed in West Berlin from continuing to pursue their occupations in West Berlin. They have thus denied to the working population under their control the elementary right of free choice of place of employment.

It is obvious that the East German authorities have taken these repressive measures because the people under their control, deeply perturbed by the threats on Berlin recently launched by Communist leaders, were fleeing in large numbers to the West.

We must protest against the illegal measures introduced on August 13 and hold you responsible for the carrying out of the relevant agreements.

Note From the Soviet Commandant at Berlin to the American, British, and French Commandants, August 18, 1961

[Translation]

In reference to your letter of 15 August 1961, I was instructed to communicate the following:

As has already been repeatedly emphasized, the command of the Soviet garrison in Berlin does not interfere with the affairs of the capital of the German Democratic Republic. The matter which you referred to me lies entirely within the competence of the Government of the German Democratic Republic in the fulfillment of the normal rights of each sovereign nation to protect its legal interests. Every government establishes on its borders a regime which it considers necessary and fitting for the situation. Consequently your remarks pertaining to these measures are entirely out of place.

Of course, the Commandants of the U.S.A., English and French sectors in West Berlin are very well aware of the reasons that provoked the need for the introduction of effective controls on the West Berlin border. It has been pointed out many times that there are based in West Berlin under the cover of the occupation powers more than diversionist, undermining, and spying organizations which are conducting their activities against the G.D.R., U.S.S.R., and other socialist governments. Undoubtedly, the Commandants are familiar with such facts as the transportation in airplanes over the air corridors from the Federal Republic of Germany to West Berlin for the purpose of participating in rallies and manifestations of West German revanchists and militarists; they are also familiar with all possible attempts of the F.R.G. Government to include West Berlin within the sphere of its military preparations. It is very widely known what role has been assigned to West Berlin in the plans of the F.R.G. and NATO for undermining the economy of the G.D.R. and for the conduct of hostile and inciting propaganda against the countries of the socialist sphere of friendship. The politicians of the F.R.G. have openly named West Berlin "the front line city" and called upon it to interfere with the peaceful work in the G.D.R. and other socialist countries.

All this was done in spite of frequent serious warnings regarding the consequences of such hostile acts. The authorities of the U.S.A., England, and France have done nothing to put an end to the use of the territory of West Berlin for such intolerable international provocations.

It is quite natural that the G.D.R. was forced, in view of such provocative acts on the part of revanchist and militarist circles, to adopt measures for stopping these activities. The aim of these measures is to protect the interests of all countries in the socialist sphere of friendship, about which these countries informed the G.D.R. in their common appeal.

As has been pointed out in the declaration of these countries as the participants of the Warsaw agreement, the whole responsibility for the situation which has arisen and for the known inconveniences which a part of the population is experiencing in connection with these defensive measures, rests fully and completely on the revanchist-militaristic circles of the F.R.G. and also on the Western Powers which perform the occupation functions in West Berlin. Consequently this responsibility rests also on you, Mr. Commandant, as the man in charge of the occupation authority. Therefore, I decisively reject your pretensions as expressed in the letter of August 15 as devoid of any basis whatsoever.

DOCUMENT 80

THE ALLIANCE FOR PROGRESS: THE CHARTER OF PUNTA DEL ESTE, AUGUST 17, 1961

In the belief that Latin-American poverty provided a fertile field for Communist propaganda, the United States sought to encourage its neighbors to help themselves. Pledging generous assistance, on August 17, 1961, it signed the Charter of Punta del Este establishing the Alliance for Progress. All American republics with the exception of Cuba participated.

PREAMBLE

We, the American Republics, hereby proclaim our decision to unite in a common effort to bring our people accelerated economic progress and broader social justice within the framework of personal dignity and political liberty.

Almost two hundred years ago we began in this Hemisphere the long struggle for freedom which now inspires people in all parts of the world. Today, in ancient lands, men moved to hope by the revolutions of our young nations search for liberty. Now we must give a new meaning to that revolutionary heritage. For America stands at a turning point in history. The men and women of our Hemisphere are reaching for the better life which today's skills have placed within

Department of State *Bulletin*, XLV (September 11, 1961), 463–466.

their grasp. They are determined for themselves and their children to have decent and ever more abundant lives, to gain access to knowledge and equal opportunity for all, to end those conditions which benefit the few at the expense of the needs and dignity of the many. It is our inescapable task to fulfill these just desires—to demonstrate to the poor and forsaken of our countries, and of all lands, that the creative powers of free men hold the key to their progress and to the progress of future generations. And our certainty of ultimate success rests not alone on our faith in ourselves and in our nations but on the indomitable spirit of free man which has been the heritage of American civilization.

Inspired by these principles, and by the principles of Operation Pan America and the Act of Bogotá, the American Republics hereby resolve to adopt the following program of action to establish and carry forward an Alliance for Progress.

TITLE I

OBJECTIVES OF THE ALLIANCE FOR PROGRESS

It is the purpose of the Alliance for Progress to enlist the full energies of the peoples and governments of the American republics in a great cooperative effort to accelerate the economic and social development of the participating countries of Latin America, so that they may achieve maximum levels of well-being, with equal opportunities for all, in democratic societies adapted to their own needs and desires.

The American republics agree to work toward the achievement of the following fundamental goals in the present decade:

1. To achieve in the participating Latin American countries a substantial and sustained growth of per capita incomes at a rate designed to attain, at the earliest possible date, levels of income capable of assuring self-sustaining development, and sufficient to make Latin American income levels constantly larger in relation to the levels of the more industrialized nations. In this way the gap between the living standards of Latin America and those of the more developed countries can be narrowed. Similarly, presently existing differences in income levels among the Latin American countries will be reduced by accelerating the development of the relatively less

developed countries and granting them maximum priority in the distribution of resources and in international cooperation in general. In evaluating the degree of relative development, account will be taken not only of average levels of real income and gross product per capita, but also of indices of infant mortality, illiteracy, and per capita daily caloric intake.

It is recognized that, in order to reach these objectives within a reasonable time, the rate of economic growth in any country of Latin America should be not less than 2.5 per cent per capita per year, and that each participating country should determine its own growth target in the light of its stage of social and economic evolution, resource endowment, and ability to mobilize national efforts for development.

2. To make the benefits of economic progress available to all citizens of all economic and social groups through a more equitable distribution of national income, raising more rapidly the income and standard of living of the needier sectors of the population, at the same time that a higher proportion of the national product is devoted to investment.

3. To achieve balanced diversification in national economic structures, both regional and functional, making them increasingly free from dependence on the export of a limited number of primary products and the importation of capital goods while seeking to attain stability in the prices of exports or in income derived from exports.

4. To accelerate the process of rational industrialization so as to increase the productivity of the economy as a whole, taking full advantage of the talents and energies of both the private and public sectors, utilizing the natural resources of the country and providing productive and remunerative employment for unemployed or part-time workers. Within this process of industrialization, special attention should be given to the establishment and development of capital-goods industries.

5. To raise greatly the level of agricultural productivity and output and to improve related storage, transportation, and marketing services.

6. To encourage, in accordance with the characteristics of each country, programs of comprehensive agrarian reform leading to the effective transformation, where required, of unjust structures and systems of land tenure and use, with a view to replacing latifundia and

dwarf-holdings by an equitable system of land tenure so that, with the help of timely and adequate credit, technical assistance and facilities for the marketing and distribution of products, the land will become for the man who works it the basis of his economic stability, the foundation of his increasing welfare, and the guarantee of his freedom and dignity.

7. To eliminate adult illiteracy and by 1970 to assure, as a minimum, access to six years of primary education for each school-age child in Latin America; to modernize and expand vocational, secondary and higher educational and training facilities, to strengthen the capacity for basic and applied research, and to provide the competent personnel required in rapidly-growing societies.

8. To increase life expectancy at birth by a minimum of five years, and to increase the ability to learn and produce, by improving individual and public health. To attain this goal it will be necessary, among other measures, to provide adequate potable water supply and drainage to not less than 70 per cent of the urban and 50 per cent of the rural population; to reduce the mortality rate of children less than five years of age to at least one-half of the present rate; to control the more serious transmissible diseases, according to their importance as a cause of sickness and death; to eradicate those illnesses, especially malaria, for which effective cures are known; to improve nutrition; to train medical and health personnel to meet at least minimum standards of competence; to improve basic health services at national and local levels; to intensify scientific research and apply its results more fully and effectively to the prevention and cure of illness.

9. To increase the construction of low-cost houses for low-income families in order to replace inadequate and deficient housing and to reduce housing shortages; and to provide necessary public services to both urban and rural centers of population.

10. To maintain stable price levels, avoiding inflation or deflation and the consequent social hardships and maldistribution of resources, bearing always in mind the necessity of maintaining an adequate rate of economic growth.

11. To strengthen existing agreements on economic integration, with a view to the ultimate fulfillment of aspirations for a Latin American common market that will expand and diversify trade among the Latin American countries and thus contribute to the economic growth of the region.

12. To develop cooperative programs designed to prevent the harmful effects of excessive fluctuations in the foreign exchange earnings derived from exports of primary products, which are of vital importance to economic and social development; and to adopt the measures necessary to facilitate the access of Latin American exports to international markets.

TITLE II

ECONOMIC AND SOCIAL DEVELOPMENT

Chapter I. Basic Requirements for Economic and Social Development

The American republics recognize that to achieve the foregoing goals it will be necessary:

1. That comprehensive and well-conceived national programs of economic and social development, aimed at the achievement of self-sustaining growth, be carried out in accordance with democratic principles.

2. That national programs of economic and social development be based on the principle of self-help—as established in the Act of Bogotá—and the maximum use of domestic resources, taking into account the special conditions of each country.

3. That in the preparation and execution of plans for economic and social development, women should be placed on an equal footing with men.

4. That the Latin American countries obtain sufficient external financial assistance, a substantial portion of which should be extended on flexible conditions with respect to periods and terms of repayment and forms of utilization, in order to supplement domestic capital formation and reinforce their import capacity; and that, in support of well-conceived programs, including the necessary structural reforms and measures for the mobilization of internal resources, a supply of capital from all external sources during the coming ten years of at least 20 billion dollars be made available to the Latin American countries, with priority to the relatively less developed countries. The greater part of this sum should be in public funds.

5. That institutions in both the public and private sectors, including labor, cooperative, commercial, industrial, and financial institutions, be strengthened and improved for increasingly effective use of

domestic resources, and that the necessary social reforms be effected to permit a fair distribution of the fruits of economic and social progress. . . .

Chapter III. Immediate and Short-Term Action Measures

1. Recognizing that a number of Latin American countries, despite their best efforts, may require emergency financial assistance, the United States will provide assistance from the funds which are or may be established for such purposes. The United States stands ready to take prompt action on applications for such assistance. Applications relating to existing situations should be submitted within the next 60 days.

2. Participating Latin American countries should immediately increase their efforts to accelerate their development, giving special emphasis (in addition to the creation or strengthening of machinery for long-term development programming) to the following objectives:

a. The completion of projects already under way and the initiation of projects for which the basic studies have been made in order to accelerate their financing and execution.

b. The implementation of new projects which are designed:

   i. To meet the most pressing social needs and benefit directly the greatest number of people;
   ii. To concentrate efforts within each country in the less developed or more depressed areas in which particularly serious social problems exist;
   iii. To utilize idle capacity or resources, particularly underemployed manpower;
   iv. To survey and assess natural resources.

c. The facilitation of the preparation and execution of longterm programs through measures designed:

   i. To train teachers, technicians, and specialists;
   ii. To provide accelerated training to workers and farmers;
   iii. To improve basic statistics;
   iv. To establish needed credit and marketing facilities;
   v. To improve services and administration.

272 — The Cold War

3. The United States will assist in the realization of these short-term measures with a view to achieving concrete results from the Alliance for Progress at the earliest possible moment. In connection with the measures set forth above, and in accordance with the statement of President Kennedy, the United States will provide assistance under the Alliance, including assistance for the financing of short-term measures, totalling more than one billion dollars in the year ending March 1962. . . .

DOCUMENT 81

DECLARATION ON THE NEUTRALITY OF LAOS, JULY 23, 1962

Warfare in Indo-China did not cease with the conclusion of the 1954 Geneva agreements. The Pathet Lao, a pro-Communist group, not only refused to give up the provinces it controlled, but intermittently waged war on the government of Laos. After an international conference consisting of fourteen nations had met for some fourteen months, an arrangement for the neutralization of the country was finally worked out at Geneva (July 23, 1962). However, the agreement was broken almost immediately.

The Governments of the Union of Burma, the Kingdom of Cambodia, Canada, the People's Republic of China, the Democratic Republic of Viet-Nam, the Republic of France, the Republic of India, the Polish People's Republic, the Republic of Viet-Nam, the Kingdom of Thailand, the Union of Soviet Socialist Republics, the United Kingdom of Great Britain and Northern Ireland and the United States of America, whose representatives took part in the International Conference on the Settlement of the Laotian Question, 1961–1962;

Welcoming the presentation of the statement of neutrality by the Royal Government of Laos of July 9, 1962, and taking note of this statement, which is, with the concurrence of the Royal Government of Laos, incorporated in the present Declaration as an integral part thereof, and the text of which is as follows:

United States Treaties and Other International Agreements, **XIV**, Part I (Washington, 1963), 1105–1107.

THE ROYAL GOVERNMENT OF LAOS,

Being resolved to follow the path of peace and neutrality in conformity with the interests and aspirations of the Laotian people, as well as the principles of the Joint Communiqué of Zurich dated June 22, 1961, and of the Geneva Agreements of 1954, in order to build a peaceful, neutral, independent, democratic, unified and prosperous Laos,

Solemnly declares that:

(1) It will resolutely apply the five principles of peaceful coexistence in foreign relations, and will develop friendly relations and establish diplomatic relations with all countries, the neighbouring countries first and foremost, on the basis of equality and of respect for the independence and sovereignty of Laos;

(2) It is the will of the Laotian people to protect and ensure respect for the sovereignty, independence, neutrality, unity, and territorial integrity of Laos;

(3) It will not resort to the use or threat of force in any way which might impair the peace of other countries, and will not interfere in the internal affairs of other countries;

(4) It will not enter into any military alliance or into any agreement, whether military or otherwise, which is inconsistent with the neutrality of the Kingdom of Laos; it will not allow the establishment of any foreign military base on Laotian territory, nor allow any country to use Laotian territory for military purposes or for the purposes of interference in the internal affairs of other countries, nor recognise the protection of any alliance or military coalition, including SEATO.

(5) It will not allow any foreign interference in the internal affairs of the Kingdom of Laos in any form whatsoever;

(6) Subject to the provisions of Article 5 of the Protocol, it will require the withdrawal from Laos of all foreign troops and military personnel, and will not allow any foreign troops or military personnel to be introduced into Laos;

(7) It will accept direct and unconditional aid from all countries that wish to help the Kingdom of Laos build up an independent and autonomous national economy on the basis of respect for the sovereignty of Laos;

(8) It will respect the treaties and agreements signed in conformity with the interests of the Laotian people and of the policy

of peace and neutrality of the Kingdom, in particular the Geneva Agreements of 1962, and will abrogate all treaties and agreements which are contrary to those principles.

This statement of neutrality by the Royal Government of Laos shall be promulgated constitutionally and shall have the force of law.

The Kingdom of Laos appeals to all the States participating in the International Conference on the Settlement of the Laotian Question, and to all other States, to recognise the sovereignty, independence, neutrality, unity and territorial integrity of Laos, to conform to these principles in all respects, and to refrain from any action inconsistent therewith.

Confirming the principles of respect for the sovereignty, independence, unity and territorial integrity of the Kingdom of Laos and non-interference in its internal affairs which are embodied in the Geneva Agreements of 1954;

Emphasising the principle of respect for the neutrality of the Kingdom of Laos;

Agreeing that the above-mentioned principles constitute a basis for the peaceful settlement of the Laotian question;

Profoundly convinced that the independence and neutrality of the Kingdom of Laos will assist the peaceful democratic development of the Kingdom of Laos and the achievement of national accord and unity in that country, as well as the strengthening of peace and security in South-East Asia;

1. Solemnly declare, in accordance with the will of the Government and people of the Kingdom of Laos, as expressed in the statement of neutrality by the Royal Government of Laos of July 9, 1962, that they recognise and will respect and observe in every way the sovereignty, independence, neutrality, unity and territorial integrity of the Kingdom of Laos.

2. Undertake, in particular, that

(*a*) they will not commit or participate in any way in any act which might directly or indirectly impair the sovereignty, independence, neutrality, unity or territorial integrity of the Kingdom of Laos;

(*b*) they will not resort to the use or threat of force or any other measure which might impair the peace of the Kingdom of Laos;

(*c*) they will refrain from all direct or indirect interference in the internal affairs of the Kingdom of Laos;

(*d*) they will not attach conditions of a political nature to any assistance which they may offer or which the Kingdom of Laos may seek;

(*e*) they will not bring the Kingdom of Laos in any way into any military alliance or any other agreement, whether military or otherwise, which is inconsistent with her neutrality, nor invite or encourage her to enter into any such alliance or to conclude any such agreement;

(*f*) they will respect the wish of the Kingdom of Laos not to recognise the protection of any alliance or military coalition, including SEATO;

(*g*) they will not introduce into the Kingdom of Laos foreign troops or military personnel in any form whatsoever, nor will they in any way facilitate or connive at the introduction of any foreign troops or military personnel;

(*h*) they will not establish nor will they in any way facilitate or connive at the establishment in the Kingdom of Laos of any foreign military base, foreign strong point or other foreign military installation of any kind;

(*i*) they will not use the territory of the Kingdom of Laos for interference in the internal affairs of other countries;

(*j*) they will not use the territory of any country, including their own for interference in the internal affairs of the Kingdom of Laos.

3. Appeal to all other States to recognise, respect and observe in every way the sovereignty, independence and neutrality, and also the unity and territorial integrity, of the Kingdom of Laos and to refrain from any action inconsistent with these principles or with other provisions of the present Declaration.

4. Undertake, in the event of a violation or threat of violation of the sovereignty, independence, neutrality, unity or territorial integrity of the Kingdom of Laos, to consult jointly with the Royal Government of Laos and among themselves in order to consider measures which might prove to be necessary to ensure the observance of these principles and the other provisions of the present Declaration.

5. The present Declaration shall enter into force on signature and together with the statement of neutrality by the Royal Government of

Laos of July 9, 1962, shall be regarded as constituting an international agreement. The present Declaration shall be deposited in the archives of the Governments of the United Kingdom and the Union of Soviet Socialist Republics, which shall furnish certified copies thereof to the other signatory States and to all the other States of the world. . . .

DOCUMENT 82

THE SECOND CUBAN CRISIS: PRESIDENT KENNEDY'S RADIO-TELEVISION ADDRESS, OCTOBER 22, 1962

When aerial photography revealed the installation of Russian ballistic missiles in Cuba, President Kennedy decided to call a halt. In a radio and television address on October 22, 1962, he announced a quarantine of all offensive weapons bound for Cuba and called for a dismantling of the Russian installations already there.

GOOD EVENING, MY FELLOW CITIZENS:

This Government, as promised, has maintained the closest surveillance of the Soviet military build-up on the Island of Cuba. Within the past week, unmistakable evidence had established the fact that a series of offensive missile sites is now in preparation on that imprisoned island. The purpose of these bases can be none other than to provide a nuclear strike capability against the Western Hemisphere.

Upon receiving the first preliminary hard information of this nature last Tuesday morning at 9 A.M., I directed that our surveillance be stepped up. And having now confirmed and completed our evaluation of the evidence and our decision on a course of action, this Government feels obliged to report this new crisis to you in fullest detail.

The characteristics of these new missile sites indicate two distinct types of installations. Several of them include medium-range ballistic missiles, capable of carrying a nuclear warhead for a distance of more than 1,000 nautical miles. Each of these missiles, in short, is capable of striking Washington, D.C., the Panama Canal, Cape Canaveral,

The Parliament of the Commonwealth of Australia, *Papers Presented to Parliament Relating to Cuba*, October–November, 1962 (Canberra, 1963), 9–11.

Mexico City, or any other city in the southeastern part of the United States, in Central America or in the Caribbean area.

Additional sites not yet completed appear to be designed for intermediate range ballistic missiles—capable of travelling more than twice as far—and thus capable of striking most of the major cities in the Western Hemisphere, ranging as far north as Hudson's Bay, Canada, and as far south as Lima, Peru. In addition, jet bombers, capable of carrying nuclear weapons, are now being uncrated and assembled in Cuba, while the necessary air bases are being prepared.

This urgent transformation of Cuba into an important strategic base —by the presence of these large, long-range and clearly offensive weapons of sudden mass destruction—constitutes an explicit threat to the peace and security of all the Americas, in flagrant and deliberate defiance of the Rio Pact of 1947, the traditions of this Nation and Hemisphere, the Joint Resolution of the 87th Congress, the Charter of the United Nations, and my own public warnings to the Soviets on September 4 and 13. This action also contradicts the repeated assurances of Soviet spokesmen, both publicly and privately delivered, that the arms build-up in Cuba would retain its original defensive character, and that the Soviet Union had no need or desire to station strategic missiles on the territory of any other nation.

The size of this undertaking makes clear that it had been planned for some months. Yet only last month, after I had made clear the distinction between any introduction of ground-to-ground missiles and the existence of defensive anti-aircraft missiles, the Soviet Government publicly stated on September 11 that, and I quote, "the armaments and military equipment sent to Cuba are designed exclusively for defensive purposes," and there is, and I quote the Soviet Government, "no need for the Soviet Union to shift its weapons . . . for a retaliatory blow to any other country, for instance Cuba," and that, and I quote the Soviet Government, "the Soviet Union has so powerful rockets to carry these nuclear warheads that there is no need to search for sites for them beyond the boundaries of the Soviet Union," That statement was false.

Only last Thursday, as evidence of this rapid offensive build-up was already in my hand, Soviet Foreign Minister Gromyko told me in my office that he was instructed to make it clear once again, as he said his Government had already done, that Soviet assistance to Cuba, and I quote "pursued solely the purpose of contributing to the defence capabilities of Cuba," that, and I quote him, "training by Soviet specialists of Cuban nationals in handling defensive armaments was by no means offensive," and that "If it were otherwise," Mr. Gromyko went on, "the Soviet Government would never become involved in rendering such assistance." That statement also was false.

Neither the United States of America nor the world community of nations can tolerate deliberate deception and offensive threats on the part of any nation, large or small. We no longer live in a world where only the actual firing of weapons represents a sufficient challenge to a nation's security to constitute maximum peril. Nuclear weapons are so destructive, and ballistic missiles are so swift, that any substantially increased possibility of their use or any sudden change in their deployment may well be regarded as a definite threat to peace.

For many years, both the Soviet Union and the United States—recognizing this fact—have deployed strategic nuclear weapons with great care, never upsetting the precarious status quo which ensured that these weapons would not be used in the absence of some vital challenge. Our own strategic missiles have never been transferred to the territory of any other nation under a cloak of secrecy and deception. And our history—unlike that of the Soviets since we ended World War II—demonstrates that we have no desire to dominate or conquer any other nation or impose our system upon its people. Nevertheless, American citizens have become adjusted to living daily on the bulls eye of Soviet missiles located inside the U.S.S.R. or in submarines. In that sense, missiles in Cuba add to an already clear and present danger—although, it should be noted, the nations of Latin America have never previously been subjected to a potential nuclear threat.

But this secret, swift, extraordinary build-up of Communist missiles—in an area well-known to have a special and historical relationship to the United States and the nations of the Western Hemisphere, in violation of Soviet assurances, and in defiance of American and hemispheric policy—this sudden, clandestine decision to station strategic weapons for the first time outside of Soviet soil—is a deliberately provocative and unjustified change in the status quo which cannot be accepted by this country and if our courage and our commitments are ever to be trusted again by either friend or foe.

The 1930's taught us a clear lesson: aggressive conduct, if allowed to go unchecked and unchallenged, ultimately leads to war.

This Nation is opposed to war. We are also true to our word. Our unswerving objective, therefore, must be to prevent the use of these missiles against this or any other country, and to secure their withdrawal or elimination from the Western Hemisphere.

Our policy has been one of patience and restraint, as befits a peaceful and powerful nation, which leads a world-wide alliance. We have been determined not to be diverted from our central concerns by mere irritants and fanatics. But now further action is required—and it is under way—and these actions may only be the beginning. We will not prematurely or unnecessarily risk the course of world-wide nuclear war in which even the fruits of victory would be ashes in our mouth—but neither will we shrink from that risk at any time it must be faced.

Acting, therefore, in the defense of our own security and of the entire Western Hemisphere, and under the authority entrusted to me by the Constitution as endorsed by the Resolution of the Congress, I have directed that the following initial steps be taken immediately:

First: To halt this offensive build-up, a strict quarantine on all offensive military equipment under shipment to Cuba is being initiated. All ships of any kind bound for Cuba, from whatever nation or port, will, if found to contain cargoes of offensive weapons, be turned back. This quarantine will be extended, if needed, to other types of cargo and carriers. We are not at this time, however, denying the necessities of life as the Soviets attempted to do in their Berlin Blockade of 1948.

Second: I have directed the continued and increased close surveillance of Cuba and its military build-up. The Foreign Ministers of the OAS, in their communique of October 6, rejected secrecy on such matters in this hemisphere. Should these offensive military preparations continue, thus increasing the threat to the hemisphere, further action will be justified. I have directed the Armed Forces to prepare for any eventualities—and I trust that, in the interest of both the Cuban people and the Soviet technicians at the sites, the hazards to all concerned of continuing this threat will be recognized.

Third: It shall be the policy of this nation to regard any nuclear missile launched from Cuba against any nation in the Western Hemisphere as an attack by the Soviet Union on the United States, requiring a full retaliatory response upon the Soviet Union.

Fourth: As a necessary military precaution, I have reinforced our

Base at Guantanamo, evacuated to-day the dependents of our personnel there and ordered additional military units on a stand-by on an emergency basis.

Fifth: We are calling tonight for an immediate meeting of the Organization of Consultation under the Organization of American States, to consider this threat to hemispheric security and to invoke Articles 6 and 8 of the Rio Treaty in support of all necessary action. The United Nations Charter allows for regional security arrangements —and the nations of this hemisphere decided long ago against the military presence of outside powers. Our other allies around the world have also been alerted.

Sixth: Under the Charter of the United Nations, we are asking tonight that an emergency meeting of the Security Council be convoked without delay to take action against this latest Soviet threat to world peace. Our Resolution will call for the prompt dismantling and withdrawal of all offensive weapons in Cuba, under the supervision of U.N. observers, before the quarantine can be lifted.

Seventh and Finally: I call upon Chairman Khrushchev to halt and eliminate this clandestine, reckless and provocative threat to world peace and to stable relations between our two Nations. I call upon him further to abandon this course of world domination, and to join in an historic effort to end the perilous arms race and to transform the history of man. He has an opportunity now to move the world back from the abyss of destruction—by returning to his Government's own words that it had no need to station missiles outside its own territory, and withdrawing these weapons from Cuba—by refraining from any action which will widen or deepen the present crisis —and then by participating in a search for peaceful and permanent solutions.

This Nation is prepared to present its case against this Soviet threat to peace, and our own proposals for a peaceful world, at any time and in any forum—in the OAS, in the United Nations, or in any other meeting that could be useful—without limiting our freedom of action. We have in the past made strenuous efforts to limit the spread of nuclear weapons. We have proposed the elimination of all arms and military bases in a fair and effective disarmament treaty. We are prepared to discuss new proposals for the removal of tensions on both sides—including the possibilities of a genuinely independent Cuba, free to determine its own destiny. We have no wish to war with the Soviet Union—for we are a peaceful people who desire to live in peace with all other peoples.

But it is difficult to settle or even discuss these problems in an atmosphere of intimidation. That is why this latest Soviet threat—or any other threat which is made either independently or in response to our actions this week—must and will be met with determination. Any hostile move anywhere in the world against the safety and freedom of peoples to whom we are committed—including in particular the brave people of West Berlin—will be met by whatever action is needed.

Finally, I want to say a few words to the captive people of Cuba, to whom this speech is being directly carried by special radio facilities. I speak to you as a friend, as one who knows of your deep attachment to your Fatherland, as one who shares your aspirations for liberty and justice for all. And I have watched, and the American people have watched, with deep sorrow how your nationalist revolution was betrayed—and how your Fatherland fell under foreign domination. Now your leaders are no longer Cuban leaders inspired by Cuban ideals. They are puppets and agents of an international conspiracy which has turned Cuba against your friends and neighbors in the Americas—and turned it into the first Latin American Country to become a target for nuclear war—the first Latin American Country to have these weapons on its soil.

These new weapons are not in your interest. They contribute nothing to your peace and well-being. They can only undermine it. But this country has no wish to cause you to suffer or to impose any system upon you. We know that your lives and land are being used as pawns by those who deny you freedom.

Many times in the past, the Cuban people have risen to throw out tyrants who destroyed their liberty. And I have no doubt that most Cubans today look forward to the time when they will be truly free— free from foreign domination, free to choose their own leaders, free to select their own system, free to own their own land, free to speak and write and worship without fear or degradation. And then shall Cuba be welcomed back to the society of free nations and to the associations of this hemisphere.

My fellow citizens: Let no one doubt that this is a difficult and dangerous effort on which we have set out. No one can foresee precisely what course it will take or what costs or casualties will be in-

curred. Many months of sacrifice and self-discipline lie ahead—
months in which both our patience, and our will, will be tested—
months in which many threats and denunciations will keep us aware
of our dangers. But the greatest danger of all would be to do nothing.

The path we have chosen for the present is full of hazards, as all
paths are—but it is the one most consistent with our character and
courage as a Nation and our commitments around the world. The
cost of freedom is always high—but Americans have always paid it.
And one path we shall never choose, and that is the path of surrender or submission.

Our goal is not the victory of might but the vindication of right—
not peace at the expense of freedom, but both peace and freedom,
here in this hemisphere, and, we hope, around the world. God willing, that goal will be achieved.

Thank you and good night.

DOCUMENT 83

THE SECOND CUBAN CRISIS: MESSAGE OF OCTOBER 28, 1962, FROM PREMIER KHRUSHCHEV TO PRESIDENT KENNEDY

*The firm stand of the United States resulted in a Soviet retreat. Amid
charges and countercharges, meetings of the Security Council and the
O.A.S., Premier Khrushchev, in response to a personal message by
President Kennedy, agreed to withdraw the offensive weapons from Cuba.
His message of October 28, 1962, spelled out his decision.*

I have received your message of 27th October, 1962, and express
my satisfaction and gratitude for the sense of proportion and understanding of the responsibility borne by you for the preservation of
peace throughout the world which you have shown.

With great understanding I think of your concern and the anxiety
of the U.S. people to the effect that the weapons you call "offensive"
are really menacing weapons. Both you and we realize what kind of
weapons they are.

To complete the liquidation of the conflict dangerous for the cause

---

Papers Presented to Parliament Relative to Cuba, October–November, 1962,
33–34.

of peace, in order to give confidence to the peoples striving for peace, to reassure the people of America who, I am sure, want peace, as much as the people of the Soviet Union, the Soviet Government, in addition to the previous order about the cessation of further works pertaining to the disposition of military equipment, has given a new order about dismantling this equipment, which you call "offensive," its packing and withdrawing back to the Soviet Union.

Mr. President, I would like to repeat once more what I have already stated in my previous letters to you—that the Soviet Government rendered its economic assistance, as well as its aid with arms to the Government of the Republic of Cuba, since Cuba, the Cuban people were living under a constant danger of an invasion of Cuba. A piratic ship has shelled Havana. It was alleged that irresponsible Cuban emigres have shelled it. This is possibly the case. But the question arises: From where did they shoot? After all these Cubans have no territory, they are people who fled from their homeland, they have no means for conducting warfare. It means that somebody put these weapons in their hands for the purpose of shelling Havana, of carrying out acts of piracy in the Caribbean Sea, in territorial waters of Cuba. Indeed, it is absolutely inconceivable in our time not to notice the piratic ship, especially taking into account a great number of American ships in the Caribbean Sea which, in fact, is completely under observation and control. Nevertheless, piratic ships are free to wander about Cuba, to shell it, to commit piratic attacks at peaceful cargo vessels. Indeed, they are known to have shelled even a British freighter. In short, Cuba was under a constant threat of aggressive forces who did not conceal their intentions to invade the Cuban territory.

The Cuban people desire to build up their life in their own interests, without interfering from outside. This is its right and the Cuban people must not be blamed for the desire to be the masters of their country, to dispose of the fruits of their labour.

The danger of invading Cuba and all the other ventures which result in creating tension as regards Cuba, are designed to engender uncertainty in the Cuban people, to intimidate them, to prevent them from building a new life undisturbed.

Mr. President, I want once more to state clearly that we could not be indifferent to that and the Soviet Government decided to help

Cuba with means of defence against aggression. These were only the means for defensive purposes. We have sent there defence means which you call "means of offence," have supplied them there to prevent the aggression against Cuba, to prevent reckless actions.

With respect and confidence I regard your statement set forth in your message of 27th October, 1962, that Cuba will not be attacked, will not be invaded, not only by the United States, but also by other countries of the western hemisphere, as pointed in your message. So the motives which prompted us to render Cuba our assistance of this nature, are no longer applicable. Therefore, we have given the order to our officers (and the said means, as I have informed you, are in the hands of Soviet officers) to carry out the necessary measures as regards discontinuing the construction of the mentioned installations, their dismantling and withdrawing to the Soviet Union.

As I have already informed you in the letter of 27th October, we are both ready to come to an agreement that representatives of the U.N.O. may verify the dismantling of these means. Thus, if taking for a basis your assurances you have made, and our orders on dismantling, all the necessary conditions for the elimination the conflict arisen, are on hand.

I note with satisfaction that you have responded to my call as to eliminate the dangerous situation mentioned, as well as to create conditions for more thoughtful assessment of the international situation fraught with great dangers in our age of thermo-nuclear weapons, rocket technology, space ships, global rockets and other lethal weapons.

All people are concerned with maintaining peace. Therefore, we who are invested with trust and great responsibility, should not allow the situation to be aggravated and should remove those hotbeds where there has been created the dangerous situation fraught with grave consequences for the cause of peace. And if we succeed, along with the aid of other people of good will, in liquidating this tense situation, we should also take care that there should not arise other dangerous conflicts which might lead to a world thermo-nuclear catastrophe.

In conclusion I wish to dwell on regulating relations between NATO and States—parties of the Warsaw Treaty, that has already been mentioned. We spoke of this long ago and are ready to continue an exchange of opinions with you on this question and to find a reasonable solution.

We also wish to continue an exchange of views on the prohibition of atomic and thermo-nuclear weapons, on general disarmament and on other questions dealing with lessening of international tension.

Mr. President, I trust your statement, but on the other hand I want to mention that there are irresponsible people who would like to undertake the invasion of Cuba and thus to unleash a war. Taking practical steps and declaring the dismantling and evacuation of the said equipment from Cuba, then in doing that at the same time we wish to create the confidence of the Cuban people in the fact that we are with them, that we do not decline our responsibility of granting help to the Cuban people. We are convinced that peoples of other countries, like yourself, Mr. President, will understand me correctly. We do not threaten, we desire only peace. Our country is on the rise now. Our people are enjoying the fruits of their peaceful labour. After the October revolution they have achieved tremendous successes, have created the greatest material, spiritual and cultural treasures. Our people make use of these values and want to develop further successes, want to ensure their further development along the path of peace and social progress by their persistent labour.

I would like to remind you, Mr. President, that military aircraft of a reconnaissance type have violated the frontiers of the Soviet Union, as a result of which we have disputes with you, an exchange of Notes has taken place.

In 1960 we shot down your U2 aircraft the reconnaissance flight of which over the U.S.S.R. resulted in the break-down of the Summit conference in Paris. At that time you assumed a correct position having condemned this criminal action by the former Government of the U.S.A.

But already during the period of your tenure of the office of President there have occurred the second case of violating of our frontiers by an American U2 aircraft over Sakhalin. We have already notified you of this violation which took place on August 30. Then you told us that this violation had taken place as a result of bad weather and gave an assurance that this would not be repeated. We regarded your assurances with confidence, for in this area there was, indeed, bad weather at that time. However, if the orders had not been given to your planes to fly near our territory, then even bad weather could not have led an American aircraft into our air space. Hence it follows that this is done with the knowledge of Pentagon which tramples on international laws and violates the frontiers of other States.

An even more dangerous case took place on October 28, 1962, when your reconnaissance aircraft intruded into the territory of the Soviet Union in the north in the area of the Chukotka peninsula and flew over our territory.

The question arises, Mr. President, how should we regard this? What is it? A provocation? Your aircraft violates our frontiers, especially in such an uneasy moment which both we and you experience when everything has been placed in a state of fighting readiness. Indeed, the American plane-intruder could easily be taken for a bomber with nuclear weapons and that can push us to take a fatal step, especially bearing in mind that the U.S. Government and the Pentagon have been declaring for a long time that your bombers with atomic bombs are always on flight duty. Therefore you can imagine what a great responsibility you assume especially now, at such uneasy times which both we and you are going through.

I would like to ask you to assess this correctly and to take necessary measures to prevent this from becoming a provocation to the unleashing of war.

I would like also to express the following wish: of course, it is the matter the Cuban people is concerned with, at present, you have got no diplomatic relations with her, but I was informed by my officers staying in Cuba that the flights of American planes over Cuba are taking place.

Our concern is that there be no war in the world at all, that the Cuban people live in peace. But, besides, Mr. President it is an open secret that we have our people in Cuba. According to the agreement with the Cuban government we have there our officers, instructors who train the Cubans, mainly ordinary people, specialists, agronomists, animal husbandry experts, irrigation and soil improvement experts, ordinary workers, tractor drivers and others. We are concerned about them. I would like to ask, Mr. President, to take into account that the violation of air space of Cuba may also bring dangerous consequences. If you do not wish that, it would be advisable not to give cause for the creation of a dangerous situation. At present we must be very cautious and avoid taking such steps which will be of no use for the defence of the States involved in the conflict, but will cause irritation and even provoke a fatal step. Therefore, we must display sobriety and wisdom and refrain from such steps.

We value peace, perhaps even more than other peoples, because we went through a terrible war against Hitler. But our people will not waver in the face of any ordeal. Our people trust their own government, and we assure our people and the world public that the Soviet Government will not allow to be provoked. But if provocators unleash a war, they will not escape the responsibility for the grave consequences of the war. But we are confident that reason will triumph, war will not be unleased and there will be ensured peace and the security of peoples.

In view of the negotiations which U Thant is conducting with the representatives of the Soviet Union, the U.S.A. and the Republic of Cuba, the Soviet Government has sent to New York the First Deputy of the U.S.S.R. Foreign Minister V. Kuznetsov to assist U Thant in his noble efforts aimed at removing the dangerous situation which has arisen.

DOCUMENT 84

TREATY BANNING NUCLEAR WEAPON TESTS, AUGUST 5, 1963

After much controversy regarding nuclear testing and the effects of radioactive fallout, the major nuclear powers finally signed a ban on all but underground tests (August 5, 1963). Although China and France refused to sign the agreement, the Cold War between the Soviet Union and the West seemed to be entering a more quiescent stage.

The Governments of the United States of America, the United Kingdom of Great Britain and Northern Ireland, and the Union of Soviet Socialist Republics, hereinafter referred to as the "Original Parties,"

Proclaiming as their principal aim the speediest possible achievement of an agreement on general and complete disarmament under

Department of State *Bulletin*, XLIX (August 12, 1963), 239–240.

strict international control in accordance with the objectives of the United Nations which would put an end to the armaments race and eliminate the incentive to the production and testing of all kinds of weapons, including nuclear weapons,

Seeking to achieve the discontinuance of all test explosions of nuclear weapons for all time, determined to continue negotiations to this end, and desiring to put an end to the contamination of man's environment by radioactive substances,

Have agreed as follows:

Article I

1. Each of the Parties to this Treaty undertakes to prohibit, to prevent, and not to carry out any nuclear weapon test explosion, or any other nuclear explosion, at any place under its jurisdiction or control:

(a) in the atmosphere; beyond its limits, including outer space; or underwater, including territorial waters or high seas; or

(b) in any other environment if such explosion causes radioactive debris to be present outside the territorial limits of the State under whose jurisdiction or control such explosion is conducted. It is understood in this connection that the provisions of this subparagraph are without prejudice to the conclusion of a treaty resulting in the permanent banning of all nuclear test explosions, including all such explosions underground, the conclusion of which, as the Parties have stated in the Preamble to this Treaty, they seek to achieve.

2. Each of the Parties to this Treaty undertakes furthermore to refrain from causing, encouraging, or in any way participating in, the carrying out of any nuclear weapon test explosion, or any other nuclear explosion, anywhere which would take place in any of the environments described, or have the effect referred to, in paragraph 1 of this Article.

Article II

1. Any Party may propose amendments to this Treaty. The text of any proposed amendment shall be submitted to the Depositary Governments which shall circulate it to all Parties to this Treaty. Thereafter, if requested to do so by one-third or more of the Parties,

the Depositary Governments shall convene a conference, to which they shall invite all the Parties, to consider such amendment.

2. Any amendment to this Treaty must be approved by a majority of the votes of all the Parties to this Treaty, including the votes of all of the Original Parties. The amendment shall enter into force for all Parties upon the deposit of instruments of ratification by a majority of all the Parties, including the instruments of ratification of all of the Original Parties.

Article III

1. This Treaty shall be open to all States for signature. Any State which does not sign this Treaty before its entry into force in accordance with paragraph 3 of this Article may accede to it at any time.

2. This Treaty shall be subject to ratification by signatory States. Instruments of ratification and instruments of accession shall be deposited with the Governments of the Original Parties—the United States of America, the United Kingdom of Great Britain and Northern Ireland, and the Union of Soviet Socialist Republics—which are hereby designated the Depositary Governments.

3. This Treaty shall enter into force after its ratification by all the Original Parties and the deposit of their instruments of ratification.

4. For States whose instruments of ratification or accession are deposited subsequent to the entry into force of this Treaty, it shall enter into force on the date of the deposit of their instruments of ratification or accession.

5. The Depositary Governments shall promptly inform all signatory and acceding States of the date of each signature, the date of deposit of each instrument of ratification of and accession to this Treaty, the date of its entry into force, and the date of receipt of any requests for conferences or other notices.

6. This Treaty shall be registered by the Depositary Governments pursuant to Article 102 of the Charter of the United Nations.

Article IV

This Treaty shall be of unlimited duration.

Each Party shall in exercising its national sovereignty have the right to withdraw from the Treaty if it decides that extraordinary events, related to the subject matter of this Treaty, have jeopardized the supreme interests of its country. It shall give notice of such withdrawal to all other Parties to the Treaty three months in advance. . . .

DOCUMENT 85

CHINESE GOVERNMENT STATEMENT DENOUNCING TEST BAN, JULY 31, 1963

While the rest of the world with few exceptions rejoiced at the signing of the Nuclear Test Ban Treaty, the Chinese Communists, now at odds with their former Russian mentors, bitterly denounced it.

. . . This treaty signed in Moscow is a big fraud to fool the peoples of the world. It runs diametrically counter to the wishes of the peace-loving peoples of the world. This treaty provides them with false peace. . . . The peoples of the world demand a complete cessation of nuclear tests. This treaty leaves out a prohibition of underground tests, an omission that is particularly advantageous for the further development of nuclear weapons by United States imperialism. . . . Thus the interests of the Soviet people have been sold out, the interests of the people of the countries in the Socialist camp, including the people of China, have been sold out and the interests of all peace-loving people of the world have been sold out. . . .

DOCUMENT 86

CONGRESSIONAL RESOLUTION ON NORTH VIETNAM, AUGUST 7, 1964

In South Vietnam as in Laos, the 1954 agreements on Indo-China broke down. A Communist revolt supported by North Vietnam became a major problem for the government at Saigon, which received military and economic aid from the United States. In August, 1964, North Vietnamese forces went so far as to attack units of the American fleet in the Gulf of Tonkin. President Johnson thereupon ordered an air strike against Communist bases and asked Congress for authority to take all necessary measures to repel aggression. Congress complied with a Joint Resolution, August 7, 1964.

New York Times, July 31, 1963, 3.
New York Times, August 6, 1964, 7.

Resolved by the Senate and House of Representatives of the United States of America in Congress assembled,

Whereas naval units of the Communist regime in Vietnam, in violation of the principles of the Charter of the United Nations and of International law, have deliberately and repeatedly attacked United States naval vessels lawfully present in international waters, and have thereby created a serious threat to international peace;

Whereas these attacks are part of a deliberate and systematic campaign of aggression that the Communist regime in North Vietnam has been waging against its neighbors and the nations joined with them in the collective defense of their freedom;

Whereas the United States is assisting the peoples of Southeast Asia to protect their freedom and has no territorial, military or political ambitions in that area, but desires only that these peoples should be left in peace to work out their own destinies in their own way;

Now therefore, be it resolved, by the Senate and House of Representatives of the United States of America in Congress assembled:

The Congress approves and supports the determination of the President, as Commander in Chief, to take all necessary measures to repel any armed attack against the forces of the United States and to prevent further aggression.

Section 2—The United States regards as vital to its national interest and to world peace the maintenance of international peace and security in Southeast Asia. Consonant with the Constitution and the Charter of the United Nations and in accordance with its obligations under the Southeast Asia Collective Defense Treaty, the United States is, therefore, prepared, as the President determines, to take all necessary steps, including the use of armed force, to assist any member or protocol state of the Southeast Asia Collective Defense Treaty requesting assistance in defense of its freedom.

Section 3—This resolution shall expire when the President shall determine that the peace and security of the area is reasonably assured by international conditions created by action of the United Nations or otherwise, except that it may be terminated earlier by concurrent resolution of the Congress.

Bibliography

OFFICIAL DOCUMENTS: UNITED STATES

Congress. House of Representatives. Committee on Foreign Affairs. National and International Movements, Subcommittee No. 5, Report: *The Strategy and Tactics of World Communism*. Supplement III. Country Studies. A. *The Coup d'État in Prague*. Washington, 1948.

Congress. Senate. Committee on Foreign Relations. *A Decade of American Foreign Policy, Basic Documents, 1941–1949*. Washington, 1950. 81st Cong., 1st Ses., S. Doc. No. 123.

Congress. Senate. Committee on Foreign Relations. *Background Documents on Events Incident to the Summit Conference*. Washington, 1960. 86th Cong., 2d Ses.

Congress. Senate. Committee on Foreign Relations. *Documents on Germany, 1944–1961*. Washington, 1961. 87th Cong., 1st Ses.

Congress. Senate. Committee on the Judiciary. Subcommittee to Investigate the Administration of the Internal Security Act and Other Internal Security Laws. *Speech of Nikita Khrushchev Before a Closed Session of the XXth Congress of the Communist Party of the Soviet Union on February 25, 1956*. Washington, 1957. 85th Cong., 1st Ses.

Department of State. Department of State *Bulletin*.

Department of State. Far Eastern Series No. 28. *Korea 1945 to 1948, A Report on Political Developments and Economic Resources with Selected Documents.* Washington, 1948. Department of State Publication No. 3305.

Department of State. Far Eastern Series No. 30. *United States Relations with China with Special Reference to the Period 1944–1949.* Washington, 1949. Department of State Publication No. 3573.

Department of State. Foreign Relations of the United States. Diplomatic Papers. *The Conferences at Cairo and Teheran, 1943.* Washington, 1961. Department of State Publication No. 7187.

Department of State. Foreign Relations of the United States. Diplomatic Papers. *The Conferences at Malta and Yalta, 1945.* Washington, 1955. Department of State Publication No. 6199.

Department of State. Foreign Relations of the United States. Diplomatic Papers. *The Conference of Berlin (The Potsdam Conference), 1945.* Washington, 1960. 2 vols. Department of State Publication Nos. 7015 and 7163.

Department of State. General Foreign Policy Series 117. *American Foreign Policy, 1950–1955.* Washington, 1957. 2 vols. Department of State Publication No. 6446.

Department of State. *The Geneva Conference of Heads of Government, July 18–23, 1955.* Washington, 1955. Department of State Publication No. 6046.

Department of State. *United States Treaties and Other International Agreements.* Vol. XIV, Part 1. Washington, 1963.

OFFICIAL DOCUMENTS: BRITISH COMMONWEALTH OF NATIONS

Hansard. *Parliamentary Debates.* 406 H. C. Deb. 5 s. 1944

The Parliament of the Commonwealth of Australia. *Papers presented to Parliament relating to Cuba, October–November, 1962.* Canberra, 1963.

OFFICIAL DOCUMENTS: SOVIET UNION

Ministry of Foreign Affairs of the U.S.S.R. *Correspondence Between the Chairman of the Council of Ministers of the U.S.S.R. and the Presidents of the U.S.A. and the Prime Ministers of Great Britain During the Great Patriotic War of 1941–1945.* Moscow, 1957. 2 vols.

Ministry of Foreign Affairs of the U.S.S.R. *The Soviet Union and the Berlin Question (Documents).* Moscow, 1948.

Ministry of Foreign Affairs of the U.S.S.R. *The Soviet Union and the Korean Question (Documents).* Moscow, 1948.
Ministry of Foreign Affairs of the U.S.S.R. *The Soviet Union and the Question of the Unity of Germany and of the German Peace Treaty.* Moscow, 1952.

OFFICIAL DOCUMENTS: UNITED NATIONS

Security Council. *Official Records.* 5th Year, 480th Meeting, No. 22.
Security Council. *Official Records.* 11th Year. Supplement for October, November and December, 1956.

OTHER DOCUMENTS

Churchill, Winston S. *The Second World War: Triumph and Tragedy.* Boston, 1953.
Rosenman, Samuel I. (comp.). *The Public Papers and Addresses of Franklin D. Roosevelt.* Vol. XII. New York, 1950.
The New York Times.
Vital Speeches of the Day.

SELECTED STANDARD LITERATURE OF THE COLD WAR

Agar, Herbert. *The Price of Power.* Chicago, 1957.
Berger, Carl. *The Korean Knot, A Military-Political History.* Philadelphia, 1957.
Campbell, John C. *Defense in the Middle East.* New York, 1960.
Feis, Herbert. *Churchill, Roosevelt, Stalin.* Princeton, 1957.
Feis, Herbert. *Between War and Peace: The Potsdam Conference.* Princeton, 1960.
Feis, Herbert. *The China Tangle.* Princeton, 1953.
Feis, Herbert. *Japan Subdued.* Princeton, 1961.
Fleming, D. F. *The Cold War and Its Origins, 1917–1960.* New York, 1960. 2 vols.
Goldman, Eric. *The Crucial Decade and After.* New York, 1960.
Graebner, Norman. *Cold War Diplomacy, 1945–1960.* New York, 1962.
Jones, Joseph. *The Fifteen Weeks.* New York, 1955.
Kennan, George F. *Russia and the West Under Lenin and Stalin.* Boston, 1960.

Kissinger, H. A. *Nuclear Weapons and Foreign Policy*. New York, 1957.

Lukacs, John A. *A History of the Cold War*. New York, 1960.

Snell, John L. *Illusion and Necessity: The Diplomacy of Global War, 1939–1945*. Boston, 1963.

Snell, John L. *Wartime Origins of the East-West Dilemma Over Germany*. New Orleans, 1959.

Spanier, John W. *American Foreign Policy Since World War II*. New York, 1960.

Truman, Harry S. *Memoirs*. Garden City, 1955. 2 vols.

Tsou, Tang. *America's Failure in China, 1941–1950*. Chicago, 1963.